**VOLUME ONE**

**STUDY GUIDE FOR**
*Merriman's*
*A History of*
# MODERN EUROPE

## by Kathleen Nilan
*Arizona State University West*

**W. W. NORTON & COMPANY, INC.**
*New York  /  London*

Cover illustration: *Ommeganck in Brussels—Triumph of Isabella* (detail), early 17th century, by Denis van Asloot. Victoria and Albert Museum/Art Resource.

Credits: *pp. 132–133* Hardman, John, ed. and trans. "The Declaration of the Rights of Man and Citizen." In *The French Revolution: The Fall of the Ancien Regime to the Thermidorian Reaction, 1785–1795*, pp. 114–117. New York: St. Martin's Press, 1982. Reprinted by permission of St. Martin's Press. *pp. 132–133* de Gouges, Olympe. "Declaration of the Rights of Woman and Citizen." In *European Women: A Documentary History, 1789–1945*, pp. 63–66. Eds. Eleanor S. Reimer and John C. Fout. New York: Schocken Books, 1980. Reprinted by permission of Schocken Books, a division of Random House, Inc. *pp. 135–136* Wollstonecraft, Mary. *A Vindication of the Rights of Men*, pp. 7–10. Delmar, NY: Scholars' Facsimiles and Reprints, 1975. Reprinted by permission.

ISBN 0-393-96886-3 (pbk.)

W. W. Norton & Company, Inc., 500 Fifth Avenue, New York, N.Y. 10110
http://web.wwnorton.com
W. W. Norton & Company Ltd., 10 Coptic Street, London WC1A 1PU

2 3 4 5 6 7 8 9 0

# Contents

# *Preface*

*Now, what I want is Facts. Teach these boys and girls nothing but Facts. Facts alone are wanted in life. Plant nothing else, and root out everything else.*
— CHARLES DICKENS, *Hard Times*

*. . . a collection of facts is no more science than a heap of stones is a house.*
— JULES-HENRI POINCARÉ

Too many students, perhaps the victims at some time in their educational careers of a fact-obsessed Mr. Gradgrind, are convinced that history involves nothing more than the memorization of heaps of dry-as-dust facts. However, as Poincaré reminds us, the true study of history, like science, involves much more than collecting facts: it requires using facts to analyze the world of the past.

Of course, learning the basics about a historical event or development—the who, what, where, and when—is important because it allows us to begin to look for answers to the critical questions of how and why something happened in the past. But history only becomes a meaningful and engaging pursuit—a full-blooded story of the past—when the budding historian moves beyond a simple mastery of historical detail to a more sophisticated interpretation of human experience over time.

This Study Guide has been designed to provide you with an opportunity to test your knowledge of the factual information presented in John Merriman's *A History of Modern Europe* and to test your ability to make sense of these facts. Most importantly, the Study Guide is intended to allow you to engage with the text as an active apprentice to the study of history. When used conscientiously, it will help you to build your "historical imagination" on a solid foundation of both fact and analysis.

## USING THE STUDY GUIDE

As students of history soon learn, the study of history requires a considerable amount of thoughtful and attentive reading of a variety of texts. In order to make the fullest and most efficient use of your study time, begin by reading each chapter of the textbook carefully, paying attention to the specific historical information it presents. As you read, you may wish to consult the list of "people and terms to identify" (Exercise 3 in the Study Guide), marking each item as it appears in the text. Having read through the text once, return to it for a second, more rapid reading, this time focusing on the broad themes and general outline of events discussed in that particular chapter. This is a good time to highlight the most important facts and points of historical analysis: Having already familiarized yourself with the contents of the chapter, you will be better able to decide which information is most important and will be most useful to you when you return to the chapter to review for an exam.

Once you feel confident that you have thoroughly assimilated the contents of the chapter, turn to the Study Guide and work through the exercises *without reference to the text.* Try to answer as many questions as possible from memory, rather than simply copying information from the textbook into the Study Guide. This is the only way that you can be sure that you have truly mastered the material. Once you have completed the exercises, correct your work using the textbook and the study-drill answers provided at the end of the Study Guide chapter.

You will derive the maximum benefit from your work if you do it far enough in advance to be able to *review* the text and your Study Guide answers before the class meeting for which they have been assigned. This will further reinforce your knowledge of the chapter contents and will greatly improve your comprehension of classroom lectures, discussion, and other activities.

Each chapter of the Study Guide contains an outline of the corresponding textbook chapter, sets of exercises designed to test your knowledge of geography and history, and short excerpts from documents contemporary to the events narrated in the textbook. The following instructions provide guidelines for the use of these materials.

The CHAPTER OUTLINE consists of a brief summary of the key points made in each chapter. It allows you to review the material quickly and efficiently, whether in preparation for a class meeting or an exam. Have you really understood the information presented in the textbook? Test your comprehension by writing your own outline and then comparing it with the Study Guide outline. Writing a concise summary of a substantial body of information is challenging, but it will help you to understand and to remember what you have learned, and it will also help you to hone your note-taking skills.

Students of history should carry an accurate map of the world inside their head. Every chapter of the Study Guide contains a set of HISTORICAL GEOGRAPHY exercises, including one or more blank maps, a list of places to locate on these maps, and several questions. As you are reading the textbook chapter, refer frequently to the maps provided, focusing

especially on finding the places listed in the Study Guide. When you feel confident about your knowledge of this geography, complete the MAP EXERCISES *without reference to the textbook maps.* Your knowledge of historical geography will be greatly reinforced by frequent review. Every few weeks, try quizzing yourself on all of the map exercises you have completed up to that point.

The MAP QUESTIONS ask you to put your knowledge of geography to use in analyzing historical situations and developments. They refer to specific problems of geography raised by material covered in the textbook.

The names, events, and other items listed under PEOPLE AND TERMS TO IDENTIFY have been selected from among the many others presented in the textbook both for their historical importance and for their representativeness. When you "identify" each item, you should be able to do two things:

1. Briefly but thoroughly *describe* the person or thing, remembering to explain *who* was involved, *what* happened, and *where, when,* and *how* it happened.

2. Explain the *significance* of the item with reference to the broad historical trends or developments discussed in the text.

The STUDY QUESTIONS ask you to consider specific problems raised by the historical developments covered in each chapter. Once again, make every effort to answer these questions without reference to the text. You can check the accuracy of your answers after you have responded to the questions.

Illustrations provided in the textbook can help you to develop a sense of both how people in the past saw themselves and what their world looked like. The questions in the ANALYZING ART AND ARTIFACTS section of the Study Guide ask you to "read" visual images as historical documents. As you work your way through the textbook, you should make an effort to become a sophisticated reader of visual documents and to familiarize yourself with the ways in which art and material culture are transformed by changing historical circumstances.

Changes in technology—whether agricultural, industrial, military, medical, or related to communications and transportation—often have a significant impact on history, and are themselves the product of changing human needs and interests. The questions posed in the TECHNOLOGY AND HISTORY section ask you to explore the reasons why technologies change and to reflect on how these changes affect human experience.

The questions posed under the heading of HISTORICAL ANALYSIS: INTERPRETIVE ESSAYS ask you to synthesize the information presented in each chapter and to analyze large-scale historical developments. Your responses should take the form of well-organized essays that demonstrate both your mastery of the historical record and your ability to develop a sustained historical argument. While you will undoubtedly not be able to write a full-length answer to every one of these questions, preparing outlines and thinking through possible responses can be helpful preparation for exams.

When historians write history, they rely on a variety of historical documents to reconstruct the world of the past. In the HISTORICAL VOICES section of each chapter of the Study Guide, you will find two or more excerpts from works written during the historical period under discussion in the textbook chapter. You will be asked to read these documents in light of information presented in the textbook and to answer questions about the documents themselves. These documents may sometimes be challenging to read, but they will allow you to hear the people of the past express themselves in their own words and to become more knowledgeable about the distinctive ideas and perceptions of different historical eras.

Finally, the STUDY DRILLS at the end of each Study Guide chapter allow you to test your knowledge of IMPORTANT HISTORICAL FACTS. These exercises consist of multiple-choice questions, various drills testing your knowledge of historical chronology, "fill-in-the-blank" problems, and identification quizzes. The answers to all of these exercises are provided in the following section.

Throughout the Study Guide you will come across questions labeled *Historical Continuities*. Questions listed under this heading ask you to draw connections between material presented in two or more chapters and to analyze the long-term impact of important historical events. They are intended to provide you with an opportunity to review material you have already covered and to become more aware of broad historical trends.

# 1 Medieval Legacies and Transforming Discoveries

## 1. CHAPTER OUTLINE

I. CONTINUITIES FROM THE MEDIEVAL PERIOD: Although European society was beginning to experience dramatic change in 1500, it remained deeply rooted in the medieval past.

A. THE FRAGMENTATION OF EUROPE was still evident in localized political structures, divided religious loyalties, a multiplicity of legal codes, and considerable linguistic diversity. A weak and divided Europe confronted the powerful and united Islamic empire of the Ottomans.

B. THE STRUCTURE OF SOCIETY: Medieval society had consisted of three social groups: the clergy, the nobility, and a poor (and sometimes rebellious) peasantry.

C. Under FEUDALISM, powerful lords had granted land to their vassals in exchange for military support. This system began to collapse as a result of the rise of monarchical states and the outbreak of the Black Death.

D. European peasants continued to live in a SUBSISTENCE ECONOMY, producing only enough to feed themselves and to pay what they owed their lords and the Church. Serfdom was disappearing in the West, but it was on the increase in Central and Eastern Europe.

E. RELIGION AND POPULAR CULTURE: Religion permeated everyday life, and the Church still exercised considerable social and cultural control. Popular culture was shaped by Christian belief, but also by superstition and belief in magic.

II. THE EMERGENCE OF EARLY MODERN EUROPE was the result of significant changes in late medieval economic, social, and political structures.

A. A RISING POPULATION: In the mid-fourteenth century the Black Death devastated Europe. Recovery was slow, but by 1550 the population had returned to its pre-plague level and was entering a period of rapid increase.

B. AN EXPANDING ECONOMY: The continuing growth of trade and financial institutions (bills of exchange, banks) facilitated a commercial boom in the 1500s. Manufacturing increased, and some entrepreneurs sought to circumvent urban guild restrictions by transferring production to rural "cottage industry."

C. THE GROWTH OF TOWNS was linked to economic expansion. City dwellers remained a small percentage of the total population, but they played an

1

especially dynamic role in the development of early modern Europe.

D. Cities and towns claimed increasing freedom from territorial rulers, establishing a tradition of MUNICIPAL LIBERTIES that would have a significant long-term impact on European political structures.

E. THE EMERGENCE OF SOVEREIGN STATES: "New monarchies" in France, England, and Spain exercised increasing power over their territories, building powerful centralized states.

F. DEVELOPING STATE STRUCTURES: Rulers increased and centralized their power through a variety of means, including state bureaucracies (often staffed by a new service nobility), taxation, royal courts, hereditary succession, and diplomacy.

G. LIMITS TO STATE AUTHORITY: The power of European monarchs was constrained by the privileges of towns and cities, representative assemblies (which often had a say in taxation policies), and the prerogatives of nobles and clergy.

III. Dramatic changes in European culture were also brought about by three TRANSFORMING DISCOVERIES:

A. GUNPOWDER, WARFARE, AND ARMIES: The introduction of gunpowder transformed warfare, greatly decreasing the importance of the cavalry. The size of armies increased and the use of mercenaries became common.

B. THE PRINTING PRESS AND THE POWER OF THE PRINTED WORD: The availability of printed texts greatly facilitated the dissemination of ideas and stimulated a significant increase in literacy.

C. EXPLORATION AND CONQUEST OF THE NEW WORLD: The voyages of explorers like Columbus brought Europeans into contact with the Americas, with often tragic results for the native populations and for those Africans who would be brought to the New World as slaves. Spain, especially, benefited from the riches of these newly discovered territories.

IV. CONCLUSION

## 2. HISTORICAL GEOGRAPHY

**Map Exercises**

Familiarize yourself with the maps provided in your text, and then attempt to locate the following places on Blank Map 1.1.

EUROPE IN 1500

| | |
|---|---|
| Aragon | Naples |
| Austria | Ottoman Empire |
| Castile | Papal States |
| Denmark-Norway | Poland-Lithuania |
| England | Portugal |
| France | Scotland |
| Holy Roman | Sicily |
| Empire | Spain |
| Hungary | Sweden |
| Ireland | Swiss |
| Muscovy | Confederation |

BODIES OF WATER

| | |
|---|---|
| Adriatic Sea | English Channel |
| Aegean Sea | Loire River |
| Atlantic Ocean | Mediterranean Sea |
| Azov, Sea of | North Sea |
| Baltic Sea | Oder River |
| Black Sea | Po River |
| Danube River | Rhine River |
| Dnieper River | Rhône River |
| Ebro River | Seine River |
| Elbe River | Vistula River |

**Map Questions**

Locate the following regions and identify their most important component parts: the Balkans, the British Isles, "Germany," the Iberian Peninsula, "Italy," the Netherlands,* and Scandinavia.

*Also known as the Low Countries and the Benelux countries (for BElgium, NEtherlands, LUXembourg).

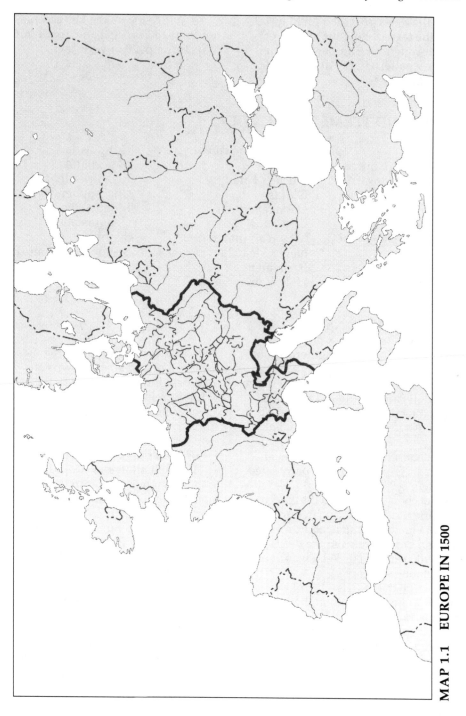

**MAP 1.1   EUROPE IN 1500**

Using the dates provided on Map 1.2 (p. 37 of the text), follow the spread of printing throughout Europe. Can you discern any pattern in the dissemination of this technology?

Be able to locate the key colonial holdings of Portugal and Spain (refer to Map 1.3 on p. 29 of your text).

## 3. PEOPLE AND TERMS TO IDENTIFY

Jacob Fugger
Roman Catholic Church/
   Eastern Orthodox
   Church
Ottoman Empire
Civil, Canon, and
   Customary Law
Peasants
Feudalism
The Black Death

Subsistence Economy
Carnival
Nuclear Family
Guilds
Cottage Industry
City-State
"Town air makes free."
New Monarchies
Parliament
Holy Roman Empire

Gunpowder
Mercenaries
Johann Gutenberg
Christopher Columbus
Montezuma
Conquistadors
Syphilis
Bishop Bartolomé de Las
   Casas

## 4. STUDY QUESTIONS

1. Why was Europe "fragmented" in 1500?
2. How was the European social order organized during the medieval period?
3. What factors led to the revival of centralized states in the late medieval period?
4. In what sense was late medieval European society and culture permeated by Christianity?
5. What changes signaled the emergence of the "early modern" period in Europe?
6. What factors influenced European population growth rates in the years between 1000 and 1700? Why was average life expectancy so short?
7. Describe the married life of an average European woman in the early modern period.
8. What specific developments encouraged and facilitated an increase in commerce and manufacturing in the sixteenth century?

9. What had stimulated the increase in the number and size of towns and cities in medieval Europe? How was the growth of towns related to economic developments?
10. *Historical Continuities:* What long-term political consequences might result from the rise of towns?
11. What allowed European monarchs to increase their power in the early modern period? What factors continued to limit their authority?
12. How was European warfare transformed by the introduction of gunpowder?
13. How did the development of printing affect the dissemination of knowledge in the early modern period?
14. What was the impact on Europe of the discovery and conquest of the New World? On the population of the New World? On the rest of the world's peoples?

## 5. ANALYZING ART AND ARTIFACTS

Study the images of rural life presented in your text (pp. 10, 12, 14, 16) and use them to describe the work lives and leisure activities of European peasants in the early modern period.

## 6. TECHNOLOGY AND HISTORY

How important was technological innovation to the transition between the medieval and early modern periods? Which technology do you think was most important?

## 7. HISTORICAL ANALYSIS: INTERPRETIVE ESSAYS

1. *Historical Continuities:* In what sense was Europe no longer "medieval" by the year 1500?

2. *Historical Continuities:* Of the three discoveries discussed in this chapter—gunpowder, printing, and the New World—which one would you consider the most important? Why? While your answer should focus on the immediate impact of the discovery, also consider its long-term implications.

3. Imagine you had been born in a rural region of Europe in 1500, but moved to an important city at the age of twenty. Write your life history.

4. What changes were taking place in European political structures during the period of transition covered in this chapter?

5. During the late medieval and early modern period, Europeans greatly increased their contacts with the outside world. What impact did these global connections have on European culture and society? On non-European cultures and societies?

## 8. HISTORICAL VOICES: OLD WORLDS AND NEW WORLDS

### A. Columbus and the People of the New World

Born in Italy, Christopher Columbus (1451–1506) grew up in Genoa and took to the Mediterranean Sea at the age of fourteen, by his own account. After nearly perishing in a sea battle with pirates during his first Atlantic voyage, Columbus washed up on the shore of Portugal. He stayed on in Lisbon and shipped out several times with Portuguese vessels, learning his way around the Atlantic wind systems during trips to England, the island of Madeira, and Portuguese trading stations along the coast of northwest Africa.

Believing, on the basis of erroneous calculations, that the Atlantic was much narrower than it really is (and that no dry land lay between Western Europe and the riches of Eastern Asia), Columbus tried to convince King John II of Portugal to fund an exploratory voyage across the Atlantic in 1483, but the king refused. Almost ten years later, Queen Isabella of Spain finally agreed to underwrite Columbus' journey.

On October 12, 1492, Columbus and his crew landed on a Caribbean island he named San Salvador. The following account from his diary relates Columbus' impressions of the "Indians" he encountered in the "New World" he believed (to his dying day) to be Asia.

FROM *The Voyages of Christopher Columbus: The Story of the Discovery of America, as told by the Discoverer*

THURSDAY, OCTOBER 11, 1492  After sundown kept due W., made twelve miles an hour, and by two hours after midnight had made ninety miles, which is twenty-two and a half leagues. The Pinta being a fast sailer kept ahead of the Admiral, and discovered land and made the signals the Admiral had ordered in such a case. This land was seen first by a sailor called Rodrigo de Triana. The Admiral at ten o'clock at night being on top of the castle or cabin, on the high poop of his vessel, saw a light, but so dim that he feared he might be deceived; he called Pedro Gutierrez, a gentleman of the King's bed chamber, and told him it looked like a light, and to look at it himself; which he did, and saw it; he also told Rodrigo Sanchez of Segovia, whom the King and Queen had sent with the fleet as a comptroller, but he failed to see it because of his position. The Admiral said he saw it once or twice afterwards, as if it were a little tallow candle that rose and sank on the waves, and which impressed a few as being an indication of land. But the Admiral felt sure that he was close to land.

Where upon, when, as was the invariable custom, the sailors had sung the *Salve Regina*, the Admiral made an impressive address to the crew, and ordered them to keep a strict watch from the forecastle, and promised to the first man who should see land, a doublet of silk in addition to the largesses promised by the Sovereigns, which was an annuity of ten thousand *maravedis*. Two hours after midnight land was seen, about two leagues off. Sail was taken in and the vessels lay to awaiting the dawn of Friday, when they found themselves near the Island of Lucayas, called in the Indian language *Guanahani*. Then were seen people entirely naked, and the Admiral entered his own boat, and Martin Alonso Pinzon and Vicente Anse (or Yanez), his brother, who was captain of the Niña, entered theirs. The Admiral held aloft the standard, and the captains displayed two banners emblazoned with a green cross, which the Admiral carried on all his vessels as banners of the enterprise. These had on either side the letters F and Y, (the initials of the monarchs, Fernando and Ysabel), surmounted by the crown, one at one extreme of the ✠ and the other at the other. On nearing the shore they saw trees that were very green, and many streams of water, and fruits in great varieties. The Admiral called to the two captains and the crews to leap ashore, and to Rodrigo Descovedo, Notary of the Armada, and Rodrigo Sanchez of Segovia, and called upon them to take oath of obedience to him, and to bear witness that he, in the presence of all, as he now did, before all others, took solemn possession of the island in the name of the King and Queen, his Sovereigns, complying with the required forms and ceremonies. Then there gathered around him a large number of the inhabitants of the island. What now follows are the precise words of the Admiral in his book, on his first voyage of discoveries of these Indies. "I" (he says), to gain their friendship, because I recognized that they were a people that from the gentleness of their disposition could be more easily converted to our Holy Faith by love than by fear; I gave some of them red caps, glass beads which they put around their necks, and other trifles which seemed to them of inestimable value. They afterwards came out to the ships in which we were, some swimming, others in light barks, bringing parrots and cotton yarn in large and small balls, and many other things, which they exchanged with us for glass beads and hawk's bells. Indeed, they took everything and gave us what they had with the greatest good will. But they appeared to me to be a people poor in everything. They went about as naked as when they were born, as did also the women, of whom I saw but one, quite young and beautifully formed. All the natives I saw were gentle and none seemed to be over thirty years of age; they were well shaped, moderate in stature; and had agreeable features; their hair was almost as coarse as horse hair and short, partly cut short above the ears while some locks were left long behind, and falling upon their shoulders. Some paint themselves black; they are of the color of the natives of the Canary Islands, neither black nor white. They paint themselves in every variety of colors; some paint only a portion of the face and some the entire body. They have no weapons nor do they know their use, and when I showed them our swords they grasped them by the blades and cut themselves with the sharp edges, not knowing any better. They have no iron; their lances are hardened at the end by fire, or pointed at the end with flint or the teeth or bone of a fish. I saw some of them who bore scars of wounds upon their bodies, and I asked them, by signs, what this meant. They made known to me that people came from neighboring islands and tried to carry them off, and that they defended themselves. I thought, and still believe, that these men came from the mainland. They must make good servants and be quite apt, as I see that they very soon say what they are told to say, and it seems to me that they can readily be made Christians; I have not noticed any religion among them. Please the Lord, when I leave here I shall take six of these natives to your Highness, so that they may learn our language. There is no kind of wild beasts, only parrots, on this island." All this was said by the Admiral.

*Source:* Christopher Columbus. *The Voyages of Christopher Columbus: The Story of the Discovery of America, as told by the Discoverer*, pp. 34–36. Trans. Marc F. Vallette. New York: Press of the Unites States Catholic Historical Society, 1892.

### Questions:

How does Columbus describe the inhabitants of San Salvador? In what ways do his comments reveal his European cultural biases?

What kind of a relationship does Columbus propose to establish between these "Indians" and their European "discoverers"?

## B. Rabelais and the New World of Knowledge

The life of François Rabelais (c. 1490–1553) reveals in microcosm both the continuities between medieval and early modern culture, and the dramatic breaks in that continuity that had begun to be apparent by 1500. Born into a comfortably affluent family, Rabelais received a solid but traditional education and entered a monastic order sometime in his youth. A budding humanist scholar, he was apparently frustrated with the intellectual narrowness of the monastery, and he left the cloistered life in 1530 to study medicine at Montpellier. While he went on to serve as the doctor of Cardinal Jean du Bellay, he was best known during his lifetime for his comic narratives of the lives of the mythical giants Gargantua and his son Pantagruel. Rabelais' criticisms of the traditionalist theologians of Paris won him their lasting enmity, and his works were persistently condemned by Church officials.

Rabelais' writing is known for its often earthy humor, but it also contains sophisticated satire and demonstrates its author's considerable erudition. Rabelais claimed that he wished to do no more than entertain—"To be called a good companion and fellow-boozer is to me pure honor and glory."—but he nonetheless insisted that the literary bones he threw his readers contained a "substantial marrow" of worldly and spiritual wisdom.

In the following extract from *Pantagruel* (1532), Gargantua offers his son advice about how to get the most out of his university studies.

### FROM *Pantagruel*, in *The Works of Rabelais*

Pantagruel studied very hard, as you may well conceive, and profited accordingly: for he had an excellent understanding, and notable wit, together with a capacity, in point of memory, equal to the measure of twelve oil-budgets, or butts of olives. And as he was there abiding, one day, he received a letter from his father, in manner as followeth:

"Most Dear Son,

. . . although my deceased father, of happy memory, Grangousier, had bent his best endeavours to make me profit in all perfection and political knowledge, and that my labour and study was fully correspondent to, yea, went beyond his desire; nevertheless, as thou may'st well understand, the time then was not so proper and fit for learning as it is at present, neither had I plenty of such good masters as thou hast had: for that time was darksome, obscured with clouds of ignorance, and savouring a little of the infelicity and calamity of the Goths, who had, wherever they set footing, destroyed all good literature, which in my age hath by the divine goodness been restored unto its former light and dignity, and that with such amendment and increase of knowledge, that now hardly should I be admitted unto the first form of the little grammar school-boys: I say, I who in my youthful days was (and that justly) reputed the most learned of that age. Which I do not speak in vain-boasting, although I might lawfully do it in writing unto thee, by the authority of Marcus Tullius, in his book of old age, and the sentence of Plutarch, in the book, entitled, How a man may praise himself without envy: but to give thee all emulous encouragement to strive yet farther.

"Now it is that the minds of men are qualified with all manner of discipline, and the old sciences revived, which for many ages were extinct: now it is, that the learned languages are to their pristine purity restored—viz., Greek (without which a man may be ashamed to account himself a scholar), Hebrew, Arabic, Chaldean, and Latin. Printing likewise is now in use, so elegant, and so correct, that better cannot be imagined, although it was found out in my time but by divine inspiration; as by a diabolical suggestion, on the other side, was the invention of ordnance. All the world is full of knowing men, of most learned school-masters, and vast libraries; and it appears to me as a truth, that neither in Plato's time, nor Cicero's, nor Papinian's, there was ever such conveniency for studying, as we see at this day there is. Nor must any adventure henceforward to come in public, or represent himself in company, that hath not been pretty well polished in the shop of Minerva. I see robbers, hangmen, free-booters, tapsters, ostlers, and such like, of the very rubbish of the people, more learned now, than the doctors and preachers were in my time.

"What shall I say? The very women and children have aspired to this praise and celestial manna of good learning: yet so it is, that at the age I am now of, I have been constrained to learn the Greek tongue, which I contemned not like Cato, but had not the leisure in my younger years to attend the study of it. And I take much delight in the reading of Plutarch's morals, the pleasant dialogues of Plato, the monuments of Pausanias, and the antiquities of Athenæus, whilst I wait the hour wherein God my creator shall call me, and command me to depart from this earth and transitory pilgrimage. Wherefore, my son, I admonish thee to employ thy youth to profit as well as thou canst, both in thy studies and in virtue. Thou art at Paris, where the laudable examples of many brave men may stir up thy mind to many gallant actions; and hast likewise for thy tutor the learned Epistemon, who by his lively and vocal documents may instruct thee in the arts and sciences.

"I intend, and will have it so, that thou learn the languages perfectly. First of all, the Greek, as Quintilian will have it: secondly, the Latin; and then the Hebrew, for the holy Scripture-sake. And then the Chaldee and Arabic likewise. And that thou frame thy style in Greek, in imitation of Plato; and for the Latin, after Cicero. Let there be no history which thou shalt not have ready in thy memory; and to help thee therein, the books of cosmography will be very conducible. Of the liberal arts of geometry, arithmetic, and music, I gave thee some taste when thou wert yet little, and not above five or six years old; proceed further in them, and learn the remainder if thou canst. As for astronomy, study all the rules thereof: let pass nevertheless the divining and judicial astrology, and the art of Lullius, as being nothing else but plain cheats and vanities. As for the civil law, of that I would have thee to know the texts by heart, and then to confer them with philosophy.

"Now in matter of the knowledge of the works of nature, I would have thee to study that exactly; so that there be no sea, river, or fountain, of which thou dost not know the fishes; all the fowls of the air; all the several kinds of shrubs and trees, whether in forest or orchard: all the sorts of herbs and flowers that grow upon the ground; all the various metals that are hid within the bowels of the earth; together with all the diversity of precious stones that are to be seen in the orient and south parts of the world: let nothing of all these be hidden from thee. Then fail not most carefully to peruse the books of the Greek, Arabian and Latin physicians; not despising the talmudists and cabalists; and by frequent anatomies get thee the perfect knowledge of the microcosm, which is man. And at some hours of the day apply thy mind to the study of the holy Scriptures: first in Greek, the New Testament with the Epistles of the Apostles; and then the Old Testament in Hebrew. In brief, let me see thee an abyss and bottomless-pit of knowledge: for from henceforward, as thou growest great and becomest a man, thou must part from this tranquility and rest of study; thou must learn chivalry, warfare, and the exercise of the field, the better thereby to defend my house and our friends, and to succour and protect them at all their needs against the invasion and assaults of evil-doers.

"Furthermore, I will that very shortly thou try how much thou hast profited, which thou canst not better do than by maintaining publicly theses and conclusions in all arts, against all persons whatsoever, and by haunting the company of learned men, both at Paris and otherwhere. But because, as the wise man Soloman saith, wisdom entereth not into a malicious mind, and that science without conscience is but the ruin of the soul; it behoveth thee to serve, to love, to fear God, and on him to cast all thy thoughts and all thy hope, and, by faith formed in charity, to cleave unto him, so that thou mayest never be separated from him by thy sins. Suspect the abuses of the world: set not thy heart upon vanity, for this life is transitory, but the word of the Lord endureth forever. Be serviceable to all thy neighbours, and love them as thyself: reverence thy præceptors; shun the conversation of those whom thou desirest not to resemble, and receive not in vain the graces which God hath bestowed upon thee. And when thou shall see that thou hast attained to all the knowledge that is to be acquired in that part, return unto me, that I may see thee, and give thee my blessing before I die. My son, the peace and grace of our Lord be with thee. Amen.

"From Utopia, the 17th day
    of the month of March.

"Thy father, Gargantua."

These letters being received and read, Pantagruel plucked up his heart, took a fresh courage to him, and was inflamed with a desire to profit in his studies more than ever; so that if you had seen him, how he took pains, and how he advanced in learning, you would have said that the vivacity of his spirit, amidst the books, was like a great fire amongst dry wood; so active it was, vigorous, and indefatigable.

*Source:* François Rabelais. "How Pantagruel, Being at Paris, Received Letters From His Father Gargantua, and the Copy of Them." From *Pantagruel,* in *The Works of Rabelais,* pp. 142–46. Derby: Moray Press, 1894.

### Questions:
According to Gargantua, how has Europe changed during his lifetime?

What kind of educational program does Gargantua outline in his letter? How do you think it differs from that of the medieval period?

To what extent does Gargantua's advice remain rooted in medieval patterns of thought and behavior?

## 9. IMPORTANT HISTORICAL FACTS: STUDY DRILLS

### A. Multiple Choice

1. Jacob Fugger became known for his involvement in
   A. farming.
   B. banking.
   C. government.
   D. manufacturing.

2. The territories that made up the Ottoman Empire included
   A. the German states.
   B. the Iberian Peninsula.
   C. Turkey and much of the Balkans and North Africa.
   D. the British Isles.

3. All of the following statements about the Black Death are true *except*
   A. It reached Western Europe in 1348.
   B. It killed at least one-third of the Western European population.
   C. It helped to bring an end to feudalism.
   D. It was a sexually transmitted disease.

4. In the days before Lent, European Christians participated in a festive round of eating, drinking, and (sometimes subversive) amusements. This was known as
   A. Christmas.
   B. popular culture.
   C. the subsistence economy.
   D. carnival.

5. Consisting of a man and woman and their children, this social structure was common in early modern England:
   A. the nuclear family
   B. the extended family
   C. the peasant household
   D. the economy of makeshifts

6. In search of cheap labor and freedom from guild restrictions, many early modern craftsmen and merchant-capitalists moved their operations out of cities, resulting in the rise of rural manufacturing in Europe. This was known as
   A. cottage industry.
   B. the guild system.
   C. urbanization.
   D. industrialization.

7. By 1100, Venice, Florence, Genoa, Milan, and Pisa had become
   A. the Byzantine Empire.
   B. the Holy Roman Empire.
   C. Italy.
   D. city-states.

8. The saying "town air makes free" meant that
   A. urban residents were licentious in their behavior.
   B. medieval cities had healthy air.
   C. living in cities released serfs from their bondage.
   D. manufactured goods were less expensive in cities.

9. The introduction of gunpowder in Europe transformed warfare in all of the following ways *except* that
   A. it allowed muskets to replace lances and the longbows in battle.
   B. it decreased the size of armies.
   C. it made the knight in armor obsolete.
   D. it made warfare far more deadly.

10. Christopher Columbus succeeded in "discovering" the New World because
    A. he had correctly calculated the distance across the Atlantic Ocean.
    B. he believed the earth was flat.
    C. he knew that unexplored territory lay across the ocean from Spain.
    D. he successfully navigated the Atlantic trade winds.

### B. Chronological Relationships

1. Place each of the following events on a timeline running from 1300 to 1550 and identify the date on which each occurred:
   The dukedom of Burgundy becomes the property of the French king.
   The first Habsburg is elected Holy Roman emperor.
   The Black Death strikes Europe.
   At the Battle of Novara, 700 men are killed in three minutes by artillery fire.

The Ottoman Turks capture Constantinople after a long siege.

Cortès lands on the coast of Mexico and goes to meet Montezuma.

Isabella and Ferdinand marry and unite the kingdoms of Castile and Aragon.

Movable metal type is first used in printing in Mainz.

Pope Alexander VI divides the non-Christian world between Portugal and Spain.

English peasants rise up in revolt.

2. Briefly explain the historical significance of each of the events listed above.

## C. Fill in the Blanks

1. After the Great Schism of 1054, European Christianity was split between the ~~Roman Catholic~~ Church and the ~~Eastern Orthodox~~ Church.

2. The fragmentation of medieval Europe was reinforced by the existence of three distinct legal systems: ~~Roman civil~~ law, derived from the Roman classical tradition; ~~customary~~ law, derived from the codification of precedents established by judges' decisions; and ~~canon~~ law, the legal code of the Catholic Church.

3. In 1500, 85 percent of the European population were ~~peasants~~, agricultural workers who lived in rural areas.

4. The medieval system by which vassals provided military service to powerful lords in exchange for land was known as ~~feudalism~~.

5. Agricultural workers who produce only enough to feed themselves (and to pay taxes to their kings and a tithe to the Church) are said to live in a ~~subsistence~~ economy.

6. In medieval and early modern Europe most production and distribution of finished goods was controlled by associations of master artisans. These ~~guilds~~ regulated entry into a trade (through apprenticeship) and set quality standards.

7. In England, royal power was limited by the existence of ~~Parliament~~, a consultative body representing the interests and concerns of leading subjects.

8. Early modern armies often consisted largely of hired soldiers, known as ~~mercenaries~~.

9. While we do not know for certain who invented movable metal type, ~~Gutenberg~~ was one of the first Germans to make use of this new technology, producing beautiful printed Bibles.

10. Often the offspring of impoverished noble families, the ~~conquistadors~~ set off from Spain and Portugal for the New World in search of adventure and wealth, bringing with them brutal warfare and epidemic diseases.

# IMPORTANT HISTORICAL FACTS: STUDY-DRILL ANSWERS

## A. Multiple Choice

1. B. banking.
2. C. Turkey and much of the Balkans and North Africa.
3. D. It was a sexually transmitted disease.
4. D. carnival.
5. A. the nuclear family.
6. A. cottage industry.
7. D. city-states.
8. C. living in cities released serfs from their bondage.
9. B. it decreased the size of armies.
10. D. he successfully navigated the Atlantic trade winds.

## B. Chronological Relationships

1348 The Black Death strikes Europe.

1381 English peasants rise up in revolt.

1438 The first Habsburg is elected Holy Roman emperor.

c.1450 Movable metal type is first used in printing in Mainz.

1453 The Ottoman Turks capture Constantinople after a long siege.

1469 Isabella and Ferdinand marry and unite the kingdoms of Castile and Aragon.

1482 The dukedom of Burgundy becomes the property of the French king.

1493    Pope Alexander VI divides the non-Christian world between Portugal and Spain.

1513    At the battle of Novara, 700 men are killed in three minutes by artillery fire.

1519    Cortès lands on the coast of Mexico and goes to meet Montezuma.

**C. Fill In The Blanks**

1. Roman Catholic/Eastern Orthodox
2. civil/customary or common/canon
3. peasants
4. feudalism
5. subsistence
6. guilds
7. Parliament
8. mercenaries
9. Johann Gutenberg
10. conquistadors

# 2 *The Renaissance*

## 1. CHAPTER OUTLINE

I. THE CITY-STATES OF THE ITALIAN PENINSULA served as the setting for the great cultural achievements of the Renaissance.
   - A. The Renaissance was made possible by the THRIVING ECONOMIES of the city-states, which drew their wealth from international trade and banking.
   - B. SOCIAL STRUCTURE: The city-states were dominated by a mixed elite of wealthy nobles, merchants, and manufacturers. The majority of the city-states' residents were poor-to-middling urban merchants, artisans, laborers, and peasants.
   - C. RENAISSANCE POLITICAL LIFE: Some city-states were "republics," constitutional oligarchies dominated by the wealthy elite; others, the *signori,* were outright hereditary despotisms. All relied increasingly on bureaucracies and mercenary soldiers (the *condottieri*).
   - D. FLORENCE: ANATOMY OF A RENAISSANCE CITY: A prosperous and culturally sophisticated city, Florence was the cradle of the Italian Renaissance.

II. Prosperity and political innovation helped to produce A DYNAMIC CULTURE in Florence and throughout the Italian peninsula.
   - A. THE REDISCOVERY OF CLASSICAL LEARNING, pioneered by the poet Petrarch, was vital to Renaissance culture. The development of printing greatly facilitated the dissemination of recovered classical texts.
   - B. FROM SCHOLASTICISM TO HUMANISM: Rejecting the theological debates of medieval scholars, Renaissance humanists promoted the cultivation of a practical knowledge of the "art of living."
   - C. THE RENAISSANCE AND RELIGION: Renaissance humanists did not reject religion, but rather sought the origins of Christianity in the classical world.
   - D. THE RENAISSANCE MAN AND WOMAN: Renaissance society celebrated the civilized and well-rounded individual. However, this "universal person" was almost invariably a man; women were rarely allowed to cultivate their individual talents.

III. Like Renaissance humanism, RENAISSANCE ART drew its inspiration from classical models.
   - A. ARCHITECTURE: Renaissance architects such as Filippo Brunelleschi applied theories of classical architecture to the construction of elegant new buildings.
   - B. PATRONAGE AND THE ARTS: Renaissance artists were supported in their creative efforts by wealthy patrons such as the Medici family.

C. RENAISSANCE ARTISTS enjoyed far greater esteem and status than their medieval precursors, who had been considered mere craftsmen.

D. PAINTING AND SCULPTURE: Renaissance artists sought to achieve a natural representation of beauty through the use of perspective and other "scientific" principles. Secular subjects became more popular, but religious images continued to dominate Renaissance art.

E. HIGH RENAISSANCE STYLE: Under the patronage of the Catholic Church, artists of the High Renaissance (1490–1530) developed a Mannerist style that was both monumental and emotional.

IV. THE END OF THE RENAISSANCE began in the late fifteenth century, as the city-states lost their vitality.

A. The ECONOMIC DECLINE of the city-states was largely the result of the rise of Ottoman power in the eastern Mediterranean and growing economic competition from other European states.

B. FOREIGN INVASION: With the weakening of the city-states, Italy became a battleground for competing French kings and Holy Roman emperors.

C. Disturbed by the inability of the city-states to defend themselves against foreign powers, and deeply pessimistic about human nature, the Florentine writer MACHIAVELLI called for a strong leader—the Prince—to unify Italy and defend it from invasion.

D. THE DECLINE OF THE CITY-STATES continued as war plagued the Italian peninsula throughout the first thirty years of the sixteenth century.

E. IMPULSES ELSEWHERE: As the city-states lost their dynamism, the economic and cultural vitality of Europe shifted toward Spain and England.

## 2. HISTORICAL GEOGRAPHY

**Map Exercises**

Familiarize yourself with the maps provided in your text, and then attempt to locate the following places on Blank Maps 2.1 and 2.2.

EUROPEAN TRADING CITIES

| | |
|---|---|
| Alexandria | Kiev |
| Amsterdam | Lisbon |
| Barcelona | London |
| Belgrade | Lyon |
| Bordeaux | Marseille |
| Bruges | Paris |
| Buda | Pest |
| Constantinople | Prague |
| (Istanbul) | Stockholm |
| Gdansk (Danzig) | Vienna |
| Jerusalem | |

ITALIAN CITY-STATES
[Locate both city and city-state, where appropriate]

| | |
|---|---|
| Bologna | Papal States |
| Ferrara | Perugia |
| Florence | Pisa |
| Genoa | Rome |
| Lucca | Savoy |
| Mantua | Sicily |
| Milan | Siena |
| Modena | Urbino |
| Naples | Venice |

**Map Questions**

Where were the major arteries of trade in Renaissance Europe?

What impact did the location of the Italian peninsula have on its economic and political life?

Where is the Iberian peninsula? What changes in political boundaries took place there during the Renaissance years?

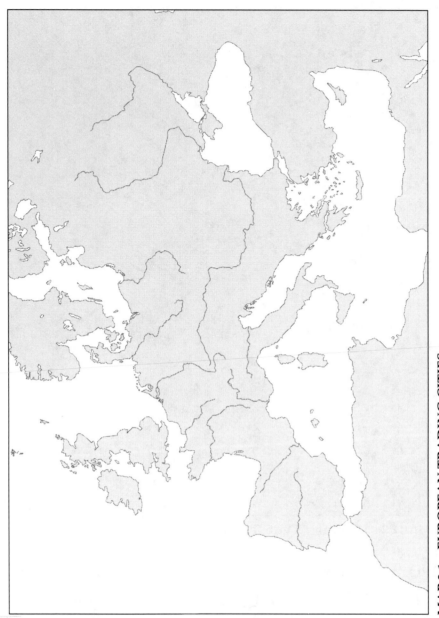

**MAP 2.1   EUROPEAN TRADING CITIES**

**MAP 2.2   ITALIAN CITY-STATES**

## 3. PEOPLE AND TERMS TO IDENTIFY

Pope Julius II
The Sistine Chapel
Renaissance
City-state
Republic
Condottieri
Signoria
Ciompi
Cosimo de' Medici

Lorenzo the Magnificent
Petrarch
Humanitas
The Courtier
Leonardo da Vinci
Filippo Brunelleschi
Michelangelo
Raphael
Neo-Platonism

Giotto di Bondone
Perspective
High Renaissance
Mannerism
Peace of Lodi
David
Girolamo Savonarola
Niccolò Machiavelli

# 4. STUDY QUESTIONS

1. Why was the Italian economy thriving in the fourteenth and fifteenth centuries?

2. How was Italian society organized? What circumstances made the ruling elite a particularly dynamic sector of this society?

3. *Historical Continuities:* What general characteristics typified the political systems of the Italian city-states, whether republics or *signoris*? How did city-state governments differ from medieval political structures?

4. What allowed Florence to play the role of "great civilizing city"?

5. Why were Renaissance scholars so eager to "rediscover" antiquity? How were classical texts made available to the reading public of the Renaissance?

6. *Historical Continuities:* Compare and contrast medieval scholasticism and Renaissance humanism. What was the relationship between the new Renaissance thought and traditional Christian theology?

7. What characteristics and abilities distinguished the "Renaissance man"? The "Renaissance woman"?

8. What elements typified the Renaissance style of architecture?

9. Who provided financial support for the production of Renaissance art? Why?

10. How did the status of the artist change during the Renaissance?

11. Why was perspective such an important element in Renaissance art?

12. Why did the economic might of the Italian city-states decline in the second half of the fifteenth century? How was this economic downswing related to the great political and military upheavals in Italy during this period?

13. Why did the Renaissance end?

# 5. ANALYZING ART AND ARTIFACTS

How does Leonardo da Vinci's use of perspective in *The Last Supper* (p. 77 of the text) work to support the religious message of this painting?

How do Renaissance portraits (pp. 59, 69, 70, and 85 of the text) express the individuality of their subjects?

Select one illustration of a work of art from the text and analyze it as a "typical" expression of the Renaissance.

# 6. TECHNOLOGY AND HISTORY

How did a new, more "scientific" model of artistic representation (demonstrated, for example, in the anatomical drawing by Leonardo da Vinci in your text, p. 65) affect the art of the Renaissance? How might this new way of viewing the human body have influenced perceptions of human existence in general?

# 7. HISTORICAL ANALYSIS: INTERPRETIVE ESSAYS

1. Why was Italy the home of the Renaissance?

2. *Historical Continuities:* In what sense was the Renaissance a "rebirth"? In what sense was it, in fact, a new departure for Europeans?

3. If Renaissance culture was typified by a new emphasis on the individual, how was this individualism expressed in the different realms of politics, social relations, the economy, and the arts?

4. If Machiavelli's Prince had come to power in 1494, what would he have done to preserve the city-states from decline?

5. What general cultural values were reflected in Renaissance art?

# 8. HISTORICAL VOICES: RENAISSANCE CULTURE AND RENAISSANCE POLITICS

## A. Castiglione and the Courtier

Baldassare Castiglione (1478–1529) was himself raised to be a courtier. As a young man he entered the service of several Renaissance rulers, including Lodovico Sforza and Francesco Gonzaga, but his happiest years were spent in Urbino, at the court of the ailing Duke Guidobaldo and his dynamic wife, Elisabetta Gonzaga. In the final years of his life he served as the pope's ambassador to Spain.

Written as an idealized transcription of conversations between members of the duke of Urbino's court, *The Courtier* (1527) provides a synthesis of Renaissance ideas about appropriate gentlemanly behavior. While it could be read as a practical guidebook for those wishing to make their way in the intrigue-ridden courts of the Italian city-states, it also served to promote the deeper Renaissance values of personal excellence and well-roundedness throughout Europe.

### FROM *The Book of the Courtier* by Baldassare Castiglione

"Then coming to the bodily frame, I say it is enough if this be neither extremely short nor tall, for both of these conditions excite a certain contemptuous surprise, and men of either sort are gazed upon in much the same way that we gaze on monsters. Yet if we must offend in one of the two extremes, it is preferable to fall a little short of the just measure of height than to exceed it, for besides often being dull of intellect, men thus huge of body are also unfit for every exercise of agility, which thing I should much wish in the Courtier. And so I would have him well built and shapely of limb, and would have him show strength and lightness and suppleness, and know all bodily exercises that befit a man of war: whereof I think the first should be to handle every sort of weapon well on foot and on horse, to understand the advantages of each, and especially to be familiar with those weapons that are ordinarily used among gentlemen; for besides the use of them in war, where such subtlety in contrivance is perhaps not needful, there frequently arise differences between one gentleman and another, which afterwards result in duels often fought with such weapons as happen at the moment to be within reach: thus knowledge of this kind is a very safe thing. Nor am I one of those who say that skill is forgotten in the hour of need; for he whose skill forsakes him at such a time, indeed gives token that he has already lost heart and head through fear.

"Moreover I deem it very important to know how to wrestle, for it is a great help in the use of all kinds of weapons on foot. Then, both for his own sake and for that of his friends, he must understand the quarrels and differences that may arise, and must be quick to seize an advantage, always showing courage and prudence in all things. Nor should he be too ready to fight except when honour demands it; for besides the great danger that the uncertainty of fate entails, he who rushes into such affairs recklessly and without urgent cause, merits the severest censure even though he be successful. But when he finds himself so far engaged that he cannot withdraw without reproach, he ought to be most deliberate, both in the preliminaries to the duel and in the duel itself, and always show readiness and daring. Nor must he act like some, who fritter the affair away in disputes and controversies, and who, having the choice of weapons, select those that neither cut nor pierce, and arm themselves as if they were expecting a cannonade; and thinking it enough not to be defeated, stand ever on the defensive and retreat,—showing therein their utter cowardice. And thus they make themselves a laughing-stock for boys, like those two men of Ancona who fought at Perugia not long since, and made everyone laugh who saw them.". . .

The Magnifico replied:

"Since I may fashion this Lady as I wish, not only am I unwilling to have her practise such vigourous and rugged manly exercises, but I would have her practise even those that are becoming to women, circumspectly and with that gentle daintiness which we have said befits her; and thus in dancing I would not see her use too active and violent movements, nor in singing or playing those abrupt and oft-repeated diminutions which show more skill than sweetness; likewise the musical instruments that she uses ought, in my opinion, to be appropriate to this intent. Imagine how unlovely it would be to see a woman play drums, fifes or trumpets, or other like instruments; and this because their harshness hides and destroys that mild gentleness which so much adorns every act a woman does. Therefore when she starts to dance or make music of any kind, she ought to bring herself to it by letting herself be urged a little, and with a touch of shyness which shall show that noble shame which is the opposite of effrontery.

"Moreover, she ought to adapt her dress to this intent, and so to clothe herself that she may not seem vain or frivolous. But since women may and ought to take more care for beauty than men,—and there are divers sorts of beauty,—this Lady ought to have the good sense to discern what those garments are that enhance her grace and are most appropriate to the exercises wherein she purposes to engage at the time, and to wear them. And if she is conscious of possessing a bright and cheerful beauty, she ought to set it off with movements, words and dress all tending towards the cheerful; so too, another, who feels that her style is gentle and serious, ought to accompany it with fashions of that sort, in order to enhance that which is the gift of nature. Thus, if she is a little more stout or thin than the medium, or fair or dark, let her seek help from dress, but as covertly as possible; and while keeping herself dainty and neat, let her always seem to give no thought or heed to it.

"And since my lord Gaspar further asks what these many things are whereof she ought to have knowledge, and in what manner she ought to converse, and whether her virtues ought to contribute to her conversation,—I say I would have her acquainted with that which these gentlemen wished the Courtier to know. And of the exercises that we have said do not befit her, I would have her at least possess such understanding as we may have of things that we do not practise; and this in order that she may know how to praise and value cavaliers more or less, according to their deserts.

"And to repeat in a few words part of what has been already said, I wish this Lady to have knowledge of letters, music, painting, and to know how to dance and make merry; accompanying the other precepts that have been taught the Courtier with discreet modesty and with the giving of a good impression of herself. And thus, in her talk, her laughter, her play, her jesting, in short, in everything, she will be very graceful, and will entertain appropriately, and with witticisms and pleasantries befitting her, everyone who shall come before her. And although continence, magnanimity, temperance, strength of mind, prudence, and the other virtues, seem to have little to do with entertainment, I would have her adorned with all of them, not so much for the sake of entertainment (albeit even there they can be of service), as in order that she may be full of virtue, and to the end that these virtues may render her worthy of being honoured, and that her every act may be governed by them."

*Source:* Baldassare Castiglione. *The Book of the Courtier*, pp. 29–30, 179–80. Trans. Leonard Eckstein Opdycke. New York: Charles Scribner's Sons, 1901.

### Questions

What characteristics typify the ideal courtier? The ideal court lady? How different are these two models from one another?

To what extent are the courtier and the court lady exemplars of the Renaissance ideal of individual excellence?

## B. Machiavelli and the Prince

Considered by many to be the founding father of modern political theory, Niccolò Machiavelli (1469–1527) lived during a period of great turmoil in Italy—and throughout Europe. Sent into exile upon the return of the Medici to power in Florence, Machiavelli wrote his most famous work, *The Prince* (written in 1513, but not published until 1532) in the hopes of winning favor with the Medici and, more importantly for political theory, of inspiring them to lead all of Italy out of the chaos provoked by constant warfare, both between city-states and against the invading armies of France, Spain, and the Holy Roman Empire.

While Machiavelli's political writings have been described as cynical, and even immoral, it is clear from a careful reading of *The Prince* that Machiavelli was, at bottom, a realist who understood that what the world recognized as virtue was often a luxury for a political leader and sometimes a disaster for his subjects. Convinced that morality and civic order could not flourish without the stability provided by strong, even brutal, rule, Machiavelli argued that the Prince must be ruthless, but also cunning, in his pursuit of power.

### FROM *The Prince* by Niccolò Machiavelli

#### OF THOSE WHO BY THEIR CRIMES COME TO BE PRINCES

... Agathocles the Sicilian came, not merely from a private station, but from the very dregs of the people, to be King of Syracuse. Son of a potter, through all the stages of his fortunes he led a foul life. His vices, however, were conjoined with so great vigour both of mind and body, that becoming a soldier, he rose through the various grades of the service to be Praetor of Syracuse. Once established in that post, he resolved to make himself Prince, and to hold by violence and without obligation to others the authority which had been spontaneously entrusted to him. Accordingly, after imparting his design to Hamilcar, who with the Carthaginian armies was at that time waging war in Sicily, he one morning assembled the people and senate of Syracuse as though to consult with them on matters of public moment, and on a preconcerted signal caused his soldiers to put to death all the senators, and the wealthiest of the commons. These being thus got rid of, he assumed and retained possession of the sovereignty without opposition on the part of the people; and although twice defeated by the Carthaginians, and afterwards besieged, he was able not only to defend his city, but leaving a part of his forces for its protection, to invade Africa with the remainder, and so in a short time to raise the siege of Syracuse, reducing the Carthaginians to the utmost extremities, and compelling them to make terms whereby they abandoned Sicily to him and confined themselves to Africa.

Whoever examines this man's actions and achievements will discover little or nothing in them which can be ascribed to Fortune, seeing, as has already been said, that it was not through the favour of any, but by the regular steps of the military service, gained at the cost of a thousand hardships and hazards, he reached the princedom which he afterwards maintained by so many daring and dangerous enterprises. Still, to slaughter fellow-citizens, to betray friends, to be devoid of honour, pity, and religion, cannot be counted as merits, for these are means which may lead to power, but which confer no glory. Wherefore, if in respect of the valour with which he encountered and extricated himself from difficulties, and the constancy of his spirit in supporting and conquering adverse fortune, there seems no reason to judge him inferior to the greatest captains that have ever lived, his unbridled cruelty and inhumanity, together with his countless crimes, forbid us to number him with the greatest men; but, at any rate, we cannot attribute to Fortune or to merit what he accomplished without either. . . .

### Of the Duty of a Prince In Respect of Military Affairs

A Prince, therefore, should have no care or thought but for war, and for the regulations and training it requires, and should apply himself exclusively to this as his peculiar province; for war is the sole art looked for in one who rules, and is of such efficacy that it not merely maintains those who are born Princes, but often enables men to rise to that eminence from a private station; while, on the other hand, we often see that when Princes devote themselves rather to pleasure than to arms, they lose their dominions. And as neglect of this art is the prime cause of such calamities, so to be a proficient in it is the surest way to acquire power. Francesco Sforza, from his renown in arms, rose from privacy to be Duke of Milan, while his descendants, seeking to avoid the hardships and fatigues of military life, from being Princes fell back into privacy. . . .

. . . A Prince, therefore, ought never to allow his attention to be diverted from warlike pursuits, and should occupy himself with them even more in peace than in war. This he can do in two ways, by practice or by study.

As to the practice, he ought, besides keeping his soldiers well trained and disciplined, to be constantly engaged in the chase, that he may inure his body to hardships and fatigue, and gain at the same time a knowledge of places, by observing how the mountains slope, the valleys open, and the plains spread; acquainting himself with the characters of rivers and marshes, and giving the greatest attention to this subject. Such knowledge is useful to him in two ways; for first, he learns thereby to know his own country, and to understand better how it may be defended; and next, from his familiar acquaintance with its localities, he readily comprehends the character of other districts when obliged to observe them for the first time. For the hills, valleys, plains, rivers, and marshes of Tuscany, for example, have a certain resemblance to those elsewhere; so that from a knowledge of the natural features of that province, similar knowledge in respect of other provinces may readily be gained. The Prince who is wanting in this kind of knowledge, is wanting in the first qualification of a good captain, for by it he is taught how to surprise an enemy, how to choose an encampment, how to lead his army on a march, how to array it for battle, and how to post it to the best advantage for a siege. . . .

## Of Cruelty and Clemency, and Whether It Is Better To Be Loved or Feared

. . . And here comes in the question whether it is better to be loved rather than feared, or feared rather than loved. It might perhaps be answered that we should wish to be both; but since love and fear can hardly exist together, if we must choose between them, it is far safer to be feared than loved. For of men it may generally be affirmed that they are thankless, fickle, false, studious to avoid danger, greedy of gain, devoted to you while you are able to confer benefits upon them, and ready, as I said before, while danger is distant, to shed their blood, and sacrifice their property, their lives, and their children for you; but in the hour of need they turn against you. The Prince, therefore, who without otherwise securing himself builds wholly on their professions is undone. For the friendships which we buy with a price, and do not gain by greatness and nobility of character, though they be fairly earned are not made good, but fail us when we have occasion to use them.

Moreover, men are less careful how they offend him who makes himself loved than him who makes himself feared. For love is held by the tie of obligation, which, because men are a sorry breed, is broken on every whisper of private interest; but fear is bound by the apprehension of punishment which never relaxes its grasp.

Nevertheless a Prince should inspire fear in such a fashion that if he do not win love he may escape hate. For a man may very well be feared and yet not hated, and this will be the case so long as he does not meddle with the property or with the women of his citizens and subjects. And if constrained to put any to death, he should do so only when there is manifest cause or reasonable justification. But, above all, he must abstain from the property of others. For men will sooner forget the death of their father than the loss of their patrimony. Moreover, pretexts for confiscation are never to seek, and he who has once begun to live by rapine always finds reasons for taking what is not his; whereas reasons for shedding blood are fewer, and sooner exhausted. . . .

## How Princes Should Keep Faith

Every one understands how praiseworthy it is in a Prince to keep faith, and to live uprightly and not craftily. Nevertheless, we see from what has taken place in our own days that Princes who have set little store by their word, but have known how to overreach men by their cunning, have accomplished great things, and in the end got the better of those who trusted to honest dealing.

Be it known, then, that there are two ways of contending, one in accordance with the laws, the other by force; the first of which is proper to men, the second to beasts. But since the first method is often ineffectual, it becomes necessary to resort to the second. A Prince should, therefore, understand how to use well both the man and the beast. And this lesson has been covertly taught by the ancient writers, who relate how Achilles and many others of these old Princes were given over to be brought up and trained by Chiron the Centaur; since the only meaning of their having for instructor one who was half man and half beast is, that it is necessary for a Prince to know how to use both natures, and that the one without the other has no stability.

But since a Prince should know how to use the beast's nature wisely, he ought of beasts to choose both the lion and the fox; for the lion cannot guard himself from the toils, nor the fox from wolves. He must therefore be a fox to discern toils, and a lion to drive off wolves.

To rely wholly on the lion is unwise; and for this reason a prudent Prince neither can nor ought to keep his word when to keep it is hurtful to him and the causes which led him to pledge it are removed. If all men were good, this would not be good advice, but since they are dishonest and do not keep faith with you, you, in return, need not keep faith with them; and no prince was ever at a loss for plausible reasons to cloak a breach of faith. Of this numberless recent instances could be given, and it might be shown how many solemn treaties and engagements have been rendered inoperative and idle through want of faith in Princes, and that he who was best known to play the fox has had the best success.

*Source:* Niccolò Machiavelli. *The Prince.* Harvard Classics, vol. 36, pp. 30–31, 50–51, 57–61. New York: P.F. Collier, 1910.

### Questions

In what sense was Agathocles the Sicilian a "good" ruler? Does Machiavelli approve or disapprove of his conduct?

What does Machiavelli mean when he says that the Prince should be both a fox and a lion?

What vices should the Prince have? How will these vices work to the benefit of the Prince's subjects?

## 9. IMPORTANT HISTORICAL FACTS: STUDY DRILLS

### A. Multiple Choice

1. The Italian city-states served as centers for the Italian Renaissance because
   A. they were isolated from the rest of Europe.
   B. they had suffered the ravages of the Black Death.
   C. they had become prosperous as a result of expanded commerce.
   D. they were ruled by powerful kings.
2. Which of the following *cannot* be found in Florence?
   A. the Duomo Cathedral
   B. the Arno River
   C. Filippo Brunelleschi's Foundling Hospital
   D. the Sistine Chapel
3. Florence was governed by
   A. the Signoria.
   B. the Papal States.
   C. the Doge.
   D. the Ciompi.
4. Renaissance humanism was typified by
   A. a fierce critique of Christianity.
   B. a rediscovery of classical Latin and Greek texts.
   C. a rejection of political activism in favor of retreat from the world.
   D. a return to medieval scholasticism.
5. Renaissance women were expected to
   A. live independent lives.
   B. serve their husbands.
   C. become scholars.
   D. train for the military.
6. Leonardo da Vinci's *Mona Lisa* was famous because
   A. it was such a realistic portrait.
   B. it was very expensive.
   C. it was a noteworthy example of religious art.
   D. it attempted to portray the soul as well as the body of its subject.
7. The "High Renaissance" took place during the years
   A. 1330–1530.
   B. 1475–1564.
   C. 1490–1530.
   D. 1550–1600.
8. The status of Renaissance artists rose because
   A. they were craftsmen.
   B. their parents were often shopkeepers or artisans.
   C. they practiced a "mechanical art."
   D. their art reflected a quest for beauty and the divine.
9. The Italian Renaissance fell into decline due to
   A. Columbus' voyages of exploration.

B. foreign invasions.

C. the continued economic primacy of the Italian city-states.

D. the Peace of Lodi.

10. Machiavelli's political thought is marked by

A. realism.

B. religious mysticism.

C. anti-Italian sentiment.

D. anti-militarism.

## B. Chronological Relationships

1. List the following events in chronological order:

Girolamo Savonarola is hanged and burned in Florence.

The Ottoman conquest of Constantinople.

The troops of Holy Roman Emperor Charles V sack Rome.

Pope Julius II commissions Michelangelo to paint the ceiling of the Sistine Chapel.

Machiavelli writes *The Prince.*

Castiglione's *Courtier* is published.

The "Reign" of Lorenzo de' Medici in Florence.

Bartholomew Dias rounds the Cape of Good Hope.

The Peace of Lodi.

The French king Charles VIII invades Italy.

2. Select one of the major artists of the High Renaissance mentioned in the text and write a one-sentence explanation of how his life might have been affected (directly or indirectly) by each of the ten events listed above.

## C. Fill in the Blanks

1. Military leaders who hired themselves out for pay, like Francesco Sforza, played an important role in the politics of the Italian city-states. These mercenary soldiers were known as _____.

2. While some Italian city-states were ruled by princely despots, others— Venice, Siena, Lucca, and Florence—

were dominated by constitutional oligarchies. The governments of these states were identified as _____.

3. A "universal man," the _____ learned to paint, sing, read both classical and modern languages, write poetry, and engage in athletic activities, all with the aim of serving and pleasing his prince.

4. During the Renaissance, wealthy individuals like Pope Leo X and Isabella d'Este used their fortunes to purchase works of art. This financial support of the creative activities of artists is known as _____.

5. _____ believed that eternal ideas existed beyond the realm of everyday life and that the human mind could transcend human nature. Their ideas had an important influence on Renaissance painters.

6. Based on mathematical laws, _____ was used by Renaissance artists to lend a greater naturalism and dimensionality to their paintings.

7. During the 1520s, Renaissance art became increasingly marked by drama and emotionalism. This style was known as _____.

8. A charismatic monk, _____ took control of Florence after the French invasion of 1494, but he was executed by his enemies in 1498.

9. Name the cities with which each of the following powerful families are usually associated:

A. Borgia _____

B. Este _____

C. Gonzaga _____

D. Medici _____

E. Sforza _____

10. Name the painters of the following works:

A. *The Birth of Venus* _____

B. The ceiling of the Sistine Chapel _____

C. *The Expulsion of Adam and Eve from Eden* _____

D. *The Last Supper* _____

E. *The Madonna di Foligno* _____

# IMPORTANT HISTORICAL FACTS: STUDY-DRILL ANSWERS

## A. Multiple Choice

1. C. they had become prosperous as a result of expanded commerce.
2. D. The Sistine Chapel
3. A. the Signoria.
4. B. a rediscovery of classical Latin and Greek texts.
5. B. serve their husbands.
6. D. it attempted to portray the soul as well as the body of its subject.
7. C. 1490–1530.
8. D. their art reflected a quest for beauty and the divine.
9. B. foreign invasions.
10. A. realism.

## B. Chronological Relationships

| | |
|---|---|
| 1453 | The Ottoman conquest of Constantinople. |
| 1454 | The Peace of Lodi. |
| 1469–1492 | The "Reign" of Lorenzo de' Medici in Florence. |
| 1487 | Bartholomew Dias rounds the Cape of Good Hope. |
| 1494 | The French king Charles VIII invades Italy. |
| 1498 | Girolamo Savonarola is hanged and burned in Florence. |
| 1508 | Pope Julius II commissions Michelangelo to paint the ceiling of the Sistine Chapel. |
| 1513 | Machiavelli writes *The Prince* |
| 1527 | Castiglione's *Courtier* is published. |
| 1527 | The troops of Holy Roman Emperor Charles V sack Rome. |

## C. Fill in the Blanks

1. condottieri
2. republics
3. courtier
4. patronage
5. neo-Platonists *mind is stronger than nature*
6. perspective
7. mannerism
8. Savonarola
9. A. Rome; B. Ferrara; C. Mantua; D. Florence; E. Milan
10. A. Botticelli; B. Michelangelo; C. Masaccio; D. Leonardo da Vinci; E. Raphael

# 3 The Two Reformations

## 1. CHAPTER OUTLINE

I. Italy long remained the only region affected by the Renaissance, but a NORTHERN RENAISSANCE began in about 1460.
   - A. NORTHERN ART AND HUMANISM: Italian artistic models and humanist scholarship were gradually disseminated throughout Northern Europe. In the north, the revival of classical learning produced a critique of scholasticism and religious abuses.
   - B. ERASMUS' HUMANISTIC CRITIQUE OF THE CHURCH was highly influential in the north, and helped stimulate the development of a distinctive Christian humanism.

II. THE ROOTS OF THE REFORMATION lay in an erosion of the power of the papacy due to the emergence of monarchical states and to the papacy's own failure to address abuses within the Catholic Church.
   - A. THE GREAT SCHISM (1378–1417) seriously undermined the authority of the papacy and allowed lay rulers to establish national churches over which they exercised considerable control.
   - B. HERETICAL AND SPIRITUAL MOVEMENTS grew up as a reaction against the inadequacies of the papacy. Both Wyclif and Hus called for a more direct relationship between the individual worshiper and God, and they were condemned by the Church for their efforts.
   - C. THE CHALLENGE OF CONCILIARISM TO PAPAL AUTHORITY: Criticism of the papacy was also voiced within the Church. A conciliar movement sought to place limits on the power of the pope, but the councils were effectively silenced in the mid-fifteenth century.
   - D. CLERICAL ABUSES AND INDULGENCES: Financial and moral abuses, especially the sale of indulgences, drew increasing criticism of the Church, but the papacy persisted in affirming its right to run the Church as it saw fit.
   - E. MARTIN LUTHER, a scholarly German monk wracked with worry about his personal unworthiness, came forward to challenge the papacy. At first he merely attacked abuses, but he soon broke entirely with the Church, emphasizing the "freedom of a Christian" and arguing that faith alone was necessary for salvation.

III. SOCIAL BACKGROUND OF THE REFORMATION IN THE GERMAN STATES: Luther's personal break with the Church soon generated a large-scale movement for religious reform.

26

A. URBAN CENTERS OF REFORM: Traditions of municipal liberties and popular participation in government facilitated the spread of religious reform in many German cities.

B. THE PROCESS OF REFORM: Middle-class clergy and ordinary members of the community worked together in support of reform. Divisions between clergy and worshipers diminished as the Lutheran idea of the "priesthood of all believers" came to be widely accepted.

C. THE PEASANTS' REVOLT: The outbreak of the Reformation in urban areas sparked a revolt among the German peasantry. Luther was sympathetic to the plight of the poor, but he also rejected this insurrection in no uncertain terms and supported the German princes who brutally crushed the revolt.

IV. THE SPREAD OF THE REFORMATION brought increasing hostilities between Catholics and "Protestants," especially as the reform movement became embroiled in imperial politics.

A. DIVISIONS WITHIN CHRISTENDOM became more decisive as the reform movement spread, and Catholic humanists such as Erasmus found themselves caught in the middle.

B. CHARLES V AND THE PROTESTANTS: Preoccupied with wars against France and the Ottoman Empire, Holy Roman Emperor Charles V, still devoutly Catholic, tolerated the spread of Protestantism, but once hostilities had ended, he moved against the Protestant princes.

C. THE PEACE OF AUGSBURG ended the conflict between Catholic and Protestant leaders in Germany. A compromise settlement, it stipulated that a state's religion would be determined by the faith of its ruler.

V. THE REFORMATION IN SWITZERLAND AND FRANCE drew on Luther's reforms, but soon produced divisions within Protestantism.

A. ZWINGLI AND REFORM: Swiss reformer Zwingli converted Zurich to Protestantism, but broke with Luther over the meaning of the Eucharist.

B. RADICAL REFORMERS like the Anabaptists refused to participate in political life, in an attempt to escape the sinful secular world. Both Catholic and Protestant rulers forcibly repressed dissident religious movements that rejected state authority.

C. JEAN CALVIN AND REFORM: The originator of the second major current of the Reformation, French reformer Calvin formulated a theology emphasizing predestination and the creation of a righteous community on earth. Accepted as the spiritual head of the Swiss city of Geneva, he imposed a strict religious orthodoxy on its citizenry.

D. CALVINIST CONVERSIONS in France and the Netherlands produced intense hostilities between Catholic rulers and their Protestant subjects.

VI. THE REFORMATION IN ENGLAND was initiated by the king, but enjoyed substantial popular support as a result of widespread discontentment with the papacy.

A. HENRY VIII AND THE BREAK WITH ROME: Henry VIII's desire for a divorce from Catherine of Aragon prompted him to cut the ties between the English Church and Rome.

B. AFTER THE BREAK WITH ROME, the Church of England remained doctrinally conservative, accepting the fundamental tenets of Lutheranism but also retaining certain elements of Catholicism.

*cuius regio eius religio*

VII. THE CATHOLIC REFORMATION was both a defensive response to the Protestant movement and an internal reform effort.
   A. The papacy answered the reformers with a RETREAT TO DOGMATISM, using the Inquisition to enforce religious conformity.
   B. IGNATIUS OF LOYOLA AND THE JESUITS served the pope as aggressive crusaders for the Catholic Reformation, reconverting Europeans and missionizing throughout the world.
   C. THE COUNCIL OF TRENT reasserted the validity of all Catholic dogma, making the split within Western Christendom irreparable.
   D. PUTTING ITS HOUSE IN ORDER: The Catholic Church also sought to end abuses condemned by Protestant reformers, disciplining the clergy and infusing new vigor into personal religious devotion.

VIII. CULTURE DURING THE TWO REFORMATIONS: Reformation brought cultural as well as religious change.
   A. THE BAROQUE STYLE— monumental, flamboyant, theatrically religious—emerged as the artistic complement to the Catholic Reformation.
   B. PRINT CULTURE helped to disseminate the Protestant reform message and to create a vernacular lay culture.
   C. LAY EDUCATION AND READING were supported by Protestant reformers, who encouraged ordinary individuals to learn to read so that they could study the Bible.
   D. Both Catholic and Protestant leaders sought to eliminate POPULAR RITUALS AND FESTIVALS, which were deemed "barbaric" pagan remnants by social and political elites.
   E. THE ROLE OF WOMEN: Protestants affirmed the dignity of family life and marriage for women, while Catholics emphasized the virtues of female chastity—but both insisted on women's subservience to men. Hostility toward popular religion and anxiety about female sexuality combined to produce witch hunts throughout Europe.

IX. THE LEGACY OF THE TWO REFORMATIONS: Protestantism raised the question of the proper relationship between church and state, with most reformers opting for the subordination of the church to the state. Lingering tensions between Catholics and Protestants would result in religious wars in the seventeenth century.

## 2. HISTORICAL GEOGRAPHY

**Map Exercises**

Familiarize yourself with the maps provided in your text, and then attempt to locate the following places on Blank Map 3.1.

URBAN CENTERS OF REFORM

Augsburg
Basel
Bologna
Cologne
Constance
Erfurt
Geneva
Hamburg
La Rochelle
Mainz
Münster
Nuremberg
Oxford
Regensburg
Rome
Speyer
Trent
Wittenberg
Worms
Zurich

RADICAL RELIGION IN THE HOLY ROMAN EMPIRE

Alsace
Austria
Bohemia
Hesse
Moravia
Netherlands
Switzerland
Thuringia
Tyrol
West Prussia
Wurttemberg

**MAP 3.1 URBAN CENTERS OF REFORM/RADICAL RELIGION IN THE HOLY ROMAN EMPIRE**

**Map Questions**

Where did the German peasants' revolt take place?

Make a list of the primarily Catholic regions in Europe and locate them on the map. Do the same for Protestant Europe, distinguishing between the centers of Calvinism and of Lutheranism.

Where in the Holy Roman Empire were radical religious movements centered?

## 3. PEOPLE AND TERMS TO IDENTIFY

Albrecht Dürer
Desiderius Erasmus
Christian Humanism
Great Schism
John Wyclif
Conciliarism
Indulgences
Martin Luther
The 95 Theses
Edict of Worms
German Peasants' Revolt

Protestants
Charles V
Schmalkaldic League
Peace of Augsburg
Huldrych Zwingli
Sacramentarian
  Controversy
Anabaptists
Jean Calvin
Predestination
Consistory

Henry VIII
Act of Supremacy
Catholic Reformation
Ignatius of Loyola
Society of Jesus (Jesuits)
Council of Trent
Confraternities
Baroque
Gianlorenzo Bernini
Printing Press

## 4. STUDY QUESTIONS

1. *Historical Continuities:* What characteristics distinguished the Northern Renaissance from the earlier Italian Renaissance?

2. Why was the papacy subject to increasing criticism in the fourteenth and fifteenth centuries? Who were its most outspoken critics?

3. What specific financial and moral abuses sparked opposition to the papacy?

4. Why did Martin Luther break with the Catholic Church? How were his personal religious concerns reflected in his theology?

5. Why did Martin Luther's personal act of defiance result in a rejection of papal authority and Catholic doctrine throughout much of Germany? Why was the Reformation most successful in the German states and Switzerland?

6. How did ordinary people demonstrate their allegiance to the Reformation?

7. What caused the German Peasant Revolt of 1525–1526?

8. How did the Reformation reinforce German particularism? *Historical Continuities:* How successful do you think the Peace of Augsburg would prove to be?

9. How did the Swiss Reformation differ from the German Reformation?

10. What distinguished Calvin's thought from that of other Protestant leaders?

11. How was Geneva governed under Calvin?

12. What caused the English Reformation? To what extent was it a genuine religious reform movement?

13. How did Counter-Reformation leaders like Ignatius of Loyola revitalize the Catholic Church during the sixteenth century?

14. In what sense was the Council of Trent a conservative response to the Protestant Reformation?

15. How did the two Reformations affect the lives of ordinary people?

16. Compare and contrast Protestant and Catholic attitudes toward women.

## 5. ANALYZING ART AND ARTIFACTS

Analyze the portraits of important Northern European religious and political figures reproduced in your textbook (pp. 93, 100, 122, and 123) as expressions of the Northern Renaissance. In what ways are they similar to Italian Renaissance portraits? How do they differ?

Contrast the Calvinist church shown in the illustration on p. 116 with Bernini's *Ecstasy of Saint Theresa* (p. 130), which served as an altarpiece in a Roman chapel. How do these two religious artifacts differ in their style and ornamentation? What is distinctively Catholic about Bernini's work? What is distinctively Protestant about the Calvinist church? What does this tell us about the differences between Protestant and Catholic religious sensibilities?

## 6. TECHNOLOGY AND HISTORY

What was the cultural impact of printing during the age of reform?

How do you think literacy and access to books affected ordinary people's religious beliefs and allegiances during the sixteenth century?

## 7. HISTORICAL ANALYSIS: INTERPRETIVE ESSAYS

1. *Historical Continuities:* What long-term factors, whether religious or otherwise, caused the Protestant Reformation?

2. Why did Martin Luther's attack on abuses in the Catholic Church result in the collapse of the unity of Western Christendom?

3. What theological doctrines separated Protestant reformers from Catholic reformers?

4. How did the religious "revolution" of the sixteenth century affect non-religious (i.e., political, social, cultural) aspects of life in Europe?

5. *Historical Continuities:* Writing as an intelligent observer of the European scene in 1555, predict what will happen in the next 200 years as the result of the Protestant and Catholic Reformations.

## 8. HISTORICAL VOICES: PROTESTANT REFORM AND CATHOLIC REFORM

### A. Martin Luther and the Protestant Critique of the Catholic Church

Destined for a career in law by his father, Martin Luther (1483–1546) rejected that worldly profession in favor of life as a monk. Yet even after he entered a monastery, Luther did not find the spiritual security he sought. It was not until he became convinced that salvation came through faith alone—and not good works—that he felt himself "to have been born again, and to have entered through open gates into paradise itself." Luther's soul-searching gradually led him away from orthodox Catholic theology, and this personal dilemma became a public scandal when he posted his 95 Theses on the church door at Wittenberg in 1517.

A fierce critic of the political and spiritual corruption of the Roman Catholic hierarchy, Luther began by attacking indulgences and finished by rejecting the very authority of the pope. In his address "To the Christian Nobility of the German Nation," written before his definitive break with the Church, Luther attacked the Catholic leadership for its refusal to respond to criticism and its failure to introduce fundamental reforms in both theology and practice. The work was both a ringing affirmation of the individual Christian's right to speak her or his conscience, and of the German states' rights to protest "Romish" tyranny.

### FROM *Address to the German Nobility* by Martin Luther

The time for silence is gone, and the time to speak has come, as we read in Ecclesiastes (iii. 7). I have, in conformity with our resolve, put together some few points concerning the *reformation of the Christian estate*, with the intent of placing the same before the *Christian nobility of the German nation*, in case it may please God to help His Church by means of the laity, inasmuch as the clergy, whom this task rather befitted, have become quite careless. . . .

#### THE THREE WALLS OF THE ROMANISTS

The Romanists have, with great adroitness, drawn three walls round themselves, with which they have hitherto protected themselves, so that no one could reform them, whereby all Christendom has fallen terribly.

Firstly, if pressed by the temporal power, they have affirmed and maintained that the temporal power has no jurisdiction over them, but, on the contrary, that the spiritual power is above the temporal.

Secondly, if it were proposed to admonish them with the Scriptures, they objected that no one may interpret the Scriptures but the Pope.

Thirdly, if they are threatened with a council, they pretend that no one may call a council but the Pope.

Thus they have secretly stolen our three rods, so that they may be unpunished, and intrenched themselves behind these three walls, to act with all the wickedness and malice, which we now witness. And whenever they have been compelled to call a council, they have made it of no avail by binding the princes beforehand with an oath to leave them as they were, and to give moreover to the Pope full power over the procedure of the council, so that it is all one whether we have many councils or no councils, in addition to which they deceive us with false pretences and tricks. So grievously do they tremble for their skin before a true, free council; and thus they have overawed kings and princes, that these believe they would be offending God, if they were not to obey them in all such knavish, deceitful artifices.

Now may God help us, and give us one of those trumpets that overthrew the walls of Jericho, so that we may blow down these walls of straw and paper, and that we may set free our Christian rods for the chastisement of sin, and expose the craft and deceit of the devil, so that we may amend ourselves by punishment and again obtain God's favour. . . .

Let us, in the first place, attack the first wall.

It has been devised that the Pope, bishops, priests, and monks are called the *spiritual estate*, princes, lords, artificers, and peasants are the *temporal estate*. This is an artful lie and hypocritical device, but let no one be made afraid by it, and that for this reason: that all Christians are truly of the spiritual estate, and there is no difference among them, save of office alone. As St. Paul says (I Cor. xii.), we are all one body, though each member does its own work, to serve the others. This is because we have one baptism, one Gospel, one faith, and are all Christians alike; for baptism, Gospel, and faith, these alone make spiritual and Christian people. . . .

The second wall is even more tottering and weak: that they alone pretend to be considered masters of the Scriptures; although they learn nothing of them all their life. They assume authority, and juggle before us with impudent words, saying that the Pope cannot err in matters of faith, whether he be evil or good, albeit they cannot prove it by a single letter. That is why the canon law contains so many heretical and unchristian, nay unnatural, laws; but of these we need not speak now. For whereas they imagine the Holy Ghost never leaves them, however unlearned and wicked they may be, they grow bold enough to decree whatever they like. But were this true, where were the need and use of the Holy Scriptures? Let us burn them, and content ourselves with the unlearned gentlemen at Rome, in whom the Holy Ghost dwells, who, however, can dwell in pious souls only. If I had not read it, I could never have believed that the devil should have put forth such follies at Rome and find a following. . . .

The third wall falls of itself, as soon as the first two have fallen; for if the Pope acts contrary to the Scriptures, we are bound to stand by the Scriptures, to punish and to constrain him, according to Christ's commandment, "Moreover, if thy brother shall trespass against thee, go and tell him his fault between thee and him alone; if he shall hear thee, thou hast gained thy brother. But if he will not hear thee, then take with thee one or two more, that in the mouth of two or three witnesses every word may be established. And if he shall neglect to hear them, tell it unto the Church; but if he neglect to hear the Church, let him be unto thee as a heathen man and a publican" (St. Matt. xviii. 15–17). Here each member is commanded to take care for the other; much more then should we do this, if it is a ruling member of the community that does evil, which by its evil-doing causes great harm and offence to the others. If then I am to accuse him before the Church, I must collect the Church together. Moreover, they can show nothing in the Scriptures giving the Pope sole power to call and confirm councils; they have nothing but their own laws; but these hold good only so long as they are not injurious to Christianity and the laws of God. Therefore, if the Pope deserves punishment, these laws cease to bind us, since Christendom would suffer, if he were not punished by a council. . . .

And now I hope the false, lying spectre will be laid with which the Romanists have long terrified and stupefied our consciences. And it will be seen that, like all the rest of us, they are subject to the temporal sword; that they have no authority to interpret the Scriptures by force without skill; and that they have no power to prevent a council, or to pledge it in accordance with their pleasure, or to bind it beforehand, and deprive it of its freedom; and that if they do this, they are verily of the fellowship of antichrist and the devil, and have nothing of Christ but the name.

*Source:* Martin Luther. *Address to the German Nobility Concerning Christian Liberty.* Harvard Classics, vol. 36, pp. 274, 277–9, 283–4, 286, 288. New York: P.F. Collier, 1910.

## Questions

What are the "three walls" of the "Romanists"? What arguments does Luther use to knock them down?

Which fundamental tenets of Protestantism can be derived from Luther's statements?

What are the *political* implications of Luther's arguments?

## B. Ignatius of Loyola and the Catholic Reformation

Saint Ignatius of Loyola (1491–1556) was born into the Spanish nobility and spent his early years as a courtier and soldier. Having been seriously wounded at the siege of Pamplona, he underwent a religious experience during his convalescence and decided to dedicate his life to the Church. He was eventually ordained as a priest and founded the Society of Jesus (the Jesuits).

As a former military man, Ignatius perceived of himself and his followers as soldiers in the service of Christ. The Jesuits served as the shock troops of the Catholic Reformation, working to reconvert Europeans and to win new converts throughout the rest of the world. Excelling in education and missionary work, the order was a key factor in the sixteenth- and seventeenth-century reform and revitalization of the Roman Catholic Church. In his "To Have the True Sentiment Which We Ought to Have in the Church Militant," taken from his longer work, *The Spiritual Exercises*, Ignatius responds to critiques of the Catholic Church (like Luther's above) and reaffirms the basic tenets of Catholic orthodoxy.

### FROM *The Spiritual Exercises* by St. Ignatius of Loyola

TO HAVE THE TRUE SENTIMENT
WHICH WE OUGHT TO HAVE IN THE CHURCH MILITANT

Let the following Rules be observed.

*First Rule.* The first: All judgment laid aside, we ought to have our mind ready and prompt to obey, in all, the true Spouse of Christ our Lord, which is our holy Mother the Church Hierarchical.

*Second Rule.* The second: To praise confession to a Priest, and the reception of the most Holy Sacrament of the Altar once in the year, and much more each month, and much better from week to week, with the conditions required and due.

*Third Rule.* The third: To praise the hearing of Mass often, likewise hymns, psalms, and long prayers, in the church and out of it; likewise the hours set at the time fixed for each Divine Office and for all prayer and all Canonical Hours.

*Fourth Rule.* The fourth: To praise much Religious Orders, virginity and continence, and not so much marriage as any of these.

*Fifth Rule.* The fifth: To praise vows of Religion, of obedience, of poverty, of chastity and of other perfections of supererogation. And it is to be noted that as the vow is about the things which approach to Evangelical perfection, a vow ought not to be made in the things which withdraw from it, such as to be a merchant, or to be married, etc.

*Sixth Rule.* To praise relics of the Saints, giving veneration to them and praying to the Saints; and to praise Stations, pilgrimages, Indulgences, pardons, Cruzadas, and candles lighted in the churches.

*Seventh Rule.* To praise Constitutions about fasts and abstinence, as of Lent, Ember Days, Vigils, Friday and Saturday; likewise penances, not only interior, but also exterior.

*Eighth Rule.* To praise the ornaments and the buildings of churches; likewise images, and to venerate them according to what they represent.

*Ninth Rule.* Finally, to praise all precepts of the Church, keeping the mind prompt to find reasons in their defence and in no manner against them.

*Tenth Rule.* We ought to be more prompt to find good and praise as well the Constitutions and recommendations as the ways of our Superiors. Because, although some are not or have not been such, to speak against them, whether preaching in public or discoursing before the common people, would rather give rise to fault-finding and scandal than profit; and so the people would be incensed against their Superiors, whether temporal or spiritual. So that, as it does harm to speak evil to the common people of Superiors in their absence, so it can make profit to speak of the evil ways to the persons themselves who can remedy them.

*Eleventh Rule.* To praise positive and scholastic learning. . . .

*Twelfth Rule.* We ought to be on our guard in making comparison of those of us who are alive to the blessed passed away, because error is committed not a little in this; that is to say, in saying, this one knows more than St. Augustine; he is another, or greater than, St. Francis; he is another St. Paul in goodness, holiness, etc.

*Thirteenth Rule.* To be right in everything, we ought always to hold that the white which I see, is black, if the Hierarchical Church so decides it, believing that between Christ our Lord, the Bridegroom, and the Church, His Bride, there is the same Spirit which governs and directs us for the salvation of our souls. Because by the same Spirit and our Lord Who gave the ten Commandments, our holy Mother the Church is directed and governed.

*Fourteenth Rule.* Although there is much truth in the assertion that no one can save himself without being predestined and without having faith and grace; we must be very cautious in the manner of speaking and communicating with others about all these things.

*Fifteenth Rule.* We ought not, by way of custom, to speak much of predestination; but if in some way and at some times one speaks, let him so speak that the common people may not come into any error, as sometimes happens, saying: Whether I have to be saved or condemned is already determined, and no other thing can now be, through my doing well or ill; and with this, growing lazy, they become negligent in the works which lead to the salvation and the spiritual profit of their souls.

*Sixteenth Rule.* In the same way, we must be on our guard that by talking much and with much insistence of faith, without any distinction and explanation, occasion be not given to the people to be lazy and slothful in works, whether before faith is formed in charity or after.

*Seventeenth Rule.* Likewise, we ought not to speak so much with insistence on grace that the poison of discarding liberty be engendered.

So that of faith and grace one can speak as much as is possible with the Divine help for the greater praise of His Divine Majesty, but not in such way, nor in such manners, especially in our so dangerous times, that works and free will receive any harm, or be held for nothing.

*Eighteenth Rule.* Although serving God our Lord much out of pure love is to be esteemed above all; we ought to praise much the fear of His Divine Majesty, because not only filial fear is a thing pious and most holy, but even servile fear—when the man reaches nothing else better or more useful—helps much to get out of mortal sin. And when he is out, he easily comes to filial fear, which is all acceptable and grateful to God our Lord: as being at one with the Divine Love.

*Source:* St. Ignatius of Loyola. "To Have the True Sentiment Which We Ought to Have in the Church Militant." In *The Spiritual Exercises,* pp. 92–94. Trans. Father Elder Mullan, S. J. New York: P. J. Kenedy & Sons, 1914.

### Questions

In what sense are these rules intended as a rebuttal of Protestant theology?

What sort of a relationship do these rules establish between the individual Catholic and the Church?

Ignatius has often been criticized for his insistence on blind obedience to the dictates of the Church (especially as expressed in Rule 13). What are the theological underpinnings of this argument? To what extent would Luther and Calvin disagree with this principle?

## 9. IMPORTANT HISTORICAL FACTS: STUDY DRILLS

### A. Multiple Choice

1. In Northern Europe, Renaissance scholarship had a strongly religious focus, and for this reason it is known as
   A. the Baroque.
   B. the Catholic Reformation.
   C. Christian Humanism.
   D. Conciliarism.
2. The Catholic Church was criticized for claiming that the faithful might shorten their stay in Purgatory through the purchase of
   A. indulgences.
   B. sacraments.
   C. saints' relics.
   D. ecclesiastical posts.
3. The "sacramentarian controversy" arose over the issue of
   A. Henry VIII's marriage.
   B. excommunication.
   C. communion.
   D. the baptism of infants.
4. One group of especially radical reformers were known as
   A. Jesuits.
   B. Christian humanists.
   C. Sectarians.
   D. Anabaptists.
5. Jean Calvin is most often associated with the doctrine of
   A. Anti-Trinitarianism.
   B. Predestination.
   C. Nominalism.
   D. Nepotism.
6. Geneva was ruled by
   A. the Schmalkaldic League.
   B. Michael Servetus.
   C. Charles V.
   D. a Consistory.
7. Between 1545 and 1563 Catholic Church leaders met to reaffirm the fundamentals of Catholic dogma in response to the Protestant Reformation. This series of meetings was known as
   A. the Council of Trent.
   B. the Great Schism.
   C. the Council of Constance.
   D. the Hanseatic League.
8. During the Catholic Reformation, laypeople were encouraged to form new devotional brotherhoods known as
   A. councils.
   B. diets.
   C. confraternities.
   D. leagues.
9. Bernini's *Ecstasy of Saint Theresa* is considered a representative work of
   A. Classical art.
   B. Baroque art.
   C. Northern Renaissance art.
   D. Christian Humanist art.
10. The printing press did everything *but*
    A. cause the Protestant Reformation.
    B. encourage the publication of vernacular literature.
    C. encourage the expansion of lay literacy.
    D. make Luther's writings available to a mass audience.

### B. Chronological Relationships

1. List the following events in chronological order and identify the date on which each occurred:
   The Foundation of the Society of Jesus
   The Formation of the Schmalkaldic League
   The Conclusion of the Council of Trent
   The Edict of Worms
   The Peace of Augsburg
   The Act of Supremacy
   The Great Schism
   The Posting of the 95 Theses
   The Trial of Michael Servetus
   The German Peasants' Revolt

2. Explain the relationship between each of the events listed above and the chronological development of the Protestant Reformation.

## C. Matching Exercise: Historical Actors

\_\_\_\_\_ Albrecht Dürer
\_\_\_\_\_ Desiderius Erasmus
\_\_\_\_\_ John Wyclif
\_\_\_\_\_ Martin Luther
\_\_\_\_\_ Charles V
\_\_\_\_\_ Huldrych Zwingli
\_\_\_\_\_ Jean Calvin
\_\_\_\_\_ Henry VIII
\_\_\_\_\_ Ignatius of Loyola
\_\_\_\_\_ Gianlorenzo Bernini

A. Though a pious Catholic, this Holy Roman emperor was too distracted by war with France and the Ottoman Empire to move against the German Protestants until the 1540s.

B. A Swiss Protestant leader, he rejected Luther's conception of communion, arguing that Christ's body and blood were only *symbolically* present in the Eucharist, and died fighting Catholic troops at the Battle of Kappel.

C. A Spanish noble, this former military man was a staunch supporter of the papacy and organized the Society of Jesus as a mainstay of the Catholic Reformation.

D. Born in France, this Protestant religious leader moved to Switzerland, where he emphasized the doctrine of predestination in his theological writings and exercised significant political power over the city of Geneva.

E. An early critic of the Church, this English cleric and scholar questioned papal authority and re-emphasized the importance of faith, prefiguring later Reformation thought and inspiring a movement whose followers became known as Lollards.

F. This king of England broke with the Catholic Church because Pope Clement VII refused to annul his marriage to Catherine of Aragon.

G. A key proponent of the Christian Humanism of the Northern Renaissance, he criticized the failings of the Roman Catholic Church, but never broke with it.

H. A great master of the baroque style, this Venetian sculptor expressed the religious intensity of the Catholic Reformation in his ornate creations.

I. An influential and successful German artist, he traveled to Italy to study the works of the artists of the Italian Renaissance.

J. His 95 Theses attacked the theoretical underpinnings of the sale of indulgences, and began the process that would lead to the Protestant break with the Catholic Church.

## IMPORTANT HISTORICAL FACTS: STUDY-DRILL ANSWERS

### A. Multiple Choice

1. C. Christian Humanism.
2. A. indulgences.
3. C. communion.
4. D. Anabaptists.
5. B. predestination.
6. D. a Consistory.
7. A. the Council of Trent.
8. C. confraternities.
9. B. Baroque art.
10. A. cause the Protestant Reformation.

### B. Chronological Relationships

1378–1417 The Great Schism
1517 The Posting of the 95 Theses
1521 The Edict of Worms
1525–1526 The German Peasants' Revolt
1531 The Formation of the Schmalkaldic League
1534 The Act of Supremacy
1539 The Foundation of the Society of Jesus
1553 The Trial of Michael Servetus
1555 The Peace of Augsburg
1563 The Conclusion of the Council of Trent

**C. Matching Exercise: Historical Actors**

I.  Albrecht Dürer

G. Desiderius Erasmus

E.  John Wyclif

J.  Martin Luther

A. Charles V

B. Huldrych Zwingli

D. Jean Calvin

F.  Henry VIII

C. Ignatius of Loyola

H. Gianlorenzo Bernini

# 4 *The Wars of Religion*

## 1. CHAPTER OUTLINE

I. THE WARS OF RELIGION IN SIXTEENTH-CENTURY FRANCE broke out during a period of economic crisis in France and of conflict between the French monarchy and the nobility.

A. A STRENGTHENED MONARCHY: Under Francis I, the French throne had greatly expanded its power at the expense of the French Catholic Church and the nobility.

B. Rapid population growth produced an ECONOMIC CRISIS in the mid-sixteenth century. Nobles of modest means suffered a loss of revenues, but taxes and tithes weighed especially heavily on peasants, who occasionally rose up in revolt against state taxation and the exactions of noble landowners.

C. FRENCH CALVINISTS AND THE CRISIS OF THE FRENCH STATE: During the reigns of Catherine de Medici's three weak sons, French nobles' desire to limit the encroaching power of the monarchy and the conversion of many among them to Calvinism combined with the economic crisis to produce chronic warfare between the noble Guise, Montmorency, and Bourbon families.

D. HENRY OF NAVARRE, a Protestant member of the Bourbon family, became heir to the French throne, but was forced to fight long and hard against the Guises before he could be crowned Henry IV.

E. RESTORING STABILITY TO FRANCE: Having converted to Catholicism for reasons of state, Henry IV sought to heal the wounds of civil war and to improve the financial standing of the monarchy. In 1598 his Edict of Nantes established Catholicism as the official religion of France, but it also extended tolerance to French Protestants, whose rights of worship it guaranteed.

F. STATEMAKING: Henry IV re-established the authority of the French monarchy through the creation of a state bureaucracy, the imposition of firm tax policies, and the encouragement of economic development.

G. LOUIS XIII AND THE ORIGINS OF ABSOLUTE RULE: Despite his personal shortcomings, Louis XIII continued his father's policy of consolidating the absolute power of the monarchy. During the ministry of Cardinal Richelieu, the French state was further centralized and tax revenues greatly increased.

II. THE THIRTY YEARS' WAR (1618–1648) devastated Central Europe. It arose out of religious divisions within the German states, but quickly came to involve the dynastic rivalries between European monarchs.

A. FACTIONALISM IN THE HOLY ROMAN EMPIRE grew naturally out of the decentralized nature of this loose confederation of approximately 1,000 separate German states. The Peace of Augsburg had ended religious war between the German princes, but it was an unstable settlement at best.

B. THE ORIGINS OF THE THIRTY YEARS' WAR: During the reign of Holy Roman Emperor Rudolf II, a staunch Catholic, hostilities between Protestant and Catholic princes began to increase in Germany. The effective authority of the emperor declined as princes rallied to a Protestant Union and a Catholic League.

C. CONFLICT IN BOHEMIA: Following the Defenestration of Prague, Bohemian Protestants rose in revolt against the Catholic Church and the Habsburg dynasty. The conflict quickly escalated, and the king of Spain entered on the Catholic side.

D. THE EXPANSION OF THE CONFLICT: The war in Germany took on international proportions as the opposing sides sought support from other European rulers. The Bohemian Protestants were defeated, but the war continued.

E. THE DANISH PERIOD: Christian IV, the Protestant king of Denmark, attacked northern Germany in hope of acquiring new territories, but he failed to enjoy the foreign support he had counted upon, and was defeated by a Catholic army under Count Johannes von Tilly. Holy Roman Emperor Ferdinand II attempted to reimpose Catholicism in regions recaptured by Catholic armies.

F. THE SWEDISH INTERLUDE: Gustavus Adolphus, the Protestant king of Sweden, then intervened at the behest of other Protestant powers. After initial dramatic successes, he was killed and his army defeated by a Catholic army under Albert Wallenstein. The Catholic forces now held the upper hand.

G. THE ARMIES OF THE THIRTY YEARS' WAR: Fighting during this period was exceptionally brutal. Soldiers, engaged either as mercenaries or as volunteers, were forced to live off the land, and often acted with great cruelty toward the civilian population.

H. THE WARS OF RELIGION AND DYNASTIC STRUGGLES (1635–1648): After 1635, the religious war became a dynastic war between France, allied with Sweden, and Austria, allied with Spain. The French won a series of important victories, but internal unrest forced French King Louis XIV to seek peace in 1648.

I. THE TREATY OF WESTPHALIA (1648) settled the religious conflicts in Germany by establishing a degree of toleration for some religious minorities but maintaining rulers' rights to determine the religion of their territories. The German states, shattered by years of war, remained fragmented, reinforcing the particularism of the region. Despite the peace settlement, dynastic rivalries would increase in the future as a result of the growth of centralized absolutist monarchies.

## 2. HISTORICAL GEOGRAPHY

**MAP 4.1  SIXTEENTH-CENTURY FRANCE**

### Map Exercises

Familiarize yourself with the maps provided in your text, and then attempt to locate the following places on Blank Maps 4.1 and 4.2.

SIXTEENTH-CENTURY FRANCE

| | | |
|---|---|---|
| *Provinces:* | Bourgogne | Maine |
| | Brittany | Normandy |
| | Champagne | Périgord |
| | Dauphiné | Picardy |
| | Gascogne | Poitou |
| | Languedoc | Provence |
| | | |
| *Cities:* | Bordeaux | Marseille |
| | Cateau-Cambrésis | Orléans |
| | | Paris |
| | La Rochelle | Toulouse |
| | Lyon | |

CENTRAL EUROPE IN 1648

| | |
|---|---|
| Austria | Poland |
| Bavaria | Pomerania |
| Bohemia | Prussia |
| Brandenburg | Saxony |
| Denmark-Norway | Silesia |
| Dutch United Provinces | Spanish Netherlands |
| Hungary | Styria |
| Mecklenburg | Sweden |
| Moravia | Transylvania |
| Palatinates (Upper and Lower) | Tyrol |

### Map Questions

In which parts of France was Protestantism most successful? In which parts did Catholicism remain the dominant religion?

Where was the Thirty Years' War fought?

How were the borders of Europe changed by the Treaty of Westphalia?

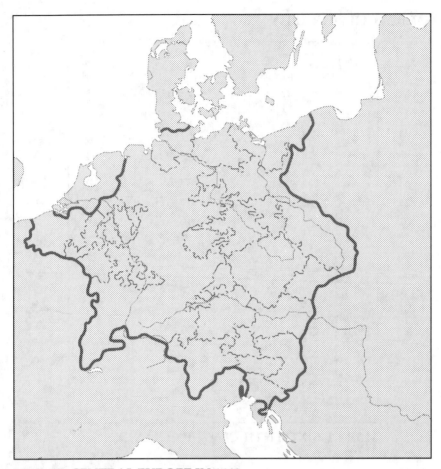

**MAP 4.2  CENTRAL EUROPE IN 1648**

## 3. PEOPLE AND TERMS TO IDENTIFY

The Defenestration of
  Prague
Huguenots
Concordat of Bologna
Poor Wretches
Catherine de Medici
Saint Bartholomew's Day
  Massacre
Politiques

French Catholic League
Henry of Navarre (Henry
  IV)
War of the Three Henrys
Edict of Nantes
Louis XIII
Cardinal Richelieu
The Thirty Years' War
Holy Roman Emperor

Emperor Ferdinand II
German Catholic
  League/Protestant
  Union
Frederick, Elector of the
  Palatinate
Albert Wallenstein
Gustavus Adolphus
The Treaty of Westphalia

## 4. STUDY QUESTIONS

1.  What made the lot of French peasants so difficult in the mid-sixteenth century?

2.  What caused the conflict between the powerful Guise, Montmorency, and Bourbon families in France?

3.  How did Henry of Navarre finally make good his claim to the French throne?

4.  In what sense was Henry IV's reign an exercise in statemaking?

5. How did Cardinal Richelieu help Louis XIII to strengthen further the French monarchy?

6. How did the reign of Rudolf II serve to weaken further the office of Holy Roman emperor?

7. What specific short-term factors led to the outbreak of the Thirty Years' War? *Historical Continuities:* What long-term conditions laid the foundations for this major conflict?

8. Why did the conflict between Catholics and Protestants within the Holy Roman Empire quickly become an international war?

9. Describe the life of a soldier during the Thirty Years' War.

10. How did the Thirty Years' War affect the populations of the German states?

11. *Historical Continuities:* What long-term impact might you expect the Thirty Years' War to have on the European state system?

## 5. ANALYZING ART AND ARTIFACTS

How was the violence of the age of religious wars represented in the art of the period? What does this tell you about perceptions of violence and disorder during this period?

How did representations of the French royal family serve to support their claim to absolute authority?

## 6. TECHNOLOGY AND HISTORY

How did the armies of the Thirty Years' War supply themselves? What sort of problems would provisioning have presented to military planners during this period? How might this problem have affected the conduct of war? What solutions were possible?

## 7. HISTORICAL ANALYSIS: INTERPRETIVE ESSAYS

1. The French monarchy emerged from the French wars of religion with increased power and authority, while the Holy Roman Empire was greatly weakened by the Thirty Years' War. What can explain this disparity between the history of French and German political structures in the sixteenth and seventeenth centuries?

2. Why did the Thirty Years' War last so long and involve so many European nations?

3. To what extent were the "Wars of Religion" fought over religion?

4. *Historical Continuities:* Write an argument in support of the following statement: "From the moment Martin Luther posted his 95 Theses in 1517, the outbreak of a European-wide war was inevitable."

5. *Historical Continuities:* Write a history of European peasant life in the years between 1500 and 1650.

## 8. HISTORICAL VOICES: RESPONSES TO THE WARS OF RELIGION

### A. Montaigne and the Freedom of Conscience

Michel Eyquem de Montaigne (1533–1592) was born in the Périgord region of France. Raised by a noble Catholic father and a Protestant mother of Spanish and Jewish origins, Montaigne had a very happy childhood and received an excellent education. Between 1557 and 1570, he pursued a career as a member of the Parlement of Bordeaux. After Montaigne inherited his father's title and château, he retreated to his famous tower study, dedicating most of the rest of his life to perfecting the "essay"—a term that he himself invented—as a literary and philosophical genre. While his short prose "experiments" address a broad range of topics, all are intended to provide at least partial answers to one fundamental question: "What do I know?"

Conservative in his support for established religion and government, Montaigne was liberal in his insistence that human beings must learn to tolerate one another's differences. In one of his most famous essays, "Of Cannibals," he suggested, with a certain bitter humor, that Europeans who killed one another over religious differences were no less savage than the "cannibals" of the New World. Similarly, in the following excerpt Montaigne returns to the problem of religious toleration, considering the merits of the apostate Roman emperor, Julian, and looking for solutions to France's religious dilemma.

## FROM *The Essays* of Michel de Montaigne

### CHAPTER XIX OF LIBERTY OF CONSCIENCE.

'Tis usual to see good intentions, if carried on without moderation, push men on to very vicious effects. In this dispute, which at this time agitates France in civil war, the best and soundest cause, no doubt, is that which maintains the ancient religion and government of the kingdom: nevertheless, amongst the good men of that party (for I do not speak of those that only make it a pretext, either to execute their own particular revenges, or to gratify their avarice, or to pursue the favour of princes; but of those who engage in the quarrel out of true zeal to religion, and a holy affection to maintain the peace and government of their country), of these, I say, we see many whom passion transports beyond the bounds of reason, and sometimes inspires with counsels that are unjust and violent, and moreover inconsiderate and rash.

It is certain that in those first times, when our religion began to gain authority with the laws, zeal armed many against all sorts of Pagan books, by which the learned suffer an exceeding great loss; a disorder that I conceive did more prejudice to letters than all the flames of the barbarians: of this Cornelius Tacitus is a very good testimony: for though the emperor Tacitus, his kinsman, had by express order furnished all the libraries in the world with his work, nevertheless one entire copy could not escape the curious search of those who desired to abolish it, for only five or six idle clauses that were contrary to our belief.

They also had the trick, easily to lend undue praises to all the emperors who did any thing for us, and universally to condemn all the actions of those who were our adversaries, as is evidently manifest in the emperor Julian, surnamed the apostate. This was, in truth, a very great and rare man; a man in whose soul philosophy was imprinted in the best characters, by which he professed to govern all his actions; and, in truth, there is no sort of virtue of which he had not left behind him very notable examples: in chastity (of which the whole course of his life has given manifest proof), we read the same of him that was said of Alexander and Scipio, that being in the flower of his age, for he was slain by the Parthians at one and thirty, of a great many very beautiful captives, he would not so much as look upon one. As to his justice, he took himself the pains to hear the parties, and although he would, out of curiosity, inquire what religion they were of, nevertheless the hatred he had to ours never gave any counterpoise to the balance. He himself made several good laws, and cut off a great part of the subsidies and taxes imposed and levied by his predecessors. . . .

In matter of religion he was wrong throughout; he was surnamed the Apostate, for having relinquished ours; though, methinks, 'tis more likely that he had never thoroughly embraced it, but had dissembled, out of obedience to the laws, till he came to the empire. He was in his own so superstitious that he was laughed at for it by those of the same opinion, of his own time, who jeeringly said that had he got the victory over the Parthians, he had destroyed the breed of oxen in the world, to supply his sacrifices. . . .

. . . he long nourished, says Marcellinus, paganism in his heart; but, all his army being Christians, he durst not own it. But in the end seeing himself strong enough to dare to discover himself, he caused the temples of the gods to be thrown open, and did his utmost to set on foot and to encourage idolatry. Which the better to effect, having at Constantinople found the people disunited, and also the prelates of the church divided amongst themselves, having convened them all before him, he gravely and earnestly admonished them to calm those civil dissensions, and that every one should freely, and without fear, follow his own religion: which he did the more sedulously solicit in hope that this licence would augment the schisms and faction of their division, and hinder the people from re-uniting, and consequently fortifying themselves against him by their unanimous intelligence and concord; having experienced by the cruelty of some Christians, "that there is no beast in the world so much to be feared by man, as man." These are very nearly his own words.

Wherein this is very worthy of consideration, that the Emperor Julian made use of the same recipe of liberty of conscience to enflame the civil dissensions, that our kings do to extinguish them. A man may say, on one side, that to give the people the reins to entertain every man his own opinion, is to scatter and sow division, and, as it were, to lend a hand to augment it, there being no sense nor correction of law to stop and hinder their career; but, on the other side, a man may also say that, to give the people the reins to entertain every man his own opinion, is to mollify and appease them by facility and toleration, and dull the point which is whetted and made sharper by rarity, novelty, and difficulty. And I think it is better for the honour and the devotion of our kings, that not having been able to do what they would, they have made a show of being willing to do what they could.

*Source:* Michel de Montaigne. "Of Liberty of Conscience." In *The Complete Works of Michael de Montaigne: Comprising His Essays, Letters and His Journey Through Germany and Italy,* pp. 337–39. Ed. William Hazlitt. New York: Worthington, 1889.

### Questions

What lessons might sixteenth-century French people draw from the life of Julian the Apostate?

What are the dangers of liberty of conscience? The benefits?

In what ways is Montaigne a typical "Renaissance man"?

## B. Simplicissimus and the Horrors of War

Little is known about the life of the German author Hans Jacob Christoph von Grimmelshausen (*c.* 1621–1676). In his later years Grimmelshausen was apparently a practicing Catholic, but he was probably born into a Protestant family. A self-taught and very prolific writer who published under a variety of pseudonyms, his most successful work was the picaresque novel *Adventurous Simplicissimus.*

Like Simplicissimus, the naive but quick-witted young narrator of his novel, Grimmelshausen lost his humble family during the Thirty Years' War and was captured by Hessian troops at the age of ten. Until the end of the war, he worked first as a serving boy and later as a soldier in different armies, traveling widely throughout Central Europe.

Grimmelshausen's novel provides one of the few accounts of the war told from the perspective of the common people, whether peasants or soldiers. It conveys with considerable humor the harsh realities of this brutal war, following Simplicissimus as he wanders from one adventure to the next. In the following passage, taken from the beginning of the novel, the young Simplicissimus returns from his shepherding duties to find his family's "castle" (in reality, a simple peasant dwelling) besieged by soldiers.

FROM *The Adventurous Simplicissimus* by Hans Jacob Christoph von Grimmelshausen

CHAPTER IV HOW SIMPLICISSIMUS'S PALACE WAS STORMED, PLUNDERED, AND RUINATED, AND IN WHAT SORRY FASHION THE SOLDIERS KEPT HOUSE THERE

Although it was not my intention to take the peace-loving reader with these troopers to my dad's house and farm, seeing that matters will go ill therein, yet the course of my history demands that I should leave to kind posterity an account of what manner of cruelties were now and again practised in this our German war: yea, and moreover testify by my own example that such evils must often have been sent to us by the goodness of Almighty God for our profit. For, gentle reader, who would ever have taught me that there was a God in Heaven if these soldiers had not destroyed my dad's house, and by such a deed driven me out among folk who gave me all fitting instruction thereupon? Only a little while before, I neither knew nor could fancy to myself that there were any people on earth save only my dad, my mother and me, and the rest of our household, nor did I know of any human habitation but that where I daily went out and in. But soon thereafter I understood the way of men's coming into this world, and how they must leave it again. I was only in shape a man and in name a Christian: for the rest I was but a beast. Yet the Almighty looked upon my innocence with a pitiful eye, and would bring me to a knowledge both of Himself and of myself. And although He had a thousand ways to lead me thereto, yet would He doubtless use that one only by which my dad and my mother should be punished: and that for an example to all others by reason of their heathenish upbringing of me.

The first thing these troopers did was, that they stabled their horses: thereafter each fell to his appointed task: which task was neither more nor less than ruin and destruction. For though some began to slaughter and to boil and to roast so that it looked as if there should be a merry banquet forward, yet others there were who did but storm through the house above and below stairs. Others stowed together great parcels of cloth and apparel and all manner of household stuff, as if they would set up a frippery market. All that they had no mind to take with them they cut in pieces. Some thrust their swords through the hay and straw as if they had not enough sheep and swine to slaughter: and some shook the feathers out of the beds and in their stead stuffed in bacon and other dried meat and provisions as if such were better and softer to sleep upon. Others broke the stove and the windows as if they had a never-ending summer to promise. Houseware of copper and tin they beat flat, and packed such vessels, all bent and spoiled, in with the rest. Bedsteads, tables, chairs, and benches they burned, though there lay many cords of dry wood in the yard. Pots and pipkins must all go to pieces, either because they would eat none but roast flesh, or because their purpose was to make there but a single meal.

Our maid was so handled in the stable that she could not come out; which is a shame to tell of. Our man they laid bound upon the ground, thrust a gag into his mouth, and poured a pailful of filthy water into his body: and by this, which they called a Swedish draught, they forced him to lead a party of them to another place where they captured men and beasts, and brought them back to our farm, in which company were my dad, my mother, and our Ursula.

And now they began: first to take the flints out of their pistols and in place of them to jam the peasants' thumbs in and so to torture the poor rogues as if they had been about the burning of witches: for one of them they had taken they thrust into the baking oven and there lit a fire under him, although he had as yet confessed no crime: as for another, they put a cord round his head and so twisted it tight with a piece of wood that the blood gushed from his mouth and nose and ears. In a word, each had his own device to torture the peasants, and each peasant his several torture. But as it seemed to me then, my dad was the luckiest, for he with a laughing face confessed what others must out with in the midst of pains and miserable lamentations: and such honour without doubt fell to him because he was the householder. For they set him before a fire and bound him fast so that he could neither stir hand nor foot, and smeared the soles of his feet with wet salt, and this they made our old goat lick off, and so tickle him that he well nigh burst his sides with laughing. And this seemed to me so merry a thing that I must needs laugh with him for the sake of fellowship, or because I knew no better. In the midst of such laughter he must needs confess all that they would have of him, and indeed revealed to them a secret treasure, which proved far richer in pearls, gold, and trinkets than any would have looked for among peasants. Of the women, girls, and maidservants whom they took, I have not much to say in particular, for the soldiers would not have me see how they dealt with them. Yet this I know, that one heard some of them scream most piteously in divers corners of the house; and well I can judge it fared no better with my mother and our Ursel than with the rest. Yet in the midst of all this miserable ruin I helped to turn the spit, and in the afternoon to give the horses drink, in which employ I encountered our maid in the stable, who seemed to me wondrously tumbled, so that I knew her not, but with a weak voice she called to me, "O lad, run away, or the troopers will have thee away with them. Look to it well that thou get hence: thou seest in what plight . . ." And more she could not say.

*Source:* Hans Jacob Christoph von Grimmelshausen. "How Simplicissimus's Palace was Stormed, Plundered, and Ruinated, and in What Sorry Fashion the Soldiers Kept House Therein." In *The Adventurous Simplicissimus: Being the Description of the Life of a Strange Vagabond Named Melchior Sternfels von Fuchshaim*, pp. 28–31. London: William Heinemann, 1912.

## Questions

Who are these pillaging soldiers? Why doesn't Simplicissimus identify them for the reader?

What can we learn from this account about the impact of the Thirty Years' War on the German peasantry?

How are we to take the narrator's comments about the "profit" to be derived from the horrors of war?

# 9. IMPORTANT HISTORICAL FACTS: STUDY DRILLS

## A. Multiple Choice

1. French Protestants were known as
   A. Politiques.
   B. Huguenots.
   C. Poor Wretches.
   D. Valois.

2. In 1516, Francis I signed an agreement with the pope that greatly reduced the authority of the Catholic Church in France. The agreement was known as
   A. the Treaty of Westphalia.
   B. the Edict of Nantes.
   C. the Concordat of Bologna.
   D. the Saint Bartholomew's Day Massacre.

3. After the death of her husband, Henry II, she all but ruled France during the succeeding reigns of her three weak and ineffectual sons:
   A. Catherine de Medici
   B. Marguerite de Valois
   C. Marie de Medici
   D. Paulette

4. Angered by Henry III's concessions to the Huguenots, certain French nobles organized to combat Protestantism, forming an alliance known as
   A. the *Dévots*.
   B. the Politiques.
   C. the Sixteen.
   D. the Catholic League.

5. Saying "Paris is worth a Mass," he converted (once again) to Catholicism and ruled France as Henry IV, the "Well-Loved":
   A. Henry of Navarre
   B. Henry Tudor
   C. Henry Valois
   D. Henry, duke of Guise

6. The reign of Louis XIII was typified by
   A. a considerable strengthening of the French monarchy.
   B. constant religious warfare.
   C. decreasing taxes.
   D. a collapse of centralized state authority.

7. As Holy Roman emperor, he led the Catholic assault on Protestantism during the Thirty Years' War:
   A. Christian IV
   B. Frederick, elector of the Palatinate
   C. Gustavus Adolphus
   D. Ferdinand II

8. A minor event in itself, it signaled the start of the long and bloody Thirty Years' War:
   A. The Battle of the White Mountain
   B. The Defenestration of Prague
   C. The Edict of Restitution
   D. The Treaty of Westphalia

9. Ambitious and ruthless, this Bohemian military supplier rose to become the most powerful Catholic general of the Thirty Years' War:
   A. Count Johannes von Tilly
   B. Albert Wallenstein
   C. Maximilian of Bavaria
   D. Cleves-Jülich

10. Signed in 1648, it signaled the end of the Thirty Years' War:
    A. The Treaty of Cateau-Cambrésis
    B. The Treaty of Lubeck
    C. The Peace of Augsburg
    D. The Treaty of Westphalia

## B. Chronological Relationships

1. List in chronological order the kings of France and the Holy Roman emperors who ruled during the Wars of Religion. Include the full names of the rulers and the dates during which they reigned.
   FRANCE
   1. Francis I (1515–1547)
   2.
   3.
   4.
   5.
   6.
   7.
   GERMANY
   1. Maximilian II (1564–1576)
   2.
   3.
   4.
   5.

2. Organize the following events in chronological order and identify the date on which each occurred:
   The Edict of Nantes.
   Henry IV is assassinated by Ravaillac.
   The Saint Bartholomew's Day Massacre.
   Calvinists seize control of Lyon.
   The Treaty of Vervins.
   Formation of the Catholic League.

Henry of Navarre is crowned King Henry IV.

The Day of the Barricades.

3. The Thirty Years' War can be divided into four separate (if not entirely distinct) stages:
   A. The Bohemian
   B. The Danish
   C. The Swedish
   D. The Dynastic

Identify the stage of the war to which each of the following events belonged and the year in which each occurred:

_____ No one shows up for the pope's peace conference in Cologne.

_____ Gustavus Adolphus dies in battle at Lützen.

_____ The Treaty of Lubeck.

_____ France declares war on Philip IV of Spain.

_____ The Defenestration of Prague.

_____ Christian IV attacks the northern German states.

_____ The Battle of the White Mountain.

_____ Albert Wallenstein is dismissed and then assassinated.

## C. Fill in the Blanks

1. In the late sixteenth century, miserable peasants rose up in revolt against nobles in central and southern France. The popular nickname for these rebels was _____.

2. On August 24, 1572, Huguenot leaders, in Paris for the wedding of Henry of Navarre and Margaret of Valois, were slaughtered by Catholic nobles in what became known as the _____.

3. During the course of the French wars of religion, many individuals became tired of the anarchy and bloodshed that had resulted from the continuing conflict between Protestants and Catholics. In the interest of peace and toleration, they sought to put politics ahead of religion. These moderates were known as _____.

4. The complex series of conflicts between Henry III, Henry of Navarre, and Henry, duke of Guise, were known as _____.

5. In 1598, the _____ made Catholicism the official religion of France, but also guaranteed certain rights to France's Protestant minority.

6. Working in support of Louis XIII's bid to increase the power and authority of the French crown, _____ divided France into thirty-two districts and placed them under the control of government officials who were directly responsible to the king.

7. Selected by seven "electors," the _____ ruled over a loose confederation of approximately 1,000 autonomous and semi-autonomous German states.

8. Even before the outbreak of the Thirty Years' War in 1618, the Germans had already formed into two hostile camps, the _____ and the _____.

9. A Calvinist, the young German prince _____ served as the leader of the German Protestant forces at the outset of the Thirty Years' War.

10. _____, the dashing young king of Sweden, entered the Thirty Years' War in 1630 as a champion of the Protestant cause, but he failed to win a decisive victory and died in battle in 1632.

# IMPORTANT HISTORICAL FACTS: STUDY-DRILL ANSWERS

## A. Multiple Choice

1. B. Huguenots.
2. C. the Concordat of Bologna.
3. A. Catherine de Medici
4. D. the Catholic League.
5. A. Henry of Navarre
6. A. a considerable strengthening of the French monarchy.
7. D. Ferdinand II
8. B. The Defenestration of Prague
9. B. Albert Wallenstein
10. D. The Treaty of Westphalia

## B. Chronological Relationships

1. FRANCE
   1. Francis I (1515–1547)
   2. Henry II (1547–1559)
   3. Francis II (1559–1560)

4. Charles IX (1560–1574)
5. Henry III (1574–1589)
6. Henry IV (1589–1610)
7. Louis XIII (1610–1643)
GERMANY
1. Maximilian II (1564–1576)
2. Rudolf II (1576–1612)
3. Matthias (1612–1619)
4. Ferdinand II (1619–1637)
5. Ferdinand III (1637–1657)

2. 1562 Calvinists seize control of Lyon.
   1572 The Saint Bartholomew's Day Massacre.
   1576 Formation of the Catholic League.
   1588 The Day of the Barricades.
   1594 Henry of Navarre is crowned King Henry IV.
   1598 The Treaty of Vervins.
   1598 The Edict of Nantes.
   1610 Henry IV is assassinated by Ravaillac.

3. D. No one shows up for the pope's peace conference in Cologne (1636).
   C. Gustavus Adolphus dies in battle at Lützen (1632).
   B. The Treaty of Lubeck (1629).
   D. France declares war on Philip IV of Spain (1635).
   A. The Defenestration of Prague (1618).
   B. Christian IV attacks the northern German states (1625).
   A. The Battle of the White Mountain (1620).
   C. Albert Wallenstein is dismissed and then assassinated (1634).

## C. Fill in the Blanks

1. Poor wretches
2. Saint Bartholomew's Day Massacre
3. Politiques
4. War of the Three Henrys
5. The Edict of Nantes
6. Cardinal Richelieu
7. Holy Roman Emperor
8. Catholic League and the Protestant Union
9. Frederick, elector of the Palatinate
10. Gustavus Adolphus

# 5

## The Rise of the Atlantic Economy: Spain and England

# 1. CHAPTER OUTLINE

1. The rise of England and Spain occurred as a result of ECONOMIC EXPANSION in the sixteenth century and marked a shift in the focus of trade and manufacturing from the Mediterranean region to Northwestern Europe.
    A. INCREASED AGRICULTURAL PRODUCTIVITY and rural industry contributed to economic growth throughout Europe during this period.
    B. EXPANSION OF TRADE was stimulated by population growth and by the development of banking and other financial services.
    C. THE GLOBAL ECONOMY: A new international trading system emerged, involving Western European nations in trade with the Americas and Asia.
    D. PRICE REVOLUTION AND DEPRESSION: The economic boom brought a great increase in prices and was followed by a long depression in the seventeenth century.
II. THE RISE OF SPAIN to its position as the greatest sixteenth-century European power was complicated by the survival of semi-autonomous regions.
    A. CENTRALIZATION AND THE SPANISH MONARCHY: Despite

successful efforts by Ferdinand and Isabella to increase their power as monarchs, traditions of parliamentary autonomy were upheld by regional assemblies (Cortes).
    B. THE SPANISH ECONOMY expanded as a result of both colonial riches and the development of agriculture, manufacturing, and commerce in Spain itself.
    C. THE EXPANSION OF THE SPANISH EMPIRE was the consequence of the marriage and inheritance strategies of Spanish rulers. Habsburg King Charles V united a vast empire under Spanish rule, but he divided his kingdom between his son and brother in 1558.
    D. THE AGE OF PHILIP II: Under the reign of Charles V's son, Philip II, Spain reached the height of its power. Philip turned the might of his kingdom against the Turks, but his victory at the Battle of Lepanto concealed the weaknesses of an overextended empire.
III. THE RISE OF ENGLAND to Great Power status took place in the late sixteenth century.
    A. THE HOUSE OF TUDOR: Brought to power by Henry VII, the Tudor kings and queens sought to

consolidate the power of the throne by building an efficient bureaucracy and, in the case of Henry VIII, by wresting control over religion from the pope. After Henry VIII's establishment of the Church of England, religion became a source of considerable conflict in England—and in Wales and Ireland.

B. RELIGIOUS SETTLEMENT AND CONFLICT: Elizabeth I attempted to re-establish social unity by imposing a moderate religious settlement. Despite her efforts, religious dissent continued and state repression became more harsh.

C. TUDOR STATEMAKING: Elizabeth I increased the reach and efficiency of the English state through royal patronage, frugal economic policies, and the creation of armies to fight foreign wars. In England, a sense of national identity arose out of shared laws and language and the development of a national market economy.

D. English DEMOGRAPHIC AND ECONOMIC EXPANSION grew out of agricultural innovation, new methods of textile manufacturing, and the development of a colonial empire. London became Europe's leading center of trade.

E. ENGLISH SOCIETY IN THE TUDOR PERIOD: Differences between the gentry elite, the "middling sort," and the urban and rural poor were sharply defined. A certain amount of social mobility was possible, but was largely restricted to the gentry and the middling sort.

F. THE QUEST FOR PUBLIC ORDER: Disastrous harvests in the 1590s ended the period of economic expansion in England.

Out of fear of social disorder caused by the poor, the English upper classes supported the passage of laws designed to reinforce obedience to authority.

G. ELIZABETHAN THEATER reflected the prosperity of the English elite. The plays of Shakespeare and Marlowe expressed concern about the social problems of their era.

IV. THE DECLINE OF SPAIN was readily apparent by 1600.

A. THE DUTCH REVOLT: Angered by taxation and the religious policies of the Spanish crown, the largely Calvinist population of the Spanish Netherlands rose up in revolt in the 1560s. The insurrection dragged on into the seventeenth century, draining the Spanish economy.

B. ECONOMIC DECLINE was the root cause of the decay of Spanish power. Continuous warfare forced the monarchy to increase taxes at the very time that agricultural productivity and the population growth rate were decreasing. Spanish nobles lived lives of idleness and dissipation, contributing little to economic vitality.

C. AN EMPIRE SPREAD TOO THIN: Seriously overextended in its global commitments, the Spanish monarchy attempted to reassert its authority, but continuing warfare—especially with the rebellious Dutch, whose independence was recognized in 1648—forced tax increases, which sparked regional revolts. By the second half of the seventeenth century Spain had become a second-rate power.

V. CONCLUSION

## 2. HISTORICAL GEOGRAPHY

**MAP 5.1   SPAIN IN THE AGE OF FERDINAND AND ISABELLA**

### Map Exercises

Familiarize yourself with the maps provided in your text, and then attempt to locate the following places on Blank Map 5.1.

SPAIN IN THE AGE OF FERDINAND AND ISABELLA

Andalusia
Aragón
Barcelona
Cádiz
Castile
Catalonia
Ebro River
Galicia
Granada
Leon

Lisbon
Madrid
Navarre
Portugal
Pyrenee Mountains
Seville
Tagus River
Toledo
Valencia
Valladolid

### Map Questions

What territories were included in the Spanish Empire at the time of its greatest extent under Habsburg Emperor Charles V?

What geographic realities made it difficult for the Spanish crown to maintain control over its massive empire?

How did England's geographic location affect the nation's economy, foreign relations, and culture?

What was the "Spanish Road"? Where was it?

## 3. PEOPLE AND TERMS TO IDENTIFY

Spanish Armada
Bills of Exchange
Dutch East India Company
The Price Revolution
Isabella of Castile and
   Ferdinand of Aragon
Cortes
Potosí
Philip II

Escorial Palace
Battle of Lepanto
Henry VIII
Elizabeth I
Book of Common Prayer
Puritanism
Enclosure
Sir Thomas Gresham
The Poor Laws

William Shakespeare
The Dutch Revolt
The Duke of Alba
Grandees
*Don Quixote*
Gaspar de Guzmán, the
   duke of Olivares
The Treaty of Münster

## 4. STUDY QUESTIONS

1. *Historical Continuities:* What was the long-term significance, both real and symbolic, of the English defeat of the Spanish Armada?

2. *Historical Continuities:* What long-term factors can account for the expansion of the European economy in the sixteenth century?

3. What was the "price revolution" and how did it affect the European economy?

4. *Historical Continuities:* How did its colonial empire contribute to Spain's expanding economy?

5. How did Philip II and Henry VII build the power of the centralized Spanish and British states, respectively?

6. How did the Tudors overcome Irish and Scottish resistance to English domination?

7. How did Elizabeth I further enhance the power of the English state? In what ways was the Elizabethan monarchy more centralized and efficient than that of France or Spain?

8. What accounts for England's great economic successes in the Elizabethan period?

9. Describe the "degrees of people" in Tudor England, detailing the characteristics of the different categories of the social hierarchy.

10. How did the English ruling class respond to the disorders occasioned by economic hardship in the 1590s?

11. Why did the Spanish military fail to suppress the Dutch revolt?

12. What factors, both general and specific, caused the decline of Spanish power and wealth?

## 5. ANALYZING ART AND ARTIFACTS

How were the power and wealth of Spain and England demonstrated in buildings such as the Escorial Palace and Longeat manor house (see pp. 195 and 211 of the text)?

How did Spanish painters express the decline of Spain in their works? (See the works of Velázquez and El Greco on the first page of color plates between pp. 316 and 317 of the text.)

## 6. TECHNOLOGY AND HISTORY

To what extent was banking a new "technology"? What impact did banking and other financial institutions have on the European economy?

How did English agriculture differ from Spanish agriculture? What can explain the dynamism of the former and the stagnation of the latter?

# 7. HISTORICAL ANALYSIS: INTERPRETIVE ESSAYS

1. Why did Britain become a first-rate power and Spain a second-rate power in the period between 1550 and 1650?

2. *Historical Continuities:* How did economic factors influence the success or failure of early modern statemaking initiatives? Use examples from the English and Spanish cases, but refer back to the French initiatives discussed in Chapter 4.

3. Compare and contrast the social structures of England and Spain in the sixteenth and seventeenth centuries.

4. *Historical Continuities:* Why did the focus of European culture and economic relations shift away from the Mediterranean to the northwest?

# 8. HISTORICAL VOICES: THE RISE OF ENGLAND, THE DECLINE OF SPAIN

## A. Elizabeth I and the Rise of English Nationalism

Throughout her long reign, Elizabeth I (1533–1603) manipulated the sentiments of her subjects and of the international community as she worked to build her own power and the power of England. Using her eligibility for marriage as a lure, Elizabeth played her courtiers, and Europe's princes and kings, against one another—although there is little evidence that the "Virgin Queen" ever truly intended to relinquish her place to a husband who might wish to rule as king.

While Europe was not lacking in female rulers during this period, most members of England's ruling elite would have preferred to see a man on the throne. Keenly aware of the prejudice against women monarchs, Elizabeth persistently sought to establish a distinction between her private role as a woman and her public role as a political leader. When she mounted the throne in 1558 at the age of twenty-five, she declared that, though she had "but one body, naturally considered," God had also granted her "a Body Politic to govern."

As England awaited the arrival of the Spanish Armada in 1588, Elizabeth, now fifty-five, rode out to review her troops at Tilbury. Wearing a silver breastplate, she delivered the following brief but very famous speech. In it can be seen both the queen's ingeniously politicized use of the language of gender and her reliance on a developing sense of national loyalty that supplemented (but did not replace) English soldiers' interest in material gain.

### FROM Queen Elizabeth's Speech to the Army at Tilbury

"My loving people; we have been persuaded by some that are careful of our safety, to take heed how we commit ourselves to armed multitudes, for fear of treachery; but assure you, I do not desire to live to distrust my faithful and loving people. Let tyrants fear: I have always so behaved myself that, under God, I have placed my chiefest strength and safeguard in the loyal hearts and good-will of my subjects. And therefore I am come amongst you at this time; not as for my recreation or sport; but being resolved in the midst and heat of the battle, to live or die amongst you all; to lay down for my God and for my kingdom and for my people my honor and my blood, even in the dust. I know I have but the body of a weak and feeble woman, but I have the heart of a king; and of a king of England too; and think foul scorn that Parma or Spain, or any prince of Europe, should dare to invade the borders of my realms: to which, rather than any dishonor should grow by me, I myself will take up arms; I myself will be your general, judge and rewarder of every one of your virtues in the field.

"I know already by your forwardness, that you have deserved rewards and crowns; and we do assure you, on the word of a prince, they shall be duly paid you. In the meantime, my lieutenant-general shall be in my stead, than whom never prince commanded a more noble and worthy subject; not doubting by your obedience to my general, by your concord in the camp and your valor in the field, we shall shortly have a famous victory over those enemies of my God, of my kingdom and of my people."

*Source:* Quoted in Lucy Aikin. *Memoirs of the Court of Queen Elizabeth.* Vol. 2, pp. 228–229. London: Longman, et al., 1819.

### Questions

What is Elizabeth trying to accomplish when she calls herself a "weak and feeble woman"?

According to Elizabeth, what is the proper relationship between a monarch and her people?

What sort of sentiments is this speech meant to inspire?

### B. Miguel de Cervantes and the "Quixotic" Search for Grandeur in an Age of Decline

Spanish aspirations toward grandeur and the reality of Spanish decline are both reflected in Miguel de Cervantes' (1547–1616) deservedly famous work, *Don Quixote de la Mancha*, the first part of which was published in 1605. This novel may be read as a caustic satire of the knights-in-shining-armor literature read so avidly by the Castilian nobility, but it may also be understood as something more—as Cervantes' own world-weary lament over the Spanish Empire's loss not only of wealth and power but also of true nobility of spirit.

Don Quixote is a figure of fun, but there is a poignant quality to his exploits. When, in a famous episode, he tilts at windmills (thinking them giants) he is comic; when he attempts to save a shepherd boy from being beaten by his cruel master, his actions—however misguided and ineffectual—reveal him to be a man whose heart is in the right place.

In the following excerpts, taken from the first English-language translation (published in 1611) of the novel, we are introduced to Cervantes' unlikely hero, an aging Castilian noble of meager means but boundless aspirations.

### FROM *Don Quixote of the Mancha* by Miguel de Cervantes

There lived not long since, in a certain village of the Mancha, the name whereof I purposely omit, a gentleman of their calling that use to pile up in their halls old lances, halberds, morions, and such other armours and weapons. He was, besides, master of an ancient target, a lean stallion, and a swift greyhound. His pot consisted daily of somewhat more beef than mutton: a gallimaufry each night, collops and eggs on Saturday, lentils on Fridays, and now and then a lean pigeon on Sundays, did consume three parts of his rents. . . . The master himself was about fifty years old, of a strong complexion, dry flesh, and a withered face. He was an early riser, and a great friend of hunting. . . .

. . . [T]his gentleman, the spurts that he was idle . . . did apply himself wholly to the reading of books of knighthood, and that with such gusts and delights, as he almost wholly neglected the exercise of hunting; yea, and the very administration of his household affairs. And his curiosity and folly came to that pass, that he made away many acres of arable land to buy him books of that kind, and therefore he brought to his house as many as ever he could get of that subject. . . .

. . . [H]e plunged himself so deeply in his reading of these books, as he spent many times in the lecture of them whole days and nights; and in the end, through his little sleep and much reading, he dried up his brains in such sort as he lost wholly his judgment. His fantasy was filled with those things that he read, of enchantments, quarrels, battles, challenges, wounds, wooings, loves, tempests, and other impossible follies. . . .

Finally, his wit being wholly extinguished, he fell into one of the strangest conceits that ever madman stumbled on in this world; to wit, it seemed unto him very requisite and behooveful, as well for the augmentation of his honour as also for the benefit of the commonwealth, that he himself should become a knight-errant, and go throughout the world, with his horse and armour, to seek adventures, and practise in person all that he had read was used by knights of yore; revenging of all kinds of injuries, and offering himself to occasions and dangers, which, being once happily achieved, might gain him eternal renown. . . .

And first of all he caused certain old rusty arms to be scoured, that belonged to his great-grandfather, and lay many ages neglected and forgotten in a by-corner of his house; he trimmed and dressed them the best he might, and then perceived a great defect they had; for they wanted a helmet, and had only a plain morion; but he by his industry supplied that want, and framed, with certain papers pasted together, a beaver for his morion. . . . Then did he presently visit his horse, who (though he had more quarters than pence in a sixpence, through leanness, and more faults than Gonella's), having nothing on him but skin and bone; yet he thought that neither Alexander's Bucephalus, nor the Cid his horse Balieca, were in any respect equal to him. He spent four days devising him a name; for (as he reasoned to himself) it was not fit that so famous a knight's horse, and chiefly being so good a beast, should want a known name; . . . he finally concluded to name him Rozinante, a name in his opinion lofty, full, and significant of what he had been when he was a plain jade, before he was exalted to his new dignity; being, as he thought, the best carriage beast of the world. The name being thus given to his horse, and so to his mind, he resolved to give himself a name also; and in that thought he laboured other eight days; and, in conclusion, called himself Don Quixote. . . . And remembering that the valorous Amadis was not satisfied only with the dry name of Amadis, but added thereunto the name of his kingdom and country, to render his own more redoubted, terming himself Amadis de Gaul; so he, like a good knight, would add to his own that also of his province, and call himself Don Quixote of the Mancha, wherewith it appeared that he very lively declared his lineage and country, which he did honour, by taking it for his surname.

. . . [H]e forthwith bethought himself, that now he wanted nothing but a lady on whom he might bestow his service and affection; for the knight-errant that is loveless resembles a tree that wants leaves and fruit, or a body without a soul: and therefore he was wont to say, "If I should for my sins, or by good hap, encounter there abroad with some giant (as knights-errant do ordinarily), and that I should overthrow him with one blow to the ground, or cut him with a stroke in two halves, or finally overcome, and make him yield to me, would it not be very expedient to have some lady to whom I might present him?". . .

. . . Oh, how glad was our knight when he had made this discourse to himself, but chiefly when he had found out one whom he might call his lady! For, as it is imagined, there dwelt in the next village unto his manor, a young handsome wench, with whom he was sometime in love, although, as is understood, she never knew or took notice thereof. She was called Aldonsa Lorenzo, and her he thought fittest to entitle with the name of Lady of his thoughts, and searching a name for her that should not vary much from her own, and yet should draw and aveer somewhat to that of a princess or great lady, he called her Dulcinea del Toboso (for there she was born), a name in his conceit harmonious, strange, and significant, like to all the others that he had given to his things.

*Source:* Miguel de Cervantes. *The First Part of the Delightful History of the Most Ingenious Knight Don Quixote of the Mancha.* Trans. Thomas Shelton. Harvard Classics, vol. 14. New York: P.F. Collier, 1910.

### Questions

What is Cervantes satirizing in this passage? Why?

In what sense might Don Quixote be read as a personification of the Spanish Empire itself?

Compare Elizabeth's speech with Cervantes' description of Don Quixote. What do these two documents tell you about the relative sense of cultural vitality in England and Spain during this period?

## 9. IMPORTANT HISTORICAL FACTS: STUDY DRILLS

### A. Multiple Choice

1. The Spanish Armada was
   A. the Duke of Alba's troops.
   B. the Spanish naval force that attempted to invade England.
   C. the fleet that defeated the Turks at Lepanto.
   D. Spanish troops sent to put down the revolt of the Catalan nobles.

2. Promissory notes that could be sold to third parties, and used in place of gold and silver coins, these new financial instruments greatly facilitated the expansion of trade in the sixteenth century:
   A. joint-stock partnerships
   B. bills of exchange
   C. London Merchant Adventurers
   D. shillings

3. In the sixteenth century, a combination of the flood of silver and gold from the New World, currency debasement, and population increase caused prices to rise considerably in Europe, without a comparable increase in wages. This was known as
   A. the price revolution.
   B. economic expansion.
   C. depression.
   D. the Dutch Revolt.

4. Like the rulers of England, the Spanish monarchs found their power limited by a political assembly known as
   A. Parliament.
   B. the Star Chamber.
   C. Cortes.
   D. the Estates-General.

5. The source of rich deposits of silver, this Spanish colonial property was partly responsible for the European price revolution of the sixteenth century:
   A. Potosí
   B. Brazil
   C. Andalusia
   D. Sardinia

6. This decisive naval victory ended Turkish domination of the eastern Mediterranean, but may also have contributed to the decline of Spanish power:
   A. the Battle of Bosworth Field
   B. the Dutch Revolt
   C. the Spanish Armada
   D. the Battle of Lepanto

7. In her efforts to establish religious uniformity in England, Elizabeth I imposed
   A. the use of the Book of Common Prayer.
   B. the use of candles and incense.
   C. the Catholic Mass.
   D. Puritanism.
8. The consolidation of landholdings by English landowners was known as
   A. gleaning.
   B. enclosure.
   C. crop rotation.
   D. common land.
9. In the late sixteenth century, concern for and fear of the wandering poor in England prompted the passage of
   A. the Act of Uniformity.
   B. the Act of Supremacy.
   C. the Thirty-Nine Articles.
   D. the Poor Laws.
10. The independence of the Dutch United Provinces from the Spanish crown was officially recognized in
   A. the Treaty of Westphalia.
   B. the Treaty of Cateau-Cambrésis.
   C. the Treaty of Münster.
   D. the Amicable Grant.

## B. Chronological Relationships

1. Connect the following events with the appropriate dates:

   | 1453 | Elizabeth I dies. |
   | 1469 | The Treaty of Münster. |
   | 1516 | The Irish rebellion is crushed by English troops. |
   | 1567 | The Dutch town of Breda surrenders to Spanish troops. |
   | 1571 | The Duke of Alba is sent to put down the Dutch Revolt. |
   | 1588 | Isabella of Castile marries Ferdinand of Aragon. |
   | 1595 | Thomas More writes *Utopia*. |
   | 1603 | The Battle of Lepanto. |
   | 1625 | The Ottoman Turks take Constantinople. |
   | 1648 | The Spanish Armada fails to invade England. |

2. List in chronological order the rulers of Spain and England in the years between 1547 and 1648. Include the full names of the rulers and the dates during which they reigned.

SPAIN
1. Isabella (1474–1504) and Ferdinand (1474–1516)
2.
3.
4.
5.

ENGLAND
1. Henry VII (1485–1509)
2.
3.
4.
5.

## C. Matching Exercise: Historical Actors

_____ The Duke of Alba
_____ Elizabeth I
_____ Grandee
_____ Sir Thomas Gresham
_____ Henry VIII
_____ Isabella of Castile
_____ Don Quixote
_____ Gaspar de Guzmán, Duke of Olivares
_____ Philip II
_____ William Shakespeare

A. Often cited as one of the greatest authors of all time, this playwright was born in Stratford-upon-Avon, but won fame and fortune writing for the Globe Theater in London.
B. As chief adviser to Philip IV, this Andalusian noble attempted to revitalize the declining Spanish Empire, but only succeeded in further embroiling Spain in a war with France and in alienating the Spanish nobility. He was sent into exile in 1643.
C. Under this monarch's leadership in the second half of the sixteenth century, Spanish power reached its peak. He built the magnificent Escorial Palace and engaged Spain in a long, successful, but in the end debilitating war with the Ottoman Turks.
D. In 1469, she married the heir to the throne of Aragon, effectively uniting the two most important provinces of Spain. A staunch supporter of Catholicism, this monarch nonetheless strove to bring the Church (and its assets) under the control of the crown.

E. With the aid of his squire Pancho Sanza, this fictional Spanish nobleman sought to restore Spanish grandeur through the revival of true chivalry. A tragicomic figure, he was an expression of Spaniards' disillusionment in the face of national decline.

F. The self-proclaimed "virgin queen," this Tudor monarch sought to bring political and religious unity to England. During her long reign in the second half of the sixteenth century, the royal administration became more centralized and efficient, and a rich and vibrant literary culture flourished.

G. Appointed to put down Dutch resistance to Spanish rule, this brutal military leader imposed a reign of terror in the Netherlands, helping to transform upper-class resistance into a national revolt.

H. This entrepreneur strengthened commercial ties between the English textile trade and merchants in the Spanish Netherlands. A shrewd businessman, he successfully advised the English state on international economic transactions, and urged development of commercial ties with the American colonies.

I. A wealthy Spanish aristocrat, he dedicated his life to pleasure and the pursuit of royal favor. His life of gluttony and laziness was a symptom of (and contributed to) the decline of the Spanish Empire.

J. When the pope refused to grant him a divorce, this second Tudor king broke with Rome and established the Church of England.

## IMPORTANT HISTORICAL FACTS: STUDY-DRILL ANSWERS

### A. Multiple Choice
1. B. the Spanish naval force that attempted to invade England.
2. B. bills of exchange
3. A. the price revolution.
4. C. Cortes.
5. A. Potosí
6. D. the Battle of Lepanto
7. A. the use of the Book of Common Prayer.
8. B. enclosure.
9. D. the Poor Laws.
10. C. the Treaty of Münster.

### B. Chronological Relationships
1. 1453 The Ottoman Turks take Constantinople.
   1469 Isabella of Castile marries Ferdinand of Aragon.
   1516 Thomas More writes *Utopia*.
   1567 The Duke of Alba is sent to put down the Dutch Revolt.
   1571 The Battle of Lepanto.
   1588 The Spanish Armada fails to invade England.
   1595 The Irish rebellion is crushed by English troops.
   1603 Elizabeth I dies.

   1625 The Dutch town of Breda surrenders to Spanish troops.
   1648 The Treaty of Münster.
2. SPAIN
   1. Isabella (1474–1504) and Ferdinand (1474–1516)
   2. Charles I (1516–1556) Emperor Charles V (1519–1558)
   3. Philip II (1556–1598)
   4. Philip III (1598–1621)
   5. Philip IV (1621–1665)
   ENGLAND
   1. Henry VII (1485–1509)
   2. Henry VIII (1509–1547)
   3. Edward VI (1547–1553)
   4. Mary Tudor (1553–1558)
   5. Elizabeth I (1558–1603)

### C. Matching Exercise: Historical Actors
G. The Duke of Alba
F. Elizabeth I
I. Grandee
H. Sir Thomas Gresham
J. Henry VIII
D. Isabella of Castile
E. Don Quixote
B. Gaspar de Guzmán, Duke of Olivares
C. Philip II
A. William Shakespeare

# 6 *England and the Dutch Republic in the Seventeenth Century*

## 1. CHAPTER OUTLINE

I. CONFLICTS IN STUART ENGLAND: The Stuart kings and Parliament competed for authority, a contest which eventually resulted in the English Civil War.
   A. CONFLICTS BETWEEN JAMES I AND PARLIAMENT: The first Stuart king's policies appeared to favor Catholicism and therefore antagonized Parliament. Taxes and foreign policy also proved to be important sources of conflict.
   B. RELIGIOUS DIVISIONS: Arminians and Calvinist Puritans clashed over religious doctrines and political influence. Most English Protestants feared a "popish plot" to restore Catholicism.
   C. CHARLES I AND PARLIAMENT CLASH: King Charles I attempted to impose additional taxes, but Parliament refused to grant him funds. He ruled alone for eleven years, but was forced to recall Parliament when rebellion broke out in Scotland.
II. THE ENGLISH CIVIL WAR: Charles' dissolution of the "Short Parliament" led to conflict between supporters of royal authority and supporters of Parliament's right to protect basic English liberties.
   A. MOVING TOWARD CONFLICT: With Scotland and Ireland in revolt, a new Parliament again asserted its right to limit the power of the king. Charles attempted a coup against Parliament in 1642, but failed to capture its leaders and was forced to flee London. The political crisis now became an armed confrontation.
   B. TAKING SIDES: As Parliament's Roundheads battled the king's Cavaliers, ordinary English people chose sides. The most economically advanced regions in the south and east tended to support Parliament, but considerable regional variations were apparent.
   C. OLIVER CROMWELL AND THE NEW MODEL ARMY: After allying with the Scots, the Roundheads defeated the Cavaliers at Marston Moor under the leadership of Oliver Cromwell. In 1645, Parliament united its troops in the New Model Army.
   D. DIVISIONS WITHIN PARLIAMENT appeared at this time, pitting moderate "Presbyterians" against more militant Independents. As Cromwell's power increased, he purged the New Model Army of supporters of the Presbyterians. Having surrendered to the Scots in 1646, Charles was turned over to Parliament in 1647.

E. RADICALS: In a world "turned upside down," radicals like the Baptists, Levellers, and Diggers agitated for a variety of religious and social reforms. Many rejected hierarchical authority and called for laws that would protect the poor.

F. PARLIAMENT'S VICTORY: After the Independents gained control of Parliament, Charles was tried for treason and executed.

G. THE PURITAN REPUBLIC AND RESTORATION: Parliament then established the Commonwealth of England, with Cromwell at its head. Having defeated the Irish and the Scots, Cromwell ruled as a military dictator. After his death, a royalist Parliament sought to end political and social anarchy by inviting Charles II, a Catholic, to return and take his father's throne. With order restored, English commerce and trade entered a new period of expansion.

III. THE GLORIOUS REVOLUTION of 1688 finally brought an end to the English constitutional crisis.

A. STUART RELIGIOUS DESIGNS: Charles II's support for Catholicism revived religious conflict between the king and Parliament. When Charles' brother took the throne as James II and began to move toward a restoration of Catholicism as the state religion, a new revolt against the Stuart monarchy erupted.

B. A group of members of Parliament invited James' Protestant daughter Mary and her Dutch husband, William of Orange, to take the throne. After THE "PROTESTANT WIND" blew William's ships to England, James fled to France.

C. THE BILL OF RIGHTS, passed by Parliament in 1689 and accepted by the new rulers, William and Mary, put an end to conflicts between the crown and Parliament by creating a limited, constitutional monarchy, establishing a certain degree of religious toleration, and guaranteeing individual liberties.

IV. THE GOLDEN AGE OF THE DUTCH REPUBLIC: Having won their independence from Spain in 1648, the Dutch, like the English, resisted the establishment of a hereditary monarchy with absolute power.

A. THE STRUCTURE OF THE DUTCH STATE: The States General governed the Dutch Republic in consultation with the stadholder, but regional autonomy remained strong. An oligarchy of wealthy families monopolized political power.

B. EXPANDING ECONOMY: Dutch wealth was based on well-developed credit institutions, increasing agricultural productivity, and extensive international trade.

C. DUTCH RELIGION AND ATTITUDES: The Dutch Republic remained a haven of religious toleration throughout the seventeenth century, but Dutch society was strongly marked by an austere Calvinism.

D. SEVENTEENTH-CENTURY DUTCH CULTURE was a product of both the affluence of the Republic and its religious toleration. Artists like Rembrandt and Ruisdael often painted scenes from everyday life, reflecting the secular tendencies of Dutch culture.

V. THE DECLINE OF THE DUTCH REPUBLIC: Caught between two powerful rivals, France and England, the Dutch Republic experienced a gradual decline in the second half of the seventeenth century. War drained Dutch resources, industry and trade failed to keep up with the Republic's rivals, and Dutch culture stagnated.

## 2. HISTORICAL GEOGRAPHY

### Map Exercises

Familiarize yourself with the maps provided in your text, and then attempt to locate the following places on Blank Maps 6.1 and 6.2.

SEVENTEENTH-CENTURY ENGLAND

| | |
|---|---|
| Chester | Marston Moor |
| Edgehill | Naseby |
| Edinburgh | Nottingham |
| England | Oxford |
| Hull | Plymouth |
| Ireland | Preston |
| Isle of Wight | Scotland |
| Landsdown | Ulster |
| Lichfield | Wales |
| London | York |

SEVENTEENTH-CENTURY NETHERLANDS

| | |
|---|---|
| Amsterdam | Brabant, Duchy of |
| Antwerp | Bruges |
| Artois | Brussels |
| Cambrai | Scheldt River |
| Cateau-Cambrésis | Spanish Netherlands |
| Flanders | United Provinces (Dutch Republic) |
| Ghent | Utrecht |
| Holland | Ypres |
| Luxembourg, Duchy of | Zuider Zee |
| North Sea | |
| Rotterdam | |

### Map Questions

Where were the major battles of the English Civil War fought? From which regions of the British Isles did the Roundheads and Cavaliers draw their support?

What geographical factors shaped Dutch national experience and international relations?

Locate the European and non-European regions in which the Dutch pursued their trading and commercial interests.

## 3. PEOPLE AND TERMS TO IDENTIFY

James I
Charles I
Arminianism
William Laud, Archbishop of Canterbury
The English Civil War
"Court" vs. "Country"
Roundheads vs. Cavaliers
Church Ales

Oliver Cromwell
The New Model Army
Levellers
Commonwealth of England
The Test Act
Tories vs. Whigs
James II
William and Mary

The Protestant Wind
The Glorious Revolution
The Bill of Rights
John Locke
Dutch States General
Stadholder
Amsterdam Public Bank
Rembrandt van Rijn

## 4. STUDY QUESTIONS

1. *Historical Continuities:* In what sense was the Reformation responsible for the growing antagonism between Parliament and the Stuart kings, James I and Charles I?

2. What issues divided English Puritans and Arminians?

3. How did Oliver Cromwell come to power?

4. What sort of radical religious groups flourished during the English Civil War? Why?

5. Why did the Commonwealth become a military dictatorship? Why did it end with a restoration of the Stuart monarchy?

6. Why did the Stuart Restoration end in a "glorious" revolution? *Historical Continuities:* What long-term consequences might be expected from the creation of a constitutional monarchy in England?

7. What factors—political, economic, social, and cultural—contributed to the great prosperity of the Dutch Republic?

8. What characterizes the seventeenth-century "Dutch School" of art?

9. What caused the decline of Dutch power in the second half of the seventeenth century?

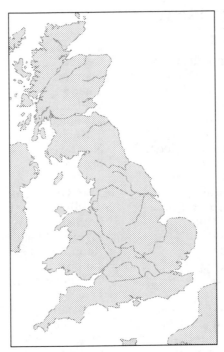

**MAP 6.1    SEVENTEENTH-CENTURY ENGLAND**

**MAP 6.2    SEVENTEENTH-CENTURY NETHERLANDS**

## 5. ANALYZING ART AND ARTIFACTS

What aspects of Dutch culture are reflected in the paintings of artists like Abraham van Beyeren, Jan Vermeer, and Rembrandt van Rijn? (See the paintings on the second page of color plates between pp. 316 and 317 of the text.)

*Historical Continuities:* How does seventeenth-century Dutch painting compare with the Italian and Spanish Baroque art of this period?

## 6. TECHNOLOGY AND HISTORY

What sorts of innovations allowed the Dutch to become preeminent in international trade during the seventeenth century?

## 7. HISTORICAL ANALYSIS: INTERPRETIVE ESSAYS

1. *Historical Continuities:* Why did seventeenth-century England and the Dutch Republic not follow the general European pattern of increasing royal absolutism?

2. Compare and contrast the English and Dutch experiences in the seventeenth century. Why did English power continue to increase after the end of the century while Dutch power went into decline?

3. Using England and the Dutch Republic as examples, describe the conditions conducive to national prosperity in the seventeenth century.

4. *Historical Continuities:* What was the political significance of the Glorious Revolution?

5. *Historical Continuities:* Using examples from other European nations, write an essay defending the Dutch practice of religious toleration.

## 8. HISTORICAL VOICES: THE GLORIOUS REVOLUTION AND THE ORIGINS OF MODERN CONSTITUTIONALISM

### A. Parliament Vindicates Ancient Rights and Liberties

Passed by Parliament in 1689, the "Act Declaring the Rights and Liberties of the Subject and Settling the Succession of the Crown," better known as the "Bill of Rights," laid the foundations for the modern British constitutional monarchy and served as a model for later constitutional settlements, most notably the American Constitution (1787) and Bill of Rights (1791), and the French Declaration of the Rights of Man and Citizen (1789).

In framing the Bill of Rights, members of Parliament claimed to be doing nothing more than "vindicating and asserting their ancient Rights and Liberties," but the provisions of this act in fact ended the long struggle for supremacy between the English monarchy and Parliament in favor of Parliament. While on the continent absolutism flourished, in Britain the monarchy would henceforth be compelled to cooperate with a legislative body representing, in theory, "all the Estates of the People of this Realm"; in practice, the interests of the landed, commercial, and (somewhat later) industrial elite.

The Bill of Rights begins with a condemnation of King James II, who was said to have "endeavor[ed] to subvert and extirpate the Protestant Religion, and the Laws and Liberties of this Kingdom." It ends by announcing the transfer of the British crown to William and Mary and by settling the question of royal succession (in the future, only Protestants could inherit the throne). The heart of the bill consists of the following declaration of fundamental rights and liberties.

### Excerpt from the English Bill of Rights

1. That the pretended Power of suspending of Laws, or the Execution of Laws, by regal Authority, without Consent of Parliament, is illegal.

2. That the pretended Power of dispensing with Laws or the Execution of Laws, by regal Authority, as it hath been assumed and exercised of late, is illegal.

3. That the Commission for erecting the late Court of Commissioners for Eclesiastical Causes, and all other Commissions and Courts of like Nature, are illegal and pernicious.*

4. That levying Money for or to the Use of the Crown, by Pretence of Prerogative, without Grant of Parliament for longer Time, or in other Manner than the same is or shall be granted, is illegal.

5. That it is the Right of the Subjects to petition the King, and all Commitments and Prosecutions for such Petitioning are illegal.

6. That the raising or keeping a Standing Army within the Kingdom in Time of Peace, unless it be with Consent of Parliament, is against Law.

7. That the Subjects which are Protestants, may have arms for their defence suitable to their conditions and as allowed by Law.

8. That Election of Members of Parliament ought to be free.

9. That the Freedom of Speech, and Debates or Proceedings in Parliament, ought not to be impeached or questioned in any Court or Place out of Parliament.

10. That excessive Bail ought not to be required, nor excessive Fines imposed; nor cruel and unusual Punishments inflicted.

11. That Jurors ought to be duly impanelled and returned, and Jurors which pass upon Men in Trials for High Treason ought to be Freeholders.

12. That all Grants and Promises of Fines and Forfeitures of particular Persons before Conviction, are illegal and void.

13. And that for Redress of all Grievances, and for the amending, strengthening, and preserving of the Laws, Parliaments ought to be held frequently.

*This body had been used by James II as a means of exercising control over the Protestant clergy and was much disliked by Parliament.

Source: "Bill of Rights." In S. M. Johnson [John Fulton]:. *Free Government in England and America*, pp. 393–394. New York: Carleton, 1864.

#### Questions

What specific abuses of royal power are addressed in these sections of the Bill of Rights?

To what extent does the Bill of Rights limit monarchical power? What powers does it grant to Parliament?

What rights does this document guarantee to ordinary British subjects?

## B. John Locke Sets the Limits of Monarchical Authority

While Parliament justified the transfer of power from James II to William and Mary on the basis of specific actions undertaken by the Stuart king, John Locke's *Two Treatises of Government* (published in 1690 but written in the years preceding the Glorious Revolution) provided a broader theoretical argument in favor of citizens' rights to change their government.

One of the most influential thinkers of his age, Locke (1632–1704) was a wide-ranging scholar who wrote not only on politics, but also on education (*Some*

*Thoughts Concerning Education,* 1693), the philosophy of knowledge (*An Essay Concerning Human Understanding,* 1689) , and religion (*A Letter Concerning Toleration,* 1689; *The Reasonableness of Christianity,* 1695). He was keenly interested in science, and was an early member of the British Royal Society (see Chapter 8).

Locke's political writings contain in germ all of the fundamental tenets of modern liberalism. Rejecting divine-right theories of government, Locke argued that human beings, and not God, establish governments in the interest of protecting their property and personal liberties. When a government violates the terms of this contract, its people have a right to replace it—just as the British had replaced James II. In the following passages from *The Second Treatise of Government,* Locke discusses the reasons why human beings create governments and identifies those circumstances that justify the revolutionary overthrow of an existing government.

### FROM **The Second** *Treatise of Government* **by John Locke**

That the aggressor, who puts himself into the state of war with another, and unjustly invades another man's right, can, by such an unjust war, never come to have a right over the conquered, will be easily agreed by all men, who will not think that robbers and pirates have a right of empire over whomsoever they have force enough to master; or that men are bound by promises, which unlawful force extorts from them. Should a robber break into my house, and, with a dagger at my throat, make me seal deeds to convey my estate to him, would this give him any title? Just such a title by his sword has an unjust conqueror who forces me into submission. The injury and the crime are equal, whether committed by the wearer of a crown, or some petty villain. The title of the offender, and the number of his followers make no difference in the offence, unless it be to aggravate it. The only difference is, great robbers punish little ones, to keep them in their obedience; but the great ones are rewarded with laurels and triumphs; because they are too big for the weak hands of justice in this world, and have the power in their own possession, which should punish offenders. What is my remedy against a robber that so broke into my house? Appeal to the law for justice.

But the conquered, or their children, have no court, no arbitrator on earth to appeal to. Then they may appeal, as Jephthah did, to Heaven, and repeat their appeal till they have recovered the native right of their ancestors, which was to have *such a legislative over them as the majority should approve, and freely acquiesce in.* . . .

The reason why men enter into society, is *the preservation of their property;* and the end why they choose and authorize a legislative, is, that there may be laws made, and rules set, as guards and fences to the properties of all the members of the society; to limit the power and moderate the dominion of every part and member of the society; for since it can never be supposed to be the will of the society that the legislative should have a power to destroy that which every one designs to secure by entering into society, and for which the people submitted themselves to legislators of their own making; whenever the legislators endeavor to take away and destroy the property of the people, or to reduce them to slavery under arbitrary power, they put themselves into a state of war with the people, who are thereupon absolved from any further obedience, and are left to the common refuge, which God hath provided for all men, against force and violence. Whensoever therefore the legislative shall transgress this fundamental rule of society, and either by ambition, fear, folly, or corruption, endeavor to grasp themselves, or put into the hands of any other, an absolute power over the lives, liberties, and estates of the people, by this breach of trust they forfeit the power the people had put into their hands for quite contrary ends, and it devolves to the people, who have a right to resume their original liberty, and, by the establishment of a new legislative (such as they shall think fit), provide for their own safety and security, which is the end for which they are in society.

To this perhaps it will be said, that the people being ignorant, and always discontented, to lay the foundation of government in the unsteady opinion and uncertain humor of the people, is to expose it to certain ruin; and no government will be able long to subsist, if the people may set up a new legislative, whenever they take offence at the old one. To this I answer, quite the contrary. People are not so easily got out of their old forms as some are apt to suggest. They are hardly to be prevailed with to amend the acknowledged faults in the frame they have been accustomed to. And if there be any original defects, or adventitious ones introduced by time, or corruption; it is not an easy thing to get them changed, even when all the world sees there is an opportunity for it. This slowness and aversion in the people to quit their old constitutions, has in the many revolutions which have been seen in this kingdom, in this and former ages, still kept us to, or, after some interval of fruitless attempts, still brought us back again to, our old legislative of king, lords, and commons; and whatever provocations have made the crown be taken from some of our princes' heads, they never carried the people so far as to place it in another line.

*Source:* John Locke. *Second Treatise of Government.* Excerpted in: S. M. Johnson [John Fulton], *Free Government in England and America*, pp. 548–549, 555–556. New York: Carleton, 1864.

### Questions

According to Locke, what gives a government legitimacy?

When do monarchs become "robbers and pirates"? When are subjects justified in replacing these rulers?

If people have a right to replace one government with another any time they feel like it, what is to prevent a society from collapsing into perpetual revolution and anarchy?

## 9. IMPORTANT HISTORICAL FACTS: STUDY DRILLS

### A. Multiple Choice

1. Supporters of royal authority, these Protestants rejected predestination and free will and willingly accepted "Catholic" rites and rituals:
   A. Puritans
   B. Levellers
   C. Arminians
   D. Diggers

2. The constitutional crisis during the reign of Charles I resulted in the appearance of two opposing factions, the supporters of absolute royal authority and the supporters of Parliament. The two camps were respectively known as
   A. Presbyterians and Independents
   B. House of Lords and House of Commons
   C. Tories and Whigs
   D. Court and Country

3. A devout Puritan, he led the Roundhead armies against the Cavaliers and ruled the Commonwealth of England as "Lord Protector" between 1649 and 1658:
   A. William Laud
   B. Oliver Cromwell

C. Titus Oates

D. John Pym

4. After Charles II attempted to end restrictions on religious worship and repeal laws that discriminated against Catholics and Dissident Protestants, Parliament responded by requiring that government officeholders take communion in the Anglican Church, a regulation known as
   A. the Petition of Right
   B. the Test Act
   C. the Grand Remonstrance
   D. the Church Ale

5. The reign of Stuart King James II ended in
   A. 1625, with his death.
   B. 1649, with his execution.
   C. 1685, with his death.
   D. 1688, with the Glorious Revolution.

6. Blown to power by a "Protestant Wind," this Dutchman shared the throne of England with his Stuart wife, reigning as
   A. William I.
   B. Charles I.
   C. James I.
   D. Charles II.

7. The passage of this legislation formally established a limited, constitutional monarchy in England and guaranteed Parliament's financial authority over government:
   A. The Glorious Revolution
   B. The Bill of Rights
   C. The Agreement of the People
   D. The National Covenant

8. This political theorist and philosopher supported the movement to limit monarchical prerogatives and argued that subjects had a right to revolt against royal tyranny when their rights had been violated:
   A. The Duke of Buckingham
   B. Thomas Hobbes
   C. John Locke
   D. Rembrandt van Rijn

9. The chief official of the Dutch Republic, he exercised influence over the government, but did not enjoy the authority of an absolute monarch:
   A. Regent
   B. Stadholder
   C. House of Orange
   D. Lord Protector

10. Housed in the town hall of the Dutch capital, it served a crucial function in Dutch financial operations:
    A. The Bourse
    B. The Dutch East India Company
    C. The Amsterdam Public Bank
    D. The States General

## B. Chronological Relationships

1. Identify the date at which each of these events occurred and select from this list of English political regimes the period during which the events took place.

   A. James I
   B. Charles I
   C. Commonwealth of England
   D. Charles II
   E. James II
   F. William and Mary

| DATE | | REGIME |
|---|---|---|
| _____ | A "Protestant Wind" blows a new king into power. | _____ |
| _____ | After 365 years, Jews are allowed to return to England. | _____ |
| _____ | Titus Oates denounces a Catholic plot against England. | _____ |
| _____ | Parliament passes the Test Act. | _____ |
| _____ | Parliament promulgates the Petition of Right. | _____ |
| _____ | After insisting that the king go to war with Spain over the Bavarian invasion of the Upper Palatinate, Parliament refuses to provide funds for the conflict. | _____ |
| _____ | The Cavaliers are defeated by the Roundheads at Marston Moor. | _____ |
| _____ | Parliament passes the Bill of Rights. | _____ |
| _____ | The king fails to denounce Louis XIV's revocation of the Edict of Nantes. | _____ |
| _____ | Oliver Cromwell conquers Ireland. | _____ |

2. Identify the date of the following events in Dutch history and arrange them in chronological order:

The Dutch Republic gains its independence.

The Union of Utrecht is formed.

William III is named stadholder.

Louis XIV attacks the Dutch Republic.

The Amsterdam Public Bank opens.

Rembrandt paints *The Night Watch*.

France imposes heavy tariffs on Dutch goods.

Spanish rule of the Netherlands begins.

A group of private investors establishes the Dutch East India Company.

The Dutch revolt begins against Spanish rule.

The first English and French newspapers are published in Amsterdam.

### C. Fill in the Blanks

1. Named the head of England's Established Church in 1633, _____ was an Arminian and supported High Church rituals often associated with Catholicism. Puritans feared he would attempt to reestablish Catholicism in England.

2. During the English Civil War, two armies fought one another for control of England. The soldiers fighting on the side of Parliament were known as the _____. The king's troops were known as the _____.

3. When villagers wanted to raise money for the local church, they held _____, sometimes rowdy drinking bouts frowned upon by the Puritans.

4. In 1645, Parliament combined three of its armies into one, the _____. Under Cromwell's leadership, the mostly Puritan "Ironsides" soon were successful in defeating royalist troops.

5. Beginning in the 1640s, radicals known as _____ began to demand major legal and political reforms that would (among other things) protect the poor and allow small property owners to participate in elections.

6. The Puritan republic established after the execution of Charles I in 1649 was known as the _____.

7. During the 1670s, two factions emerged in Parliament. The _____, descendants of the "Court" faction during the reign of Charles II, supported the full prerogatives of the king; the _____, descendants of the "Country" faction, championed parliamentary supremacy and religious toleration.

8. In 1688, the Catholic James II was replaced on the throne by his Protestant daughter, _____, and her Dutch husband, _____.

9. The Dutch Republic consisted of seven separate provinces, each of which insisted upon maintaining its local independence. The _____, a federal body that united the provinces and presided over the republic as a whole, was relatively weak.

10. The most famous artist of the Dutch "golden age," _____ earned a fortune from his painting. Despite his wealth, he lived a troubled life and painted many self-portraits reflecting his personal sense of isolation and sadness.

## IMPORTANT HISTORICAL FACTS: STUDY-DRILL ANSWERS

### A. Multiple Choice
1. C. Arminians
2. D. Court and Country
3. B. Oliver Cromwell
4. B. the Test Act
5. D. 1688, with the Glorious Revolution.

6. A. William I.
7. B. The Bill of Rights
8. C. John Locke
9. B. Stadholder
10. C. The Amsterdam Public Bank

**B. Chronological Relationships**

1.
| 1688 | A "Protestant Wind" blows a new king into power. | F |
| 1655 | After 365 years, Jews are allowed to return to England. | C |
| 1678 | Titus Oates denounces a Catholic plot against England. | D |
| 1673 | Parliament passes the Test Act | D |
| 1628 | Parliament promulgates the Petition of Right. | B |
| 1621 | After insisting that the king go to war with Spain over the Bavarian invasion of the Upper Palatinate, Parliament refuses to provide funds for the conflict. | A |
| 1645 | The Cavaliers are defeated by the Roundheads at Marston Moor. | B |
| 1689 | Parliament passes the Bill of Rights. | F |
| 1687 | The king fails to denounce Louis XIV's revocation of the Edict of Nantes. | E |
| 1649 | Oliver Cromwell conquers Ireland. | C |

2. 1516: Spanish rule of the Netherlands begins.
1566: The Dutch revolt begins against Spanish rule.
1579: The Union of Utrecht is formed.
1602: A group of private investors establishes the Dutch East India Company.
1609: The Amsterdam Public Bank opens.
1620: The first English and French newspapers are published in Amsterdam.
1642: Rembrandt paints *The Night Watch*.
1648: The Dutch Republic gains its independence.
1667: France imposes heavy tariffs on Dutch goods.
1672: Louis XIV attacks the Dutch Republic.
1672: William III is named stadholder.

**C. Fill in the Blanks**

1. William Laud, Archbishop of Canterbury
2. Roundheads, Cavaliers
3. Church ales
4. New Model Army
5. Levellers
6. Commonwealth of England
7. Tories, Whigs
8. Mary, William
9. Dutch States General
10. Rembrandt van Rijn

# 7 *The Age of Absolutism, 1650–1720*

## 1. CHAPTER OUTLINE

I. THEORIES OF ABSOLUTISM: In the face of the rise of larger territorial states and disorder caused by religious wars, political thinkers like Bodin, Hobbes, and Bossuet argued that only the rule of an absolute (but not arbitrary) monarch could prevent the collapse of society into anarchy.

II. CHARACTERIZING ABSOLUTE RULE: In practice, the emerging absolute monarchies of Europe shared a variety of characteristics.

A. MONARCHS AND NOBLES: In each absolutist state, monarchs used force and persuasion to convince nobles to accept royal authority. In exchange for their cooperation with the monarchy, nobles were granted special privileges and status. In the East, nobles exercised considerable power over both the land and the serfs who worked it.

B. EXPANDING STATE STRUCTURES, staffed by noble and non-noble bureaucrats, allowed monarchs to exercise greater control over government administration, taxation, and military conscription.

C. ABSOLUTISM AND WARFARE: Improved tax collection allowed monarchs to maintain large standing armies. "Reasons of state" increasingly replaced religion as the cause of international warfare.

D. ABSOLUTISM AND RELIGION: While absolute monarchs supported the established churches in their kingdoms (especially in Catholic states), they also moved to limit ecclesiastical authority. In France, Catholic orthodoxy was enforced by the state, but the Gallican Church rejected the pope's claim to absolute authority.

E. MONUMENTALISM IN ARCHITECTURE AND ART: Monarchs demonstrated the power and grandeur of the absolutist state through their patronage of the arts, sponsoring the construction of capital cities laid out along geometric lines and living in royal residences designed in the Louis XIV style.

III. ABSOLUTISM IN FRANCE: Capitalizing on the gains of previous French monarchs, Louis XIV made France the most powerful state in Europe in the second half of the seventeenth century.

A. THE FRONDE: TAMING "OVERMIGHTY SUBJECTS": Between 1648 and 1653, French nobles rose up in revolt against royal authority. Young King Louis XIV moved forcefully to put down the rebellion, reasserting royal authority and bringing the nobility under the control of the monarchy.

B. MERCANTILISM UNDER LOUIS XIV: Controller-General Colbert sought to make the French state self-sufficient, most notably by increasing the amount of tax revenue received by the crown. Inspired by mercantilist principles, Colbert hoped to stimulate the French economy through state support for manufacturing, the abolition of internal tolls, and improvements in transportation.

C. LOUIS XIV'S ABSOLUTISM: Louis built the power of the monarchy around his person, portraying himself as God's representative on earth. He ruled through loyal, hand-picked officials, and brought the nobility under control by placing nobles in high government positions, by recognizing noble privileges, and by creating new nobles through the sale of office.

D. LOUIS XIV AT VERSAILLES: Unwilling to live in rebellious Paris, Louis built a magnificent royal residence at Versailles. He invited favored nobles to live at this château, where they participated in the complex rituals of royal ceremony and enjoyed a rich cultural life. Playwrights like Molière and Racine provided entertainment for the court.

E. LOUIS XIV'S PERSECUTION OF RELIGIOUS MINORITIES: The increasingly pious king insisted on the primacy of Catholicism in France, revoking the Edict of Nantes and harassing Jansenists.

F. THE LIMITS OF FRENCH ABSOLUTISM: While the French ruler exercised considerable authority within his kingdom, local traditions of autonomy and the king's own compliance with God-given laws of the realm imposed limits on royal power.

IV. THE HABSBURG MONARCHY: In theory the Holy Roman Empire was united under the rule of its emperor, but in reality it was little more than a loose confederation of Central European states. Habsburg Austria was the strongest state in the empire, and its ruler almost invariably served as Holy Roman emperor, but it too consisted of a patchwork of territories. Decisive victories over the Ottoman Turks strengthened Austria's hold over Hungary, but the Habsburg ruler remained the least absolute of Europe's absolute monarchs.

V. THE RISE OF PRUSSIA: Despite unimpressive and fragmented territorial holdings, Prussia emerged as a major Central European power under the leadership of the ambitious Hohenzollern dynasty. Successive rulers forged a powerful absolutist state through the creation of a highly efficient bureaucracy and a large standing army.

VI. THE RUSSIAN AND SWEDISH EMPIRES

A. THE EXPANSION OF MUSCOVY: From modest beginnings, Muscovy grew to be the most powerful Russian state. After the brutal reign of Ivan IV and the even worse "Time of Troubles," Romanov tsars established order by repressing peasant revolts and expanded the territorial holdings of their kingdom. Russian absolutism was characterized by the institution of serfdom and by the existence of strong ties between the state and the Russian Orthodox Church.

B. THE SWEDISH EMPIRE: During the seventeenth and eighteenth centuries, Swedish rulers attempted to establish their absolute authority, but Swedish power waned as a result of Charles XII's military adventures.

C. PETER THE GREAT TURNS WESTWARD: Under Peter the Great, Russia became a large and powerful state. Borrowing technology and models of absolutism from the West, Peter built a large army, which was used to expand greatly Russia's territorial holdings, and a civil bureaucracy to administer this massive empire. A newly constructed city, St. Petersburg, served as its capital.

VII. Concerns over maintaining THE BALANCE OF POWER increasingly replaced religion as a source of conflict between absolutist European states.

  A. THE ORIGINS OF INTERNATIONAL LAW lay in an attempt by legal theorists like Grotius and Pufendorf to establish rules governing the relations between nations.

  B. LOUIS XIV'S DYNASTIC WARS, waged in the interest of territorial gain and prestige, persistently upset the balance of power and created shifting alliances between European states anxious to limit French growth and eager to take advantage of opportunities for their own expansion. Constant warfare undermined French strength and by 1715—the year of Louis XIV's death—France was no longer the preeminent European power.

VIII. Absolutism, though challenged in the late eighteenth century, provided the foundations for THE MODERN STATE.

## 2. HISTORICAL GEOGRAPHY

### Map Exercises

Familiarize yourself with the maps provided in your text, and then attempt to locate the following places on Blank Maps 7.1 and 7.2.

THE EXPANSION OF RUSSIA

| | |
|---|---|
| Archangel | Narva |
| Astrakhan | Novgorod |
| Azov | Poland-Lithuania |
| Dnieper River | Poltava |
| Don River | St. Petersburg |
| Estonia | Siberia |
| Gulf of Finland | Ukraine |
| Kiev | Ural Mountains |
| Livonia | Volga River |
| Moscow | White Sea |

EUROPE IN 1721

| | |
|---|---|
| Austria | Naples |
| Bohemia | Norway |
| Brandenburg | Ottoman Empire |
| Denmark | Papal States |
| Dutch Republic | Portugal |
| France | Prussia |
| Great Britain | Spain |
| Holy Roman Empire | Sweden |
| Hungary | Transylvania |
| Moravia | Venice |

### Map Questions

To what extent did the Austrian Empire overlap with the Holy Roman Empire?

Why were the Hohenzollern territories (Brandenburg and Prussia) problematic from a geographic perspective?

What territorial gains were made by France between 1643 and 1715?

## 3. PEOPLE AND TERMS TO IDENTIFY

| | | |
|---|---|---|
| Absolutism | Versailles | Great Elector Frederick William |
| Thomas Hobbes | Molière | Ivan the Terrible |
| Louis XIV | Revocation of the Edict of Nantes | Serfdom |
| The Fronde | Jansenism | Peter the Great |
| Mercantilism | Holy Roman Emperor Leopold I | Table of Ranks |
| Jean-Baptiste Colbert | War of the Holy League | St. Petersburg |
| "L'état, c'est moi" ["I am the state"] | Junker | Balance of Power |
| Nobles of the Sword vs. Nobles of the Robe | | The War of the Spanish Succession |

**MAP 7.1   THE EXPANSION OF RUSSIA**

## 4. STUDY QUESTIONS

1. How did the writings of sixteenth- and seventeenth-century political theorists explain and legitimize absolutist rule?

2. *Historical Continuities:* Why were the relationships between absolute monarchs and national nobilities so problematic?

3. How did absolute monarchs use religion to buttress their power?

4. What style of art did absolutist monarchs use to demonstrate and enhance their power and glory?

5. What caused the Fronde? What impact did it have on the style of rule Louis XIV pursued after he assumed personal power?

6. What is mercantilism? In what sense was it an appropriate economic policy for an absolutist monarchy?

7. What were the limits of French absolutism?

8. Why did the Austrian Empire remain the "least absolute" of the European absolutist states?

9. Why were the Hohenzollern rulers of Brandenburg-Prussia so successful in imposing their absolute rule?

10. Why were peasant revolts so common in early modern Russia?

11. How did Peter the Great build his own power and the power of the tsarist state?

12. How did the "balance of power" concept shape international relations in the years between 1650 and 1750?

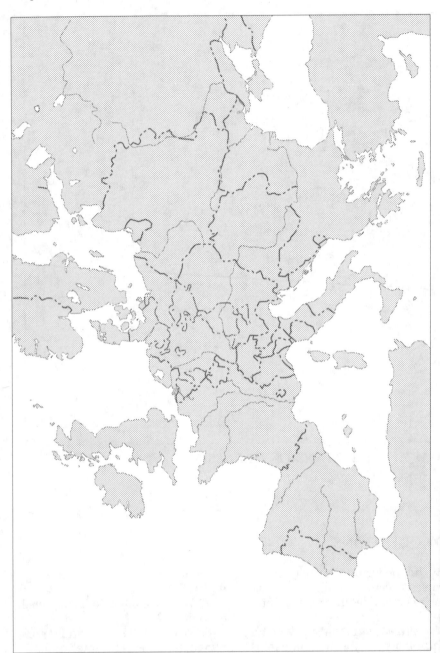

**MAP 7.2 EUROPE IN 1721**

## 5. ANALYZING ART AND ARTIFACTS

What is the Louis XIV style? How did it serve to demonstrate the power of absolute monarchs? (See pp. 285, 293, and the portrait of Louis XIV on the third page of color plates between pp. 316 and 317 in the text.)

How did St. Petersburg differ from medieval cities?

## 6. TECHNOLOGY AND HISTORY

Why did Peter the Great travel to the West? To what extent was European absolutism based on technological innovation?

## 7. HISTORICAL ANALYSIS: INTERPRETIVE ESSAYS

1. If you had inherited a kingdom in the years covered in this chapter, what would you have done to establish your absolute power as a monarch and your kingdom's status as a modern state?

2. Using the reign of Louis XIV as an example, discuss the strengths and weaknesses of royal absolutism.

3. Why was constant international warfare the (apparently) inevitable consequence of the rise of the absolutist state?

4. *Historical Continuities:* How did models of political authority evolve in the years between 1500 and 1715?

5. *Historical Continuities:* Which sectors of the European population benefited from the rise of absolutism? Which were harmed?

## 8. HISTORICAL VOICES: APPRAISING THE ABSOLUTE MONARCH

### A. A Noble of the Sword Evaluates the Reign of Louis XIV

Louis de Rouvroy, duke of Saint-Simon (1675–1755), was a soldier and courtier, but he is best known for his witty and often malicious memoirs of life at the court of Louis XIV. Although his claim to a place in the ranks of the aristocratic elite was of recent origin (his father had been named first duke of Saint-Simon by Louis XIII largely as a reward for superior horsemanship), Saint-Simon became an ardent defender of the ancient privileges of the nobility of the sword. Embittered by his failure to win a government position worthy of his prodigious talents (modesty was not one of the duke's virtues), Saint-Simon took his revenge by compiling a careful record of the petty intrigues of Louis' courtiers and of the Sun King's own inadequacies. Although Saint-Simon's personal prejudices and unrestrained vanity occasionally clouded his judgment, his descriptions of the king and his court provide a richly detailed and entertaining portrait of the culture of French absolutism.

Describing Louis XIV's death years after the event, Saint-Simon composed a detailed character study of the king and reviewed his long reign. Highly critical of the king's shortcomings, especially his treatment of the established aristocracy, Saint-Simon could not refrain from expressing admiration for the king's personal qualities and political achievements.

FROM *Memoirs of Louis XIV and the Regency* by the Duke of Saint-Simon

Louis XIV was made for a brilliant Court. In the midst of other men, his figure, his courage, his grace, his beauty, his grand mien, even the tone of his voice and the majestic and natural charm of all his person, distinguished him till his death as the King Bee, and showed that if he had only been born a simple private gentlemen, he would equally have excelled in *fêtes*, pleasures, and gallantry, and would have had the greatest success in love. . . .

. . . He wished to reign by himself. His jealousy on this point unceasingly became weakness. He reigned, indeed, in little things; the great he could never reach: even in the former, too, he was often governed. The superior ability of his early ministers and his early generals soon wearied him. He liked nobody to be in any way superior to him. Thus he chose his ministers, not for their knowledge, but for their ignorance; not for their capacity, but for their want of it. . . .

Thus we see this monarch grand, rich, conquering, the arbiter of Europe; feared and admired as long as the ministers and captains existed who really deserved the name. When they were no more, the machine kept moving some time by impulsion, and from their influence. But soon afterward we saw beneath the surface; faults and errors were multiplied, and decay came on with giant strides; without, however, opening the eyes of that despotic master, so anxious to do everything and direct everything himself, and who seemed to indemnify himself for disdain abroad by increasing fear and trembling at home. . . .

He early showed a disinclination for Paris. The troubles that had taken place there during the minority made him regard the place as dangerous; he wished, too, to render himself venerable by hiding himself from the eyes of the multitude. . . .

The frequent *fêtes*, the private promenades at Versailles, the journeys, were means on which the King seized in order to distinguish or mortify the courtiers, and thus render them more assiduous in pleasing him. He felt that of real favors he had not enough to bestow; in order to keep up the spirit of devotion, he therefore unceasingly invented all sorts of ideal ones, little preferences and petty distinctions, which answered his purpose as well.

. . . He marked well all absentees from the Court, found out the reason of their absence, and never lost an opportunity of acting toward them as the occasion might seem to justify. With some of the courtiers (the most distinguished), it was a demerit not to make the Court their ordinary abode; with others it was a fault to come but rarely; for those who never or scarcely ever came it was certain disgrace. . . .

He liked splendor, magnificence, and profusion in everything: you pleased him if you shone through the brilliancy of your houses, your clothes, your table, your equipages. Thus a taste for extravagance and luxury was disseminated through all classes of society; causing infinite harm, and leading to general confusion of rank and to ruin.

As for the King himself, nobody ever approached his magnificence. His buildings, who could number them? At the same time who was there who did not deplore the pride, the caprice, the bad taste seen in them? . . .

But he liked to subjugate nature by art and treasure. He built at Versailles, on, on, without any general design, the beautiful and the ugly, the vast and the mean, all jumbled together. His own apartments and those of the Queen, are inconvenient to the last degree, dull, close, stinking. The gardens astonish by their magnificence, but cause regret by their bad taste. . . .

*Source:* Duke of Saint-Simon. *Memoirs of Louis XIV and the Regency*, vol. 2, pp. 359–360, 364–366, 370–371. Trans. Bayle St. John. Washington & London: M. Walter Dunne, 1901.

*Questions*

Which characteristics of the king does Saint-Simon admire? Which does he criticize? To what extent are these criticisms based on Saint-Simon's anger over the king's treatment of the French nobility?

Why is Saint-Simon so critical of the king's building projects?

## B. A Western Appreciation of an Eastern Monarch

When Peter the Great toured Western Europe in 1697 and 1698, he attracted considerable attention among the nations he visited. Many of the tsar's aristocratic hosts found his personal behavior boorish and extravagant, but other commentators were flattered by his obvious appreciation for Western technology and administrative practices.

The Kingdom of Muscovy was all but unknown to Western Europeans, and travelers' sketches of life in the East were read with interest. Russia was most often depicted in these accounts as an "Asiatic" despotism dominated by brutal nobles and the superstitious clergy of the Russian Orthodox Church. Peter, on the other hand, was represented as a reforming monarch struggling against the forces of oppression and obscurantism in an effort to import more efficient economic and political models into his kingdom. Although published descriptions of Peter's bloodthirsty suppression of the rebellious palace guards (the *streltsy*) suggested that he had not entirely forsworn "barbarism" himself, Westerners generally considered his reign a great step forward for benighted Russia.

In 1723, just two years prior to Peter's death, *An Impartial History of the Life and Actions of Peter Alexowitz, the Present Czar of Muscovy* appeared in London. Purportedly written by "a British officer in the service of the Czar" (but credited to English novelist Daniel Defoe), the book smugly praised Peter for his willingness to accept the superiority of Western ways, while his opponents were condemned for their misguided and willful ignorance.

FROM *An Impartial History of the Life and Actions of Peter Alexowitz, the Present Czar of Muscovy* **by Daniel Defoe**

As to the Czar, *Evan* or *John,* he died about the Year 1691, and left the present Czar *Peter* sole Governour of the greatest Dominion in *Europe,* and in whose Reign those Dominions have received such Additions of strength from an alteration of the Conduct of the Prince, as the like cannot be shewn in the History, of any Country in the World, especially considering that it has been generally brought to pass, without any considerable Conquest of other Princes Dominions, but chiefly by altering the Economy, the Customs, Manners and Commerce of his own People.

*By this Means,* he has brought a Nation, who were before the most blind and ignorant, and the greatest contemners of Knowledge, and of all manner of Learning, to be Searchers after Wisdom, studying Sciences and eagerly bringing Home Books, Instruments, and Artists, from the most learned parts of the World for their Instruction.

*By this Means,* he has brought his Soldiery, who were before the most Scoundrel undisciplin'd Crowds, Rabbles, rather than Soldiers, and just good for nothing to be regular Disciplined Troops, Cloath'd, Arm'd and Paid like other Nations, and behaving on all Occasions in a manner sufficient to make them formidable to those who us'd to Dispise them.

*By this Means,* he has reduc'd his People in general, to a legal kind of Obedience to their Governors; not the same blind kind of Homage they us'd to pay to their Princes, who they rather worship'd than obey'd; but, a more polite Regulation; for that now the *Czar* endeavours to convince their Reason; of the real Advantages which his new Laws are to them, at the same time that he exacts their Obedience.

*By this Means,* he has regulated their Commerce, shew'd them the Profit of a vast Exportation of their own Product to other Countries, and of the Importation of the Product of other countries to them; by which their Wealth daily encreases, their People who before had little Business, now begin to get Employment, and their Lands encrease in Value. . . .

The enterprizing Genius of the *Czar,* and his early attempts to put his Empire in a posture of Defence against the Potent Neighbours who surrounded it, was not at all agreeable to the common Notions of the *Muscovites,* Building Ships of War, Entertaining Foreign Artists and Engineers, and laying Schemes according to the Manner of the other Nations of *Europe,* whose way of making War is so eminently improv'd, were all things disagreeable to them, who as they had no Knowledge of Arts and Sciences, no Mathematical understandings, or Sense of Improvement, so they Hated and Dispised all those who knew more than themselves.

Nay, so eminently were they carried out in the Esteem of their own Ignorance, that they made it a Point of Religion, and thought it a breach of the Laws of God to mingle their Customs with those of other Nations, or to bring the Usage of Foreigners among them; as if Wisdom and Knowledge were not to be search'd after to the Ends of the Earth, and it were no loss to them to be the most blind, and uninform'd Nation in the World.

But the *Czar* saw with other Eyes; it was easy to him who had a Penetrating Judgement, and a Mathematical Head, tho' uninform'd by the Knowledge of Art, to be sensible of the want of it; and when he saw the readiness of Foreign Artists, how they acted their Part by Scale and Rule, and had a whole System of things in their Heads, there needed no more for a Prince thus able to see the Defect of his own People, and the Advantage which Neighbouring Nations had over them on that account; I say there needed no more than a Sense of this, to cause him to resolve upon a general Application to the great Work of informing himself, and by degrees his People also in the useful Knowledge which flourish'd among the other Nations of *Europe*; and to bring them to receive such Notions, and such Customs as might in time render them equal to their Neighbours: If any Man were to have a true Account of the former obstinate Ignorance of the *Muscovite* Nation; how they dispis'd and refus'd all Information, how they made it Criminal to suffer any of their People to travel Abroad, much less to pretend to bring Home any experimental Knowledge, or any Customs, however good in themselves, from other Nations; one would first wonder how the *Czar* came, as it were alone; among his whole Nation, to resolve upon being better inform'd; and much more how he has been able to Conquer the obstinate Ignorance of his People. . . .

It has been said, that this insight which the *Czar* had so early receiv'd, into the Deficiency of his Country's Customs, and the Impressions of his own Ignorance, in those things, which a Prince ought to know, were first formed by Conversing early with one Monsieur *Le Fort* a *French* Gentleman, of excellent Parts and Learning, who he had Entertain'd in his Court, while he (the *Czar*) was very young, and whose Conversation he was extremely Fond of: That this Gentleman first ex[c]ited him to Great and Heroick Actions, fill'd his Mind with generous and gallant Principles, and at last recommended to him to take that happy step of Travelling incognito thro' all the polite Parts of *Europe,* that there he might see whether what he *Le Fort* had intimated to him of the exquisite Management of things in other Countries were true or not; and that he might from thence return furnish'd with Knowledge of all things relating to

Peace, War and Government, and make himself Master of what ever was Necessary to make him truly Great, and so be in time an equal Match for his (at present) more powerful Neighbours.

It is the hardest thing in the Worlds for Man to be Convinc'd of his own Defects, and till he is so Convinc'd, 'tis impossible to make him apply to Improvement; for who submits to be taught what he believes himself to know enough of.

> *If Fools could their own Ignorance discern,*
> *They'd be no longer Fools, because they'd Learn.*

But here was a Prince arriv'd to the Perfection of Knowledge, (*viz*) to know that he knew nothing; and from this original Sense of his own, and of his Peoples Deficiency, he first resolv'd to Travel, that he might Learn every thing, and then return to be the general Teacher of his own People.

Happy Humillity! he Travel'd in quest of Knowledge, that he might be qualified to be the Great School Master of his Subjects; and we shall soon see the Success in a Manner, such as the whole World can show not One Example of the like.

*Source:* "A British Officer in the Service of the Czar" [Daniel Defoe]. *An Impartial History of the Life and Actions of Peter Alexowitz, the Present Czar of Muscovy: From His Birth Down to This Present Time.* London: 1723.

### Questions

What sort of achievements are credited to Peter the Great in this document? What criticisms are leveled at his "Muscovite" opponents?

To what extent does this passage serve as a defense for absolutist rule? What does this passage tell us about British attitudes toward the East?

## 9. IMPORTANT HISTORICAL FACTS: STUDY DRILLS

### A. Multiple Choice

1. In the mid-seventeenth century, the French nobility rose up against royal authority in a revolt known as
   A. Gallicanism.
   B. the Fronde.
   C. the Taille.
   D. the Revocation of the Edict of Nantes.

2. Mercantilist theory posited that
   A. merchants should run the government.
   B. international trade should not be restricted by the state.
   C. all foreign imports should be paid for with gold.
   D. a self-sufficient nation imported more gold than it exported.

3. When Louis XIV (supposedly) said, "*L'état, c'est moi,*" he meant that
   A. his role as ruler was purely ceremonial.
   B. all governmental authority was vested in his person.
   C. he was a constitutional monarch.
   D. he shared power with the nobility.

4. In France, those who became ennobled through the purchase of a governmental office were known as
   A. nobles of the sword.
   B. nobles of the robe.
   C. Junkers.
   D. financiers.

5. Between 1669 and 1686, Louis XIV sponsored the construction of a fabulous château, intended as the symbolic expression of his absolute power. It was built at
   A. Versailles.
   B. Paris.
   C. Nantes.
   D. Burgundy.

6. When Louis XIV revoked the Edict of Nantes
   A. war broke out between England and France.
   B. Catholics revolted against his religious policies.
   C. the Paris Parlement refused to comply with his request for increased taxes.
   D. thousands of Protestants emigrated from France.

7. These religious dissidents believed that salvation came through faith and divine grace, and they advocated an ascetic withdrawal from the world:
   A. Calvinists
   B. Jansenists
   C. Catholics
   D. Jesuits

8. The Table of Ranks required that
   A. all Russian peasants remain tied to the land.
   B. all Russian Orthodox clergy come under state control.
   C. all Russian noblemen enter state service.
   D. all Russian soldiers become Cossacks.

9. In the early eighteenth century, Peter the Great built a new capital city at
   A. St. Petersburg.
   B. Moscow.
   C. Narva.
   D. Azov.

10. During the years between 1650 and 1750, the greatest perceived threat to the European "balance of power" was
    A. religious heresy.
    B. French expansionism.
    C. mercantilism.
    D. colonialism.

**B. Chronological Relationships**

1. Identify the date of the following events in French history and arrange them in chronological order:

   The Treaty of the Pyrenees ends the war between Spain and France and fixes the border between the two kingdoms.

   By order of Louis XIV, the Jansenist abbey of Port-Royal is burned to the ground.

   Colbert establishes the French East India Company.

   Louis XIV revokes the Edict of Nantes.

   Louis XIV becomes king at the age of four.

   The construction of the château of Versailles is begun.

   Mazarin dies, and Louis XIV takes personal responsibility for governing France.

   Hyacinthe Rigaud paints a portrait of Louis XIV.

   Louis XIV dies, and the French throne passes to Louis XV.

   Outbreak of the Fronde revolt.

2. Identify the date of the following events and list them in chronological order:

   Peter the Great establishes the Table of Ranks.

   The Russian army captures the mouth of the Neva River from Sweden.

   The reign of Ivan the Terrible begins.

   The Great Northern War begins.

   Serfdom is officially established in Russia.

   Catherine the Great becomes empress of Russia.

   The Treaty of Nystad ends Swedish supremacy in the Baltic region.

   Peter the Great begins his "Great Tour" of Western Europe.

   Stephen Razin, the leader of a Russian peasant revolt, is executed.

   Russia's Time of Troubles begins.

**C. Matching Exercise: Historical Actors**

_____ Thomas Hobbes
_____ Louis XIV
_____ Jean-Baptiste Colbert
_____ Molière
_____ Great Elector Frederick William
_____ Holy Roman Emperor Leopold I
_____ Junker
_____ Ivan the Terrible
_____ Serf
_____ Peter the Great

A. As ruler of Brandenburg and Prussia, he consolidated his power over his dispersed territories through the creation of a standing army.

B. This Habsburg monarch and ardent Catholic led a "Holy League" against the Turks in 1686.

C. This tsar was extraordinarily brutal, but his death in 1584 brought even harder times to Russia.

D. A proponent of mercantilism, this French controller-general helped Louis XIV to finance his expensive building projects and wars.

E. This Prussian noble accepted the royal authority of the Hohenzollern monarchs in exchange for a guarantee that his privileges (including freedom from taxation) would be maintained.

F. This French king took the sun as his emblem, and created the model

absolutist monarchy during his long reign.

G. This French playwright wrote comedies (like *Tartuffe*) for the entertainment of nobles living at the royal residence of Versailles.

H. This tsar travelled in Western Europe and borrowed Western political models and technology in his efforts to build a strong absolutist monarchy in Russia.

I. This Eastern European agricultural laborer was bound to the land and was granted few (if any) rights by his king.

J. This English political theorist wrote *Leviathan*, in which he argued that only an absolutist monarch could prevent society from lapsing into a brutal "state of nature."

## IMPORTANT HISTORICAL FACTS: STUDY-DRILL ANSWERS

### A. Multiple Choice
1. B. the Fronde.
2. D. a self-sufficient nation imported more gold than it exported.
3. B. all governmental authority was vested in his person.
4. B. nobles of the robe.
5. A. Versailles.
6. D. thousands of Protestants emigrated from France.
7. B. Jansenists
8. C. all Russian noblemen enter state service.
9. A. St. Petersburg.
10. B. French expansionism.

### B. Chronological Relationships
1. 1643 Louis XIV becomes king at the age of four.
   1648 Outbreak of the Fronde revolt.
   1659 The Treaty of the Pyrenees ends the war between Spain and France and fixes the border between the two kingdoms.
   1661 Mazarin dies, and Louis XIV takes personal responsibility for governing France.
   1664 Colbert establishes the French East India Company.
   1669 The construction of the château of Versailles is begun.

1685 Louis XIV revokes the Edict of Nantes.
1701 Hyacinthe Rigaud paints a portrait of Louis XIV.
1709 By order of Louis XIV, the Jansenist abbey of Port-Royal is burned to the ground.
1715 Louis XIV dies, and the French throne passes to Louis XV.
2. 1530 The reign of Ivan the Terrible begins.
   1584 Russia's Time of Troubles begins.
   1649 Serfdom is officially established in Russia.
   1670 Stephen Razin, the leader of a Russian peasant revolt, is executed.
   1697 Peter the Great begins his "Great Tour" of Western Europe.
   1700 The Great Northern War begins.
   1703 The Russian army captures the mouth of the Neva River from Sweden.
   1721 The Treaty of Nystad ends Swedish supremacy in the Baltic region.
   1722 Peter the Great establishes the Table of Ranks.
   1762 Catherine the Great becomes empress of Russia.

**C. Matching Exercise: Historical Actors**

J.   Thomas Hobbes

F.   Louis XIV

D.  Jean-Baptiste Colbert

G.  Molière

A.  Great Elector Frederick William

B.   Holy Roman Emperor Leopold I

E.   Junker

C.   Ivan the Terrible

I.    Serf

H.  Peter the Great

# 8
## The New Philosophy of Science

## 1. CHAPTER OUTLINE

I. CHANGING VIEWS OF THE UNIVERSE: The Scientific Revolution was less the result of new technologies than of new ways of thinking about the world. Scientists like Copernicus questioned received knowledge and helped to develop the scientific method.

 A. ANCIENT AND MEDIEVAL SCIENCE: Medieval European understanding of the cosmos and of the laws of motion was based largely on theologically inspired readings of the writings of Aristotle and Ptolemy, who posited an earth-centered universe and the existence of a "mover" behind every motion.

 B. COPERNICUS CHALLENGES THE ARISTOTELIAN VIEW OF THE UNIVERSE: Based on his own observations of the heavens and mathematical analyses, Copernicus argued that the sun was at the center of the universe and that the earth orbited the sun.

 C. THE UNIVERSAL LAWS OF THE HUMAN BODY: Rejecting classical author Galen's medical theories, scientists like Vesalius and Harvey used dissection and direct observation to develop a new understanding of the human body.

 D. BRAHE AND KEPLER EXPLORE THE HEAVENS: Using Brahe's careful and systematic astronomical observations, Kepler postulated three laws of planetary motion. He argued that the sun was at the center of the universe, and that the orbits of the planets were "imperfect" ellipses.

 E. FRANCIS BACON AND SCIENTIFIC METHOD: Rejecting the theological orientation of medieval science, Bacon argued that the truths of the universe could be discovered through inductive reasoning—using observation and experimentation to arrive at general principles.

 F. GALILEO AND SCIENCE ON TRIAL: With the help of scientific method and the telescope, Galileo formulated a theory of motion that further undermined the Aristotelian model of the universe. In 1633 he was condemned by the Inquisition for his espousal of the Copernican system.

II. DESCARTES AND NEWTON: COMPETING THEORIES OF SCIENTIFIC KNOWLEDGE

 A. DESCARTES AND DEDUCTIVE REASONING: Reversing Bacon's method, Descartes argued that scientific knowledge could be found through deductive reasoning—using mathematical logic, and not observation, to formulate general principles and arrive at conclusions.

 B. THE NEWTONIAN SYNTHESIS: Combining the findings of Bacon and Descartes, Newton formulated a scientific method based on both theory and experimentation. He demonstrated that the laws of motion can be described through mathematical formulas, and he proposed a theory of universal gravitation.

III. THE CULTURE OF SCIENCE that developed as a result of the activities of scientists like Galileo and Newton produced a "republic of science."

  A. THE DIFFUSION OF SCIENTIFIC METHOD: Traveling scientists such as Comenius and learned associations such as the Royal Society of London promoted the dissemination of the new scientific knowledge, especially among the educated elites of Western Europe.

  B. THE USES OF SCIENCE: The revolution in scientific thought eventually produced a wide range of technological innovations. Convinced of the commercial and military benefits to be derived from the new science, European governments sponsored scientific research and promoted the development of practical applications.

  C. Despite the great successes of the new knowledge, SCIENCE AND RELIGION continued to clash, especially in Catholic countries. Individual Catholics contributed to the advancement of science, but the more liberal ethos of Protestant states such as England was especially conducive to scientific inquiry.

IV. CONSEQUENCES OF THE SCIENTIFIC REVOLUTION: The new thought called into doubt not only ancient and medieval scientific theories but also fundamental tenets of religion. The scientific method could be applied not only to the study of nature but also to the study of human societies.

## 2. HISTORICAL GEOGRAPHY

**Map Exercise**

Draw diagrams of the universe representing the Ptolemaic and Copernican systems.

**Map Questions**

What principles govern the Ptolemaic model of the universe? The Copernican?

How did Kepler's calculations correct the Copernican model?

## 3. PEOPLE AND TERMS TO IDENTIFY

Galileo Galilei
The Ptolemaic System
Nicholas Copernicus
Galen
William Harvey
Tycho Brahe

Johannes Kepler
Francis Bacon
Telescope
René Descartes
Induction vs.
  Deduction

"I think, therefore I am"
  ["*Cogito ergo sum*"]
Isaac Newton
Universal Gravitation
Republic of Science
Royal Society of London

## 4. STUDY QUESTIONS

1. *Historical Continuities:* What religious significance did the Ptolemaic system hold for early modern Christians?

2. How did the Copernican system differ from the Ptolemaic? Why was Copernicus' correction of Ptolemy considered so "revolutionary"?

3. What did Brahe and Kepler contribute to the emerging understanding of the cosmos?

4. How did Galileo's ideas about motion differ from the orthodox Aristotelian position?

5. Why was Galileo tried and condemned by the Inquisition?

6. How did Descartes' and Newton's approaches to scientific inquiry differ? What premises do the two approaches share?

7. What is the Newtonian synthesis?

8. How was the new science disseminated to a wider public?

9. How did different religious denominations respond to the new science?

## 5. ANALYZING ART AND ARTIFACTS

*Historical Continuities:* Discuss the relationship between Renaissance art and the scientific study of human anatomy. In what ways might Vesalius be considered a Renaissance artist?

## 6. TECHNOLOGY AND HISTORY

How important was technological innovation to the Scientific Revolution?

Why was the Scientific Revolution so productive of technological innovation?

What role did the telescope play in disproving the Ptolemaic model of the universe?

## 7. HISTORICAL ANALYSIS: INTERPRETIVE ESSAYS

1. As a special envoy of Peter the Great, you have traveled throughout Europe in pursuit of the latest scientific knowledge. Write a summary report to the tsar, explaining what benefits the absolutist state might derive from the scientific method.

2. Draw up an official indictment of Galileo for presentation at his trial before the Inquisition.

3. *Historical Continuities:* In what sense might the new scientific method be considered one of the most revolutionary developments of the premodern period?

4. Write a defense of Cartesianism.

## 8. HISTORICAL VOICES: THE SCIENTIFIC METHOD(S)

The modern "scientific method" developed in large part as a rejection of medieval science, which had focused its efforts on cataloguing the components of the natural world and explaining their functioning and purpose on the basis of axioms drawn from authoritative texts such as the Bible or the writings of classical scholars such as Ptolemy and Galen.

Both Francis Bacon (1561–1626) and René Descartes (1596–1650) sought to free the human mind from preconceived ideas—or "idols," to use Bacon's term— and to formulate new, more systematic approaches to the acquisition of knowledge. Bacon, who was especially wary of the human tendency to leap to premature conclusions, formulated an

inductive method based on the orderly accumulation of data and the careful, unbiased interpretation of this evidence. This essentially empirical approach promoted experimentation as a cure for idle theorizing. Descartes, on the other hand, elaborated a deductive method modeled on mathematics. Beginning from a position of "radical doubt"—the rejection of anything one could not know with absolute certainty—Descartes proposed to use his reason to establish certain fundamental truths, which could then be applied to the explanation of natural phenomena. Deeply skeptical about the validity of the sensory perceptions used by Baconian scientists in their acquisition of data, Cartesians relied instead upon the mind's ability to reason and analyze.

Despite the contrast between induction and deduction, the differences between the two methods were more a matter of emphasis than of fundamental incompatibility. Like other scientific "revolutionaries" of the period, Bacon and Descartes shared the belief that a rigorous and systematic study of nature would make possible considerable progress in both science and philosophy—in Bacon's words, "Knowledge and human power are synonymous." In this sense, they were both heirs to the optimism of Renaissance humanism.

## A. Francis Bacon and the Inductive Approach

In the following aphorisms excerpted from the *Novum Organum*, or "New Instrument," published in 1620, Bacon presents his critique of the old scientific method—and of reliance on ancient authorities.

### FROM *Novum Organum* by **Francis Bacon**

Man, as the minister and interpreter of nature, does and understands as much as his observations on the order of nature, either with regard to things or the mind, permit him, and neither knows nor is capable of more.

2. The unassisted hand and the understanding left to itself possess but little power. Effects are produced by the means of instruments and helps, which the understanding requires no less than the hand; and as instruments either promote or regulate the motion of the hand, so those that are applied to the mind prompt or protect the understanding. . . .

8. Even the effects already discovered are due to chance and experiment, rather than to the sciences; for our present sciences are nothing more than peculiar arrangements of matters already discovered, and not methods for discovery or plans for new operations. . . .

19. There are and can exist but two ways of investigating and discovering truth. The one hurries on rapidly from the senses and particulars to the most general axioms, and from them, as principles and their supposed indisputable truth, derives and discovers the intermediate axioms. This is the way now in use. The other constructs its axioms from the senses and particulars, by ascending continually and gradually, till it finally arrives at the most general axioms, which is the true but unattempted way. . . .

84. . . . the reverence for antiquity, and the authority of men who have been esteemed great in philosophy, and general unanimity, have retarded men from advancing in science, and almost enchanted them. . . .

The opinion which men cherish of antiquity is altogether idle and scarcely affords with the term. For the old age and increasing years of the world should in reality be considered as antiquity, and this is rather the character of our own times than of the less advanced age of the world in those of the ancients; for the latter, with respect to ourselves, are ancient and elder, with respect to the world modern and younger. And as we expect a greater knowledge of human affairs, and more mature judgment from an old man than from a youth, on account of his experience, and the variety and number of things he has seen, heard, and meditated upon, so we have reason to expect much greater things of our own age (if it knew but its strength and would essay and exert it) than from antiquity, since the world has grown older, and its stock has been increased and accumulated with an infinite number of experiments and observations.

We must also take into our consideration that many objects in nature fit to throw light upon philosophy have been exposed to our view, and discovered by means of long voyages and travels, in which our times have abounded. It would, indeed, be dishonorable to mankind, if the regions of the material globe, the earth, the sea, and stars, should be so prodigiously developed and illustrated in our age, and yet the boundaries of the intellectual globe should be confined to the narrow discoveries of the ancients.

With regard to authority, it is the greatest weakness to attribute infinite credit to particular authors, and to refuse his own prerogative to time, the author of all authors, and, therefore, of all authority. For truth is rightly named the daughter of time, not of authority. It is not wonderful, therefore, if the bonds of antiquity, authority, and unanimity, have so enchained the power of man, that he is unable (as if bewitched) to become familiar with things themselves. . . .

95. Those who have treated of the sciences have been either empirics or dogmatical. The former like ants only heap up and use their store, the latter like spiders spin out their own webs. The bee, a mean between both, extracts matter from the flowers of the garden and the field, but works and fashions it by its own efforts. The true labor of philosophy resembles hers, for it neither relies entirely nor principally on the powers of the mind, nor yet lays up in the memory the matter afforded by the experiments of natural history and mechanics in its raw state, but changes and works it in the understanding. We have good reason, therefore, to derive hope from a closer and purer alliance of these faculties (the experimental and rational) than has yet been attempted.

*Source:* Francis Bacon. *Novum Organum.* In *Advancement of Learning and Novum Organum.* New York: Colonial Press, 1900.

### Questions

According to Bacon, what is wrong with old approaches to science?

In what sense are modern scientists the true "ancients"?

Who are the ants, spiders, and bees? To what extent does the bee represent a synthesis of the Baconian and Cartesian methods?

### B. René Descartes and the Deductive Approach

Descartes' *Discourse on the Method of Rightly Conducting the Reason, and Seeking Truth in the Sciences* (published in 1637) had a profound impact not only on modern science but also on modern philosophy, especially on the European continent. In the following very famous passages of the *Discourse,* Descartes describes the basic tenets of his method and explains how he arrived at the "first principle" of his philosophy.

### FROM *Discourse on the Method of Rightly Conducting the Reason, and Seeking Truth in the Sciences* by René Descartes

Good sense is, of all things among men, the most equally distributed; for every one thinks himself so abundantly provided with it, that those even who are the most difficult to satisfy in everything else, do not usually desire a larger measure of this quality than they already possess. And in this it is not likely that all are mistaken: the conviction is rather to be held as testifying that the power of judging aright and of distinguishing truth from error, which is properly what is called good sense or reason, is by nature equal in all men; and that the diversity of our opinions, consequently, does not arise from some being endowed with a larger share of reason than others, but solely from this, that we conduct our thoughts along different ways, and do not fix our attention on the same objects. . . .

I will not hesitate, however, to avow my belief that it has been my singular good fortune to have very early in life fallen in with certain tracks which have conducted me to considerations and maxims, of which I have formed a method that gives me the means, as I think, of gradually augmenting my knowledge, and of raising it by little and little to the highest point which the mediocrity of my talents and the brief duration of my life will permit me to reach. . . .

I had become aware, even so early as during my college life, that no opinion, however absurd and incredible, can be imagined, which has not been maintained by some one of the philosophers; and afterwards in the course of my travels I remarked that all those whose opinions are decidedly repugnant to ours are not on that account barbarians and savages, but on the contrary that many of these nations make an equally good, if not better, use of their reason than we do. . . .

Among the branches of philosophy, I had, at an earlier period, given some attention to logic, and among those of the mathematics to geometrical analysis and algebra. . . . I was induced to seek some other method which would comprise the advantages of the three and be exempt from their defects. And as a multitude of laws often only hampers justice, so that a state is best governed when, with few laws, these are rigidly administered; in like manner, instead of the great number of precepts of which logic is composed, I believed that the four following would prove perfectly sufficient for me, provided I took the firm and unwavering resolution never in a single instance to fail in observing them.

The first was never to accept anything for true which I did not clearly know to be such; that is to say, carefully to avoid precipitancy and prejudice, and to comprise nothing more in my judgment than what was presented to my mind so clearly and distinctly as to exclude all ground of doubt.

The second, to divide each of the difficulties under examination into as many parts as possible, and as might be necessary for its adequate solution.

The third, to conduct my thoughts in such order that, by commencing with objects the simplest and easiest to know, I might ascend by little and little, and, as it were, step by step, to the knowledge of the more complex. . . .

And the last, in every case to make enumerations so complete, and reviews so general, that I might be assured that nothing was omitted.

The long chains of simple and easy reasonings by means of which geometers are accustomed to reach the conclusions of their most difficult demonstrations, had led me to imagine that all things, to the knowledge of which man is competent, are mutually connected in the same way, and that there is nothing so far removed from us as to be beyond our reach, or so hidden that we cannot discover it, provided only we abstain from accepting the false for the true, and always preserve in our thoughts the order necessary for the deduction of one truth from another. . . .

. . . I had long before remarked that, in relation to practice, it is sometimes necessary to adopt, as if above doubt, opinions which we discern to be highly uncertain, as has been already said; but as I then desired to give my attention solely to the search after truth, I thought that a procedure exactly the opposite was called for, and that I ought to reject as absolutely false all opinions in regard to which I could suppose the least ground for doubt, in order to ascertain whether after that there remained aught in my belief that was wholly indubitable. . . . I, convinced that I was as open to error as any other, rejected as false all the reasonings I had hitherto taken for demonstrations. . . . But immediately upon this I observed that, whilst I thus wished to think that all was false, it was absolutely necessary that I, who thus thought, should be somewhat; and as I observed that this truth, I think, therefore I am [*Cogito Ergo Sum*], was so certain and of such evidence that no ground of doubt, however extravagant, could be alleged by the skeptics capable of shaking it, I concluded that I might, without scruple, accept it as the first principle of the philosophy of which I was in search.

*Source:* René Descartes. *Discourse on the Method of Rightly Conducting the Reason, and Seeking Truth in the Sciences.*

### Questions

Why does Descartes insist that all human beings are equally endowed with reason?

What is the Cartesian method? How does it differ from Bacon's approach?

Is *cogito ergo sum* an adequate first principle?

## 9. IMPORTANT HISTORICAL FACTS: STUDY DRILLS

### A. Multiple Choice

1. According to the second-century Greek astronomer Ptolemy
   A. the sun is at the center of the universe.
   B. the earth is at the center of the universe.
   C. God and the angels are at the center of the universe.
   D. the universe has no center.

2. Copernicus rejected Ptolemy's argument that
   A. the orbit of the planets is round.
   B. the earth does not move.
   C. the universe is finite.
   D. the stars are embedded in crystalline spheres.

3. The inductive method championed by Francis Bacon was based on
   A. observation and experimentation.
   B. hypothesizing.
   C. theological argumentation.
   D. the findings of Aristotle and Ptolemy.

4. Tried and condemned by the Italian Inquisition for his argument that the earth moves around the sun, he remained under house arrest until his death in 1642:

   A. Johannes Kepler
   B. Giordano Bruno
   C. Galileo Galilei
   D. Isaac Newton

5. According to Descartes, a systematic understanding of the cosmos can be derived from
   A. experimentation.
   B. Ptolemy's *Almagest*.
   C. God.
   D. general principles.

6. The "Newtonian synthesis" was achieved through the combination of:
   A. Aristotelian and Ptolemaic theories about the cosmos.
   B. thinking substance and extended substance.
   C. theology and metaphysics.
   D. induction and deduction.

7. Founded in 1662, this learned society played an important role in disseminating the new scientific knowledge to the educated public:
   A. The Royal Society of London
   B. The Republic of Science
   C. The Inquisition
   D. The University of Cambridge

**B. Chronological Relationships**

1. Identify the author of each of the following scientific texts and arrange them in chronological order:

    *Dialogue Concerning Two World Systems—Ptolemaic and Copernican*

    *Almagest*

    *Concerning the Revolution of the Celestial Spheres*

    *Principia, The Mathematical Principles of Natural Philosophy*

    *On the Fabric of the Human Body*

    *Discourse on Method*

**C. Matching Exercise: Historical Scientists and Theories**

Identify the scientist who originated each proposition.

A. Nicholas Copernicus
B. Tycho Brahe
C. Johannes Kepler
D. Francis Bacon
E. Galileo
F. René Descartes
G. Isaac Newton
H. William Harvey
I. Baruch Spinoza

_____ The orbits of the planets are elliptical.

_____ Observation and experimentation can reveal the truth about the natural world.

_____ The heart functions as a mechanical pump.

_____ Universal gravitation explains physical motion in the heavens and on earth.

_____ A conclusion can be deduced from a set of premises.

_____ Human understanding is the product of introspection.

_____ The sun, not the earth, is at the center of the universe.

_____ Observation of a "nova" proves the universe is not unchanging.

_____ The theory of inertia explains physical motion on the earth.

## IMPORTANT HISTORICAL FACTS: STUDY-DRILL ANSWERS

**A. Multiple Choice**

1. B. the earth is at the center of the universe.
2. B. the earth does not move.
3. A. observation and experimentation.
4. C. Galileo Galilei
5. D. general principles.
6. D. induction and deduction.
7. A. The Royal Society of London

**B. Chronological Relationships**

1. Ptolemy, *Almagest* (2nd century A.D.)

    Copernicus, *Concerning the Revolution of the Celestial Spheres* (1543)

    Vesalius, *On the Fabric of the Human Body* (1543)

    Galileo, *Dialogue Concerning Two World Systems—Ptolemaic and Copernican* (1632)

    Descartes, *Discourse on Method* (1637)

    Newton, *Principia, The Mathematical Principles of Natural Philosophy* (1687)

**C. Matching Exercise: Historical Scientists**

C. The orbits of the planets are elliptical.

D. Observation and experimentation can reveal the truth about the natural world.

H. The heart functions as a mechanical pump.

G. Universal gravitation explains physical motion in the heavens and on earth.

F. A conclusion can be deduced from a set of premises.

I. Human understanding is the product of introspection.

A. The sun, not the earth, is at the center of the universe.

B. Observation of a "nova" proves the universe is not unchanging.

E. The theory of inertia explains physical motion on the earth.

# 9 Eighteenth-Century Economic and Social Change

## 1. CHAPTER OUTLINE

I. The organization of eighteenth-century European society remained much as it had been in the past, but significant changes—including a decreased emphasis on hereditary status and increased possibilities for social mobility—were also occurring. THE SOCIAL ORDER consisted of a privileged elite made up of:

A. NOBLES, a hereditary caste that drew its wealth and status from land ownership, service to the crown, and seigneurial rights like tax exemption.

B. THE BRITISH LANDED ELITE, in particular, enjoyed great power and wealth, although many "gentry" could not claim noble status.

C. CLERGY members, all of whom enjoyed a certain degree of privilege and status as representatives of the Church, but many of whom were poor.

D. A non-privileged majority made up of: THE "MIDDLING SORT," a new and dynamic urban middle-class including in its ranks entrepreneurs, merchants, manufacturers, professionals, and craftsmen.

E. PEASANTS, the often impoverished rural agricultural workers who made up the bulk of the European population. Peasants' status and conditions varied significantly throughout Europe. In the West, some wealthier peasants owned their own land; in the East, many peasants were bound to the land as serfs.

II. THE BEGINNINGS OF THE INDUSTRIAL REVOLUTION lay not so much in technological innovation as in an interrelated increase in agricultural productivity and the population growth rate.

A. STAGNATION AND GROWTH IN AGRICULTURE: In Western Europe, and especially in England, agricultural productivity was increased through crop rotation, the cultivation of new foods, and the enclosure of common land. Agricultural societies promoted the dissemination and implementation of new agricultural techniques. On the continent, and especially in Central and Eastern Europe, the modernization of agricultural production came slowly, if at all.

B. European POPULATION GROWTH was greatly stimulated by increases in agricultural production and by other factors, such as less deadly warfare. While disease and epidemics continued to kill many, average life expectancies increased significantly during the eighteenth century.

C. MANUFACTURING: GUILDS AND DOMESTIC INDUSTRY: In the early modern period, privileged guilds enjoyed monopolies on the production and sale of many goods manufactured in urban areas. Domestic industry developed in the sixteenth and seventeenth centuries as merchants sought to circumvent guild restrictions by transferring production to the countryside.

D. Although their role has sometimes been exaggerated, new INVENTIONS also contributed to the Industrial Revolution. In the long run, the most important of these was James Watt's steam engine. Others included the use of coke and the "puddling and rolling" process in iron production; the flying shuttle, spinning jenny, water frame, and power loom in textile production; and the transfer of production from the home and small workshop to the factory.

E. The EXPANDING BRITISH ECONOMY allowed Britain to take the lead in industrialization. British advantages included political unity and linguistic uniformity, substantial colonial trade, well-developed financial institutions, an improved transportation system, and government support for (but not interference with) business.

F. The rest of Europe lagged behind Britain, but EXPANDING CONTINENTAL ECONOMIES signaled a general move toward industrialization, especially in the West.

III. Important SOCIAL CHANGES resulted from the expansion of the economy and the increase in population growth.

A. THE GROWTH OF TOWNS AND CITIES, with London and Paris as the most noteworthy examples, resulted in an increased urbanization—and "urbanity"—of the European population.

B. SOCIAL MOVEMENT WITHIN THE ELITE increased as rich commoners bought ennobling titles or offices, or simply relied on their wealth (and the purchase of land) to establish a claim to elite status.

C. THE CHANGING CONDITION OF THE POOR: Economic expansion and urbanization did not necessarily improve the lives of poor Europeans, who often lived on the edge of starvation.

IV. During the eighteenth century, SOCIAL CONTROL became a concern of upper-class Europeans, who feared the unruly behavior of the lower orders.

A. Legislation PROTECTING PROPERTY was passed by the British Parliament in the hopes of controlling property violations like poaching.

B. The SUBORDINATION AND SOCIAL CONTROL of poor people and criminals were achieved through the confinement of beggars and vagrants in workhouses and the imposition of harsh criminal penalties (especially in Britain) for theft.

V. The eighteenth century was A CENTURY OF CONTRASTS. While early modern social and economic patterns were still dominant, significant changes were also taking place.

## 2. HISTORICAL GEOGRAPHY

**Map Exercises**

Familiarize yourself with the maps provided in your text, and then attempt to locate the following places on Blank Map 9.1.

EIGHTEENTH-CENTURY CITIES

| | |
|---|---|
| Amsterdam | La Rochelle |
| Berlin | Lisbon |
| Bordeaux | Liverpool |
| Bristol | London |
| Cadiz | Madrid |
| Constantinople | Milan |
| Glasgow | Moscow |

| | |
|---|---|
| Nantes | Rome |
| Naples | St. Petersburg |
| Palermo | Venice |
| Paris | Vienna |

**Map Questions**

Which regions in Europe were the most heavily urbanized in 1780? Which regions had the highest population density?

Which European nations were most heavily engaged in colonial trade by 1775? Which European cities served as centers for this trade?

## 3. PEOPLE AND TERMS TO IDENTIFY

| | | |
|---|---|---|
| Kleinjogg | Journeyman's "Tour of France" | Sale of Title and Office |
| Social Mobility | Domestic Industry | Ségur Law |
| Seigneurial Rights | Spinning Jenny | The Combination Act of 1721 |
| Gentry | Factory | Poaching |
| Bourgeoisie | Macadamization | The Great Confinement |
| Pugachev Rebellion | Adam Smith | Chauffeurs |
| Crop Rotation | Urbanization | |
| Enclosure | Urbanity | |
| Thomas Malthus | | |

## 4. STUDY QUESTIONS

1. Describe the organization of the "society of orders." What specific characteristics distinguished each of the different orders?

2. In what sense were the nobility and the clergy privileged orders?

3. How did the conditions of Eastern European peasants differ from those of peasants in the West?

4. How did English farmers increase agricultural productivity in the eighteenth century?

5. What caused the "demographic revolution" of the eighteenth century? *Historical Continuities:* In light of earlier population trends (c. 1500–1700), what made the population growth rate of the 1700s "revolutionary"?

6. What caused the development of "domestic industry"? How did it contribute to revolutionizing industrial production?

7. How important was technological change to the Industrial Revolution?

8. Why did manufacturers gradually shift production from small workshops and homes into factories? *Historical Continuities:* How did the shift from domestic production to factory production affect the lives of working men and women?

9. Why did the Industrial Revolution come to Great Britain first?

10. What caused the urbanization of eighteenth-century Europe? How did it affect European social relations?

11. Compare the conditions of life of the urban rich and the urban poor in the eighteenth century.

12. How did the ruling elite of Europe seek to control the impoverished (and presumably disgruntled) lower orders?

**MAP 9.1 EIGHTEENTH-CENTURY CITIES**

## 5. ANALYZING ART AND ARTIFACTS

How were members of the different social orders represented in the art of the eighteenth century? How were differences in status, lifestyle, and material culture indicated? What do these illustrations tell you about relations *between* the orders?

## 6. TECHNOLOGY AND HISTORY

Why did enclosure result in increased agricultural production?

How was textile production transformed by technological innovations during the course of the eighteenth century?

Why was the invention of the steam engine of such significance?

## 7. HISTORICAL ANALYSIS: INTERPRETIVE ESSAYS

1. How were changes in the eighteenth-century European social order related to changes in the economy?

2. Write both a pro and a con response to the following statement: "The Industrial Revolution was caused by technological innovation."

3. Imagine you are a Russian noble traveling through France and England in the mid-eighteenth century. Describe the differences you see between your homeland and Western Europe.

4. *Historical Continuities:* Compare and contrast economic and social conditions in the eighteenth century with those prevailing in Europe at the start of the early modern period (circa 1500).

5. *Historical Continuities:* On the basis of the information provided in this chapter, develop an argument in support of the proposition: "Revolution was inevitable by the end of the eighteenth century."

## 8. HISTORICAL VOICES: NEW APPROACHES TO AGRICULTURE AND COMMERCE

### A. A Philosophical Peasant Promotes Agricultural Reform

While commerce and manufacturing brought increasing affluence to certain European nations during the eighteenth century, most government administrators and economic theorists continued to believe that a nation's economic and political stability was dependent upon the success of its agricultural production. Thus in his *Rural Economy,* Arthur Young (1741–1820), a very influential English advocate of improved farming techniques, argued that a "judicious rural economy is one of the chief supports of the prosperity of a state."

In 1773, Young published an English translation of the Swiss doctor Hirzel's account of the simple but very successful farming methods of the "rural Socrates,"

Jakob Gujer or "Kleinjogg." The work was intended to demonstrate that even an ordinary peasant could, through hard work and intelligent planning, make the smallest farm a miracle of productivity. At the same time, it idealized individuals like Kleinjogg as noble savages, unsullied by urban sophistication or "superficial knowledge of books."

Throughout Dr. Hirzel's work, Kleinjogg is praised not only for his diligence, but also for his rustic good sense, the product not of "art," but of "native genius and reflection." In the following excerpt from *The Rural Socrates,* Hirzel relates Kleinjogg's thoughts about the relative merits of cows and horses, and quotes "our philosopher" on the ideal relationship between the peasant, the state, and the church.

### FROM *The Rural Socrates* by M. Hirzel

His cows are small, according to the breed in that district, but well fed, and yield plenty of milk. . . . The profits of the dairy are consumed in the family. According to his calculation, exclusive of grass in the summer months, they eat two loads of hay each cow annually. His oxen are strong and well made, . . . Though they are hard worked, they are in good plight. Their allowance is three loads of hay per ox. Kleinjogg finds it answer to buy two or three lean bullocks every year, and fatten them for market. . . .

Kleinjogg finds his horse more expensive than serviceable, and seems determined to sell him, and lay out the purchase money in bullocks. A horse, he says, is a very expensive animal. He requires the same quantity of hay as the ox, besides oats to the amount of a pistole a year. The value of a horse decreases with years; whereas an ox, when old and past labour, may be fattened and sold to his master's benefit. In a word, he computes, that two oxen may be maintained to one horse*; and, it may be added, horse dung is not near so beneficial to land as that of horned cattle.

The advantages Kleinjogg derives from his cattle, are, first, milk and butter, for family uses: secondly, work: thirdly, manure. He very rationally considers the last article as the fundamental basis of improvement of soil; consequently he has applied the whole force of his care and industry towards its accumulation; and has so well succeeded, that, from his small number of beasts, he collects yearly, about a hundred tumbrel loads. . . .

. . . "You cannot conceive, Sir," he often repeated, "how many grievances would be redressed, if the government and the labouring hand mutually concurred in promoting the general good. Our estates want only to be cultivated with more understanding and industry to supply a sufficient quantity of corn for our use; but unfortunately we err greatly in our sentiments on this subject. The peasant is seldom enlightened enough to discern his real advantages. It must be then from the magistrate, who is appointed by the state to watch over the good of the community, that we hope for relief. It is they who should prescribe to cultivators the best methods of husbandry, and exert the authority lodged in their hands, to oblige the idle to work, or punish their obstinacy. The public officers should attentively inspect the conduct of every individual, leading back to their duty such subjects who have deviated from it, by reprimands, menaces, and salutary correction. The clergy might be peculiarly instrumental in this laudable work, would they be only more assiduous in admonishing their parishioners, either from the pulpit or in their pastoral visits, to the uniform practice of the duties of Christianity: would they inculcate without ceasing, that the essence of piety consists in exactly performing towards our neighbours what justice dictates, or in other words, to render to every one his due. . . .

*This determination of our cultivator is very remarkable, and should be attended to by all English farmers and others, who have an opportunity of making a choice between horses and oxen for the works of husbandry. This peasant attended to the minutiae of the comparison with an accuracy unattainable in his superiors. He worked them, fed them, and performed every office relative to them himself. How particularly judicious therefore must be his ideas of the matter! The proportion of *two* to *one* is a prodigious superiority to oxen, absolutely decisive: it is the discovery of a proportion that was greatly wanted in husbandry, and should be kept in memory as a point of knowledge.

Source: M. Hirzel. *The Rural Socrates: or, a Description of the Economical and Moral Conduct of a Country Philosopher*. 2nd ed. 1764. Published in Arthur Young, *Rural Economy: or, Essays on the Practical Parts of Husbandry*, 2nd ed., pp. 264–265. London: 1773.

*Questions*

Why is Kleinjogg thinking of selling his horse? Why does Hirzel consider this reasoning praiseworthy?

According to Kleinjogg, how might magistrates and the clergy help the peasantry to increase agricultural productivity and improve conditions in rural regions?

## B. Adam Smith and the Free-Market Economy

The Industrial Revolution was the result not only of improvements in agricultural production and new approaches to manufacturing, but also of significant changes in European economic thought. As commerce and manufacturing expanded, new ideas about economic relations began to emerge, especially among the merchants and industrialists of the British Isles. Older mercantilist thinking began to give way to a confident belief in the possibility of sustained economic expansion and a desire for greater individual freedom in national and international trade and commerce.

Adam Smith (1723–1790), a key figure in the Scottish Enlightenment (see Chapter 10), became the most influential proponent of this "classical" economic liberalism. In his *Inquiry into the Nature and Causes of the Wealth of Nations,* published in 1776, Smith championed free trade against mercantilist protectionism, arguing that artificial constraints like tariff barriers should be abolished in favor of the free play of "natural" economic laws.

Like other Enlightenment thinkers, Smith was cautiously optimistic about the beneficial effects of individual "self-love" on the larger society. In an open and competitive market, the selfishness of merchants and manufacturers would encourage them to maximize their profits by producing and distributing goods that were better and cheaper than those of their competitors, directly benefiting the consumer and society as a whole. On the other hand, although Smith called for sharp limits on government intervention in the economy, he nevertheless believed that the state had an important role to play in building the prosperity of a nation.

### FROM *An Inquiry into the Nature and Causes of the Wealth of Nations* by Adam Smith

. . . As every individual . . . endeavours as much as he can both to employ his capital in the support of domestic industry, and so to direct that industry that its produce may be of the greatest value; every individual necessarily labours to render the annual revenue of the society as great as he can. He generally, indeed, neither intends to promote the public interest, nor knows how much he is promoting it. By preferring the support of domestic to that of foreign industry, he intends only his own security; and by directing that industry in such a manner as its produce may be of the greatest value, he intends only his own gain, and he is in this, as in many other cases, led by an invisible hand to promote an end which was no part of his intention. . . .

. . . though it were certain that in the case of a free trade between France and England, for example, the balance would be in favour of France, it would by no means follow that such a trade would be disadvantageous to England, or that the general balance of its whole trade would thereby be turned more against it. If the wines of France are better and cheaper than those of Portugal, or its linens than those of Germany, it would be more advantageous for Great Britain to purchase both the wine and the foreign linen which it had occasion for of France, than of Portugal and Germany. Though the value of the annual importations from France would thereby be greatly augmented, the value of the whole annual importations would be diminished, in proportion as the

French goods of the same quality were cheaper than those of the other two countries. . . .

. . . a great part of them might be re-exported to other countries, where, being sold with profit, they might bring back a return equal in value, perhaps, to the prime cost of the whole French goods imported. What has frequently been said of the East India trade might possibly be true of the French; that though the greater part of East India goods were bought with gold and silver, the re-exportation of a part of them to other countries, brought back more gold and silver to that which carried on the trade than the prime cost of the whole amounted to. . . .

. . . lastly, there is no certain criterion by which we can determine on which side what is called the balance between any two countries lies, or which of them exports to the greatest value. National prejudice and animosity, prompted always by the private interest of particular traders, are the principles which generally direct our judgment upon all questions concerning it. . . .

By such maxims as these, however, nations have been taught that their interest consisted in beggaring all their neighbours. Each nation has been made to look with an invidious eye upon the prosperity of all the nations with which it trades, and to consider their gain as its own loss. Commerce, which ought naturally to be, among nations, as among individuals, a bond of union and friendship, . . . has become the most fertile source of discord and animosity.

. . . According to the system of natural liberty, the sovereign has only three duties to attend to; three duties of great importance, indeed, but plain and intelligible to common understandings: first, the duty of protecting the society from the violence and invasion of other independent societies; secondly, the duty of protecting, as far as possible, every member of the society from the injustice or oppression of every other member of it, or the duty of establishing an exact administration of justice; and, thirdly, the duty of erecting and maintaining certain public works and certain public institutions, which it can never be for the interest of any individual, or small number of individuals, to erect and maintain; because the profit could never repay the expence to any individual, or small number of individuals, though it may frequently do much more than repay it to a great society.

*Source:* Adam Smith, *An Inquiry into the Nature and Causes of the Wealth of Nations,* vol. 2, bk. 4, ch. 2, pp. 189–190; bk. 4, ch. 3, pp. 219–221; bk. 4, ch. 3, pp. 252–253; vol. 3, bk. 4, ch. 9, pp. 42–43. London: T. Cadell and W. Davis, 1805.

### Questions

What is the "invisible hand"?

Why should the British government allow free trade with France?

According to Smith, what are the proper functions of government?

To what extent do Kleinjogg and Smith agree or disagree about state intervention in the economy?

## 9. IMPORTANT HISTORICAL FACTS: STUDY DRILLS

### A. Multiple Choice

1. During the eighteenth century, social mobility seems to have been on the increase. This meant that

   A. it was easier to move out of the order or estate into which one had been born.

   B. people moved more often.

C. relations between people became more relaxed.

D. the masses, or "mob," became a more important part of European society.

2. Europeans increased crop yields through crop rotation, which involved
   A. the use of newly invented rototillers.
   B. turning plants to aerate their roots.
   C. replenishing the soil by alternating the planting of grain and nitrogen-rich fodder.
   D. leaving land fallow every second or third year.

3. The argument that increases in population growth rates would eventually outstrip increases in agricultural productivity, resulting in widespread hardship, is known as
   A. birth control.
   B. Malthusianism.
   C. economic liberalism.
   D. the population explosion.

4. Invented circa 1764, it allowed great increases in the production of the thread used in textile production:
   A. the water frame
   B. the spinning jenny
   C. the steam engine
   D. the power loom

5. Manufacturers originally moved production into factories because
   A. workers preferred to work away from their homes.
   B. it was impossible to use a spinning jenny at home.
   C. it was easier to supervise workers when they were under one roof.
   D. they were required to by law.

6. The transportation of British goods was made easier by a new process of road surfacing which was named after its inventor,
   A. John Macadam.
   B. Thomas Malthus.
   C. Richard Arkwright.
   D. James Watt.

7. The good taste demonstrated by affluent city dwellers became known as
   A. civility.
   B. civilization.
   C. urbanization.
   D. urbanity.

8. The Ségur Law of 1782 was intended to
   A. punish poachers.
   B. reserve elite military posts for nobles of the sword.
   C. punish men who attempted to elope with wealthy heiresses.
   D. outlaw workers' strikes.

9. The incarceration of paupers, beggars, and vagrants by the French state during the first half of the eighteenth century was known as
   A. brigandage.
   B. the Great Confinement.
   C. social control.
   D. the Black Act.

10. If you had hot feet and empty pockets, you had probably fallen victim to
    A. a noble of the robe.
    B. a chauffeur.
    C. macadamization.
    D. puddling and rolling.

**B. Chronological Relationships**

1. *Population Growth:* Using the figures provided in Table 9.1 (p. 371 of the text), draw a line or bar graph comparing the different nations' population growth rates over the course of the eighteenth century. How had the size of these populations changed during this period? Which nations experienced the most dramatic growth?

2. *Technological Change in Textile Production:* List the following developments in chronological order and identify the date of their occurrence.

   _____ A rudimentary power loom is invented.

   _____ Richard Arkwright invents the mechanized water frame.

   _____ U.S. cotton is being used in Lancashire textile mills.

   _____ A farmer invents the spinning mule.

   _____ John Kay patents the flying shuttle.

   _____ James Hargreaves invents the spinning jenny.

   Why were these technological innovations developed in this particular order?

## C. Fill in the Blanks

1. Continental nobles enjoyed privileges known as _____. These included dispensing justice in their own courts and charging fees to grind grain at their mills, bake bread at their ovens, or squeeze grapes at their presses.
2. Non-noble owners of landed estates in Britain were accorded the status of _____.
3. In 1773–1774, a Cossack claiming to be Tsar Peter III led millions of Russian peasants against their lords in what became known as the _____.
4. _____ involved the fencing in of common lands and open fields by individual owners in Britain.
5. French journeymen perfected their craft by going on a _____, traveling from city to city over the course of several years in order to learn a variety of specialized skills.
6. Merchants wishing to circumvent urban guild monopolies transferred manufacturing to the countryside, resulting in the rise of _____ or the "putting-out system."
7. _____ is said to occur when the percentage of a nation's population living in cities is on the increase.
8. In France, kings sometimes filled their treasuries through the _____, which enabled wealthy bourgeois to enter the bureaucratic and military elite without abolishing the distinction between nobles and commoners.
9. Under the terms of the _____, a law established by Parliament in _____, striking British workers could be jailed without benefit of a trial.
10. In the early modern period, hunting was often a privilege of the rich, who saw to it that stiff penalties were imposed for _____, the illegal taking of fish or game from private property.

## IMPORTANT HISTORICAL FACTS: STUDY-DRILL ANSWERS

### A. Multiple Choice

1. A. it was easier to move out of the order or estate into which one had been born.
2. C. replenishing the soil by alternating the planting of grain and nitrogen-rich fodder.
3. B. Malthusianism.
4. B. the spinning jenny
5. C. it was easier to supervise workers when they were under one roof.
6. A. John Macadam.
7. D. urbanity.
8. B. reserve elite military posts for nobles of the sword.
9. B. the Great Confinement.
10. B. a chauffeur.

### B. Chronological Relationships

1. See p. 103 for bar graph.
2. 1733    John Kay patents the flying shuttle.

c. 1764 James Hargreaves invents the spinning jenny.
1769    Richard Arkwright invents the mechanized water frame.
c. 1779 A farmer invents the spinning mule.
1784    A rudimentary power loom is invented.
1790s   U.S. cotton is being used in Lancashire textile mills.

### C. Fill in the Blanks

1. seigneurial rights
2. gentry
3. Pugachev Rebellion
4. enclosure
5. Tour of France
6. domestic industry
7. urbanization
8. sale of title and office
9. Combination Act of 1721
10. poaching

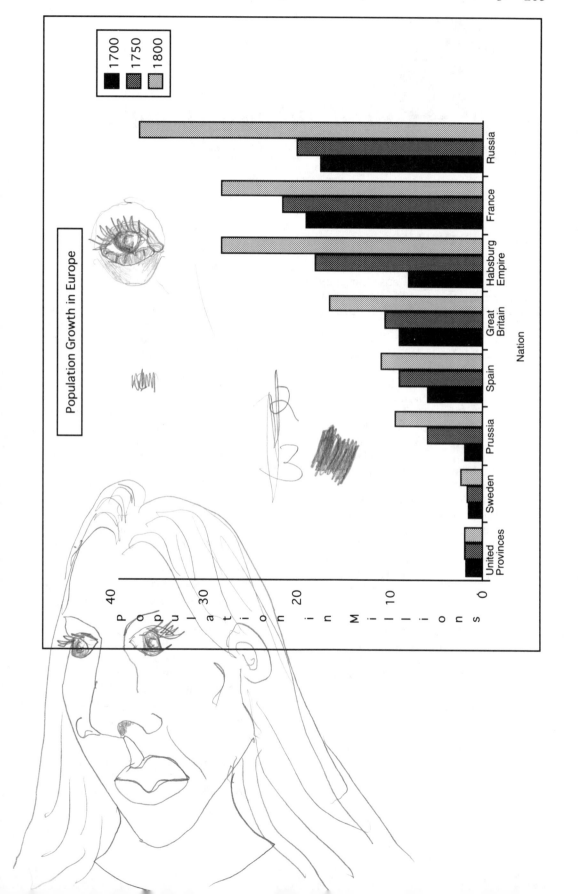

Population Growth in Europe

# 10 *Enlightened Thought and the Republic of Letters*

## 1. CHAPTER OUTLINE

I. ENLIGHTENED IDEAS were revolutionary in the sense that they challenged many of the fundamental tenets of centuries-old European thought.

  A. INTELLECTUAL INFLUENCES ON ENLIGHTENED THOUGHT: The origins of the Enlightenment lay in the Scientific Revolution. Philosopher-scientists like Locke and Buffon inspired Enlightenment thinkers to apply the scientific method to philosophy and the study of politics and society.

  B. Enlightenment intellectuals formed an informal international community, but significant differences existed between the members of THE REPUBLIC OF IDEAS.

    1. MONTESQUIEU critiqued the political and social injustices of life in the West in the *Persian Letters,* and argued that the methods of scientific inquiry could be applied to the study of laws and government in *The Spirit of the Laws,* which favored British constitutionalism over French monarchical "despotism."

    2. VOLTAIRE was also an Anglophile, but he counted on enlightened monarchs to bring political reform to the continent. He was a fierce critic of the Church, and attacked fanaticism and superstition in works such as the *Philosophical Dictionary.*

    3. DENIS DIDEROT served as the editor of the *Encyclopedia,* a great compendium of Enlightenment thought that included entries written by most of the major Enlightenment philosophes.

    4. Although he was one of the most influential Enlightenment thinkers, Jean-Jacques ROUSSEAU was atypical in many ways. His political ideas, as presented in *The Social Contract,* were very radical (he favored republican forms of government), and his emphasis on emotion and nature linked him to late eighteenth-century romanticism.

II. THE DIFFUSION AND EXPANSION OF THE ENLIGHTENMENT was the result not only of new ideas, but also of new developments in European culture and society.

  A. RELIGIOUS ENTHUSIASM AND SKEPTICISM: Movements like Pietism and Methodism revealed a continuing concern with religion, but many Europeans had lost interest in organized religion by the end of the eighteenth century.

  B. Increased literacy among the European middle classes created an EXPANSION OF THE CULTURAL

BASE. This was reflected in the growing popularity of newspapers and lending libraries, and in significant increases in the sale of historical works and other Enlightenment literature.

C. Eighteenth-century European PAINTING and MUSIC—as represented by rococo painting and the works of composers such as Mozart—were shaped both by the increasing secularization of society and by the growth of a middle-class audience.

D. THE SPREAD OF ENLIGHTENED IDEAS was effected through institutions like salons, academies, and Masonic lodges, although state and Church censorship served as an obstacle to the greater dissemination of Enlightenment thought.

III. Many Enlightenment philosophes put their hopes in ENLIGHTENED ABSOLUTISM to bring about major reforms in European society and politics.

A. The REFORM OF JURISPRUDENCE was promoted by Enlightenment authors such as Beccaria (who called for rational penalties for criminal acts and an end to the death penalty and torture), and was implemented by many eighteenth-century rulers.

B. EDUCATIONAL REFORM was a key element in the Enlightenment program, and was sponsored by monarchs who wished to "civilize" their people (and to provide the state with trained civil servants).

C. Although religious intolerance continued to plague Europe—especially in the case of the much-persecuted Jewish population—RELIGIOUS TOLERATION became more prominent, partly as the result of Enlightenment ideas but also because eighteenth-century monarchs wished to increase their power at the expense of the established churches.

D. FREDERICK THE GREAT promoted himself as the model "enlightened" monarch, but his real concern was with increasing his own power as an absolute ruler.

E. RURAL REFORM was initiated by certain "enlightened" monarchs, but again more in the interests of the power and wealth of the state than out of humanitarian concern for peasants and serfs.

F. ENLIGHTENED STATECRAFT proved a disappointment to the philosophes, who found that monarchs such as Frederick the Great and Catherine the Great were willing to compromise reform efforts if they conflicted with monarchical power.

IV. CURRENTS OF THE LATE ENLIGHTENMENT

A. ENLIGHTENMENT THOUGHT AND ECONOMIC FREEDOM: Enlightened economic theorists such as Quesnay and Smith rejected mercantilism in favor of a new ("classical") economic liberalism.

B. In the late eighteenth century, Enlightenment rationalism and universalism began to be challenged by a concern with emotion and subjectivity—as reflected in the GERMAN IDEALISM of Immanuel Kant—and with a growing interest in the national and ethnic bases of individual identity.

C. THE ENLIGHTENMENT AND PUBLIC OPINION: Public opinion made its appearance as an important social and political force during the course of the eighteenth century.

D. FORBIDDEN PUBLICATIONS AND THE UNDERMINING OF AUTHORITY: In France, state authorities sought to control the spread subversive ideas through banning books, but their efforts failed to stem the flood of works attacking the monarchy, aristocracy, and Church.

V. The LEGACY OF THE
   ENLIGHTENMENT included the
   promotion of reason as a tool for
   intellectual inquiry, a belief in human
   progress, and a commitment to the
   freedom and dignity of the individual.

While the philosophes did not see
themselves as revolutionaries, their
ideas would, in the long run,
revolutionize the society and politics
of Europe and the world.

## 2. HISTORICAL GEOGRAPHY

### Map Exercises

Familiarize yourself with the maps
provided in your text, and then attempt to
locate the following places on Blank Map
10.1.

EIGHTEENTH-CENTURY FRANCE

| | |
|---|---|
| Aix | Marseille |
| Amiens | Nantes |
| Angers | Paris |
| Arras | Poitiers |
| Avignon | Reims |
| Bordeaux | La Rochelle |
| Dijon | Rouen |
| Grenoble | Strasbourg |
| Lille | Toulouse |
| Lyon | Tours |

THE REPUBLIC OF IDEAS

| | |
|---|---|
| Amsterdam | Madrid |
| Basel | Milan |
| Brussels | Moscow |
| Copenhagen | Munich |
| Dublin | Naples |
| Geneva | Prague |
| Genoa | St. Petersburg |
| Lisbon | Turin |
| London | Warsaw |

### Map Questions

Judging by the diffusion of the
*Encyclopedia,* where in Europe was
Enlightenment thought most influential?

## 3. PEOPLE AND TERMS TO IDENTIFY

Philosophe
Science of Man
*Tabula Rasa*
Georges-Louis Buffon
Republic of Letters
Montesquieu
Voltaire
*Écrasez l'infâme!*
Denis Diderot
*The Encyclopedia*

Jean-Jacques Rousseau
Methodism
Lending Libraries
William Hogarth
Wolfgang Amadeus
   Mozart
Salons
Enlightened
   Absolutism
Beccaria

Joseph II's Edict of
   Toleration
Frederick II ("The Great")
   of Prussia
Catherine the Great's
   Charter of the Nobility
Physiocrats
Laissez-faire
Immanuel Kant

## 4. STUDY QUESTIONS

1. *Historical Continuities:* In what sense
might the Enlightenment be considered a
continuation of the Scientific Revolution?
How did the ideas of Locke and Buffon
serve to link the natural science of the
seventeenth century with the "science of
man" of the eighteenth century?

2. What distinctive ideas did
Montesquieu contribute to the social and
political thought of the eighteenth
century?

3. What did Voltaire mean by "*écrasez
l'infâme!*"? In what sense were his
attitudes toward religion representative of
Enlightenment thought in general?

4. Why might the *Encyclopedia* be
considered the most important and
representative Enlightenment publication?

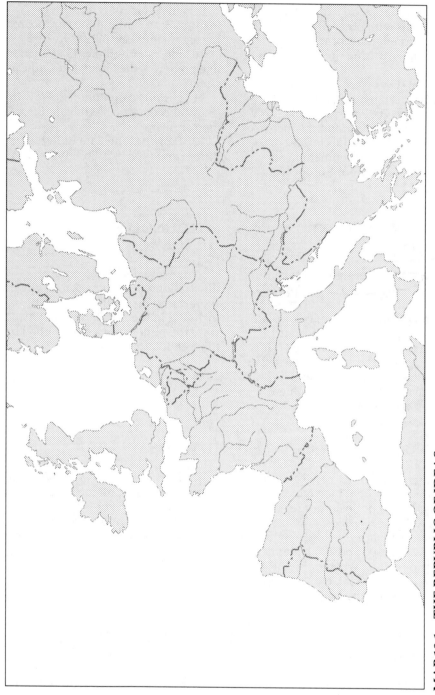

**MAP 10.1    THE REPUBLIC OF IDEAS**

5. Why did Rousseau's ideas lead him into arguments with other philosophes?

6. How did religious practice and attitudes change during the eighteenth century?

7. In what ways were eighteenth-century European reading habits, art, and music shaped by the growing secularization of society and the increased cultural role of the middle classes?

8. How were Enlightenment ideas disseminated throughout European society?

9. What sorts of reforms were instituted by "enlightened" monarchs of the eighteenth century? Why?

10. How "enlightened" were monarchs like Frederick the Great and Catherine the Great?

11. *Historical Continuities:* How does classical economic liberalism differ from mercantilism?

12. How did the Late Enlightenment differ from the High Enlightenment?

## 5. ANALYZING ART AND ARTIFACTS

To what extent was eighteenth-century portraiture "enlightened"? (See pp. 406, 413, 422, and the Boucher and Reynolds portraits on the third page of color plates between pp. 316 and 317 of the text.)

What characterized the rococo style?

What social concerns are addressed in Hogarth's works? (See p. 421 and *The Marriage Contract* on the fourth page of color plates between pp. 316 and 317.)

## 6. TECHNOLOGY AND HISTORY

Why were detailed technical illustrations, such as the engraving reproduced on p. 409 of the text, included in the *Encyclopedia*? Why were the philosophes so intrigued by the technology of industry?

## 7. HISTORICAL ANALYSIS: INTERPRETIVE ESSAYS

1. What made conflict between Voltaire and Frederick the Great inevitable?

2. Why did the philosophes reject organized religion?

3. *Historical Continuities:* Reviewing the period between 1500 and 1700, identify those developments (whether intellectual, political, religious, social, etc.) that made the Enlightenment possible.

4. *Historical Continuities:* Write an essay arguing that the Enlightenment caused the French Revolution of 1789.

5. *Historical Continuities:* How "enlightened" is contemporary American society?

## 8. HISTORICAL VOICES: THE ENLIGHTENMENT ATTACK ON TYRANNY AND FANATICISM

### A. Montesquieu Critiques Despotism

Montesquieu (1689–1755) was the most influential political theorist of the Enlightenment. His *The Spirit of the Laws*, published in 1748, was read widely throughout Europe and the Americas, and had a lasting impact on modern political theory and practice. Political leaders as diverse as Thomas Jefferson and Catherine

the Great claimed to be guided by the "first principles" set down in Montesquieu's work.

In *The Spirit of the Laws*, Montesquieu divided human governments into three basic types: republican, monarchical, and despotic. In a republic, "the body, or only a part of the people, is possessed of the supreme power." In the former case, the republic is a democracy; in the latter, an aristocracy. In a monarchy, "a single person governs by fixed and established laws." In a despotic government, "a single person directs everything by his own will and caprice." Each of these forms of government is distinguished by a set of laws and political conventions appropriate to its distinctive nature. Thus, while the motivating principle of a republic is said to be virtue, the motivating principle of a monarchy is honor, and of despotism fear.

Imbued with the Enlightenment ideals of rationality and relativism, Montesquieu insisted that he had not "drawn [his] principles from [his] prejudices, but from the nature of things." However, it is also clear that his description of despotism was meant as a critique of this illiberal and unconstitutional form of government. In the following passages from *The Spirit of the Laws*, Montesquieu describes various of the characteristics of despotism, providing a theoretical justification for later rebellions against "despotic" rulers like George III and Louis XVI.

### FROM *The Spirit of the Laws,* by Montesquieu

When the savages of Louisiana are desirous of fruit, they cut the tree to the root, and gather the fruit. This is an emblem of despotic government. . . .

From the nature of despotic power it follows that the single person, invested with this power, commits the execution of it also to a single person. A man whom his senses continually inform that he himself is everything and that his subjects are nothing, is naturally lazy, voluptuous, and ignorant. In consequence of this, he neglects the management of public affairs. But were he to commit the administration to many, there would be continual disputes among them; each would form intrigues to be his first slave; and he would be obliged to take the reins into his own hands. It is, therefore, more natural for him to resign it to a vizier, and to invest him with the same power as himself. The creation of a vizier is a fundamental law of this government. . . .

A moderate government may, whenever it pleases, and without the least danger, relax its springs. It supports itself by the laws, and by its own internal strength. But when a despotic prince ceases for one single moment to uplift his arm, when he cannot instantly demolish those whom he has intrusted with the first employment, all is over: for as fear, the spring of this government, no longer subsists, the people are left without a protector. . . .

In despotic states, the nature of government requires the most passive obedience; and when once the prince's will is made known, it ought infallibly to produce its effect.

Here they have no limitations or restrictions, no mediums, terms, equivalents, or remonstrances; no change to propose: man is a creature that blindly submits to the absolute will of the sovereign.

In a country like this they are no more allowed to represent their apprehensions of a future danger than to impute their miscarriage to the capriciousness of fortune. Man's portion here, like that of beasts, is instinct, compliance, and punishment.

Little does it then avail to plead the sentiments of nature, filial respect, conjugal or parental tenderness, the laws of honor, or want of health; the order is given, and that is sufficient. . . .

As education in monarchies tends to raise and ennoble the mind, in despotic governments its only aim is to debase it. Here it must necessarily be servile; even in power such an education will be an advantage, because every tyrant is at the same time a slave.

Excessive obedience supposes ignorance in the person that obeys: the same it supposes in him that commands, for he has no occasion to deliberate, to doubt, to reason; he has only to will.

In despotic states, each house is a separate government. As education, therefore, consists chiefly in social converse, it must be here very much limited; all it does is to strike the heart with fear, and to imprint on the understanding a very simple notion of a few principles of religion. Learning here proves dangerous, emulation fatal; and as to virtue, Aristotle cannot think that there is any one virtue belonging to slaves; if so, education in despotic countries is confined within a very narrow compass.

Here, therefore, education is in some measure needless: to give something, one must take away every thing, and begin with making a bad subject in order to make a good slave.

For why should education take pains in forming a good citizen, only to make him share in the public misery? If he loves his country, he will strive to relax the springs of government; if he miscarries he will be undone; if he succeeds, he must expose himself, the prince, and his country to ruin.

*Source:* Montesquieu. *The Spirit of Laws.* Trans. Thomas Nugent, vol. 1: bk. 2, ch. 5, p. 18; bk. 3, ch. 9, p. 26; bk. 4, ch. 3, p. 32-33; bk. 5, ch. 13, p. 57. New York: P.F. Collier and Son, 1900.

### Questions
What are the personality traits of a despot? Why?

Why is fear a necessary principle of a despotic government?

What kind of subjects must a despot have? What kind of education should they receive?

## B. Voltaire Attacks Established Religions

If Montesquieu is remembered for his political thought, Voltaire (1694–1778) attained much of his notoriety for his enlightened critique of organized religion. Celebrated for the wit and elegance of his writing and for his dedication to the cause of justice, Voltaire was a determined opponent of superstitious belief and religious intolerance. A deist, Voltaire believed in a benevolent Supreme Being, but he rejected the hairsplitting theology and elaborate rituals of the established European churches. This attitude is captured in Voltaire's wry summary of the centuries-old debate over one of the core beliefs of Christianity, transubstantiation: "Those who are called Papists [Catholics]eat God without bread, the Lutherans eat bread and God, while the Calvinists, who came soon after them, eat bread without eating God."

As this quote demonstrates, Voltaire's "rational" approach to religion was in fact deeply hostile to traditional practice and belief. Like Montesquieu, whose bald description of despotism constituted an implicit critique of this form of government, Voltaire often couched his fierce condemnation of organized religion in purportedly objective discussions of the crimes and follies committed in the name of religion, especially by members of the clergy. In a similar vein, Voltaire made use of examples from a wide range of world religions as a means of supporting his argument that, while local practices vary, all religions share certain underlying concerns. This religious relativism was eminently impartial, but it was, at the same time, highly subversive of Christian claims to a monopoly on religious truth.

Throughout his many years as an Enlightenment publicist, Voltaire simultaneously condemned religious "fanaticism" and promoted a natural, simple, and tolerant deism. In the following excerpts from *The Philosophical Dictionary*, this dual project is readily apparent.

From *A Philosophical Dictionary* by Voltaire

### FANATICISM

Fanaticism is the effect of a false conscience, which makes religion subservient to the caprices of the imagination, and the excesses of the passions. . . .

What can be said in answer to a man who says he will rather obey God than men, and who consequently feels certain of meriting heaven by cutting your throat?

When once fanaticism has gangrened the brain of any man the disease may be regarded as nearly incurable. I have seen Convulsionaries who, while speaking of the miracles of St. Paris, gradually worked themselves up to higher and more vehement degrees of agitation till their eyes became inflamed, their whole frames shook, their countenances became distorted by rage, and had any man contradicted them he would inevitably have been murdered. . . .

### RELIGION (SECTION II)

Last night I was meditating; I was absorbed in the contemplation of nature, admiring the immensity, the courses, the relations of those infinite globes, which are above the admiration of the vulgar.

I admired still more the intelligence that presides over this vast machinery. I said to myself: A man must be blind not to be impressed by this spectacle; he must be stupid not to recognize its author; he must be mad not to adore him. What tribute of adoration ought I to render him? Should not this tribute be the same throughout the extent of space, since the same Supreme Power reigns equally in all that extent?

Does not a thinking being, inhabiting a star of the Milky Way, owe him the same homage as the thinking being on this little globe where we are? Light is the same to the dog-star as to us; morality, too, must be the same. . . .

After our own holy religion, which indubitably is the only good one, what religion would be the least objectionable?

Would it not be that which should be the simplest; that which should teach much morality and very few dogmas; that which should tend to make men just, without making them absurd; that which should not ordain the belief of things impossible, contradictory, injurious to the Divinity, and pernicious to mankind; nor dare to threaten with eternal pains whosoever should possess common sense? Would it not be that which should not uphold its belief by the hand of the executioner, nor inundate the earth with blood to support unintelligible sophisms; that in which an ambiguous expression, a play upon words, and two or three supported charters, should not suffice to make a sovereign and a god of a priest who is often incestuous, a murderer, and a poisoner; which should not make kings subject to this priest; that which should teach only the adoration of one God, justice, tolerance, and humanity.

*Source:* Voltaire. "Fanaticism" and "Religion." In *A Philosophical Dictionary,* vol. 9, pp. 5 and 18; vol. 13, pp. 63–64, 84–85. In *The Works of Voltaire: A Contemporary Version.* Trans. William F. Fleming. New York: E. R. DuMont, 1901.

### Questions

What does Voltaire mean by "fanaticism"? How might religious "fanatics" respond to Voltaire's description of their activities?

Describe Voltaire's God.

What form would the ideal religion take, according to Voltaire? In what ways would this ideal religion differ from Christianity (at least as practiced by eighteenth-century Europeans)?

## 9. IMPORTANT HISTORICAL FACTS: STUDY DRILLS

### A. Multiple Choice

1.  When John Locke said that each person is born a *tabula rasa*, he meant that
    A.  human beings are stupid.
    B.  human beings have trouble remembering things.
    C.  human beings are stained by original sin.
    D.  human beings are born without any preconceived ideas.
2.  When Voltaire said "*Écrasez l'infâme!*" ["Crush the horrible thing!"], the thing he wanted to crush was
    A.  the Church.
    B.  taxation.
    C.  the Monarchy.
    D.  Jean Calas.
3.  The *Encyclopedia* sold least well in
    A.  England.
    B.  France.
    C.  Portugal.
    D.  Russia.
4.  The enthusiastic religiosity promoted by John Wesley was known as
    A.  Pietism.
    B.  Methodism.
    C.  Anglicanism.
    D.  Mesmerism.
5.  The ideas of the Enlightenment reached the general public through all of the following *except*
    A.  lending libraries.
    B.  newspapers.
    C.  Masonic Lodges.
    D.  the Inquisition.
6.  The intelligent and witty women who hosted informal gatherings of Enlightenment thinkers in their homes would have been known as
    A.  salonières.
    B.  academicians.
    C.  republicans.
    D.  "your highness."
7.  Frederick the Great and Catherine the Great both claimed to be proponents of
    A.  despotism.
    B.  enlightened absolutism.
    C.  constitutionalism.
    D.  democracy.
8.  Joseph II's Edict of Toleration increased the rights of
    A.  Russian Catholics.
    B.  the Jesuits.
    C.  Austrian Jews and Protestants.
    D.  non-nobles.
9.  Catherine the Great's Charter of the Nobility did all of the following *except*
    A.  allow Russian nobles to travel without the empress's permission.
    B.  give Russian nobles immunity from arrest.
    C.  free the Russian serfs.
    D.  formalize relations between the Russian state and the nobility.
10. In economic theory, the term *laissez-faire* is most often associated with
    A.  mercantilism.
    B.  free market competition.
    C.  protectionist tariffs.
    D.  state intervention.

### B. Chronological Relationships

1.  Identify the author and date of publication and list in chronological order each of the following works:
    *Candide*
    *The Spirit of the Laws*
    *An Essay Concerning Human Understanding*
    *The Social Contract*
    *The Encyclopedia*
    *The History of the Decline and Fall of the Roman Empire*
    *The Magic Flute*
    *On Crimes and Punishment*
    *Critique of Pure Reason*
    *Émile*
2.  Create an Enlightenment timeline using the following heading:

EARLY                                 HIGH                                LATE

1690 - - - - - - - - - - - - - - - - - - - 1748 - - - - - - - - - - - - - - - - - - 1778 - - - - - - - - - - - - - - 1800

Include representative Enlightenment individuals (e.g., Jean-Jacques Rousseau, 1712–1778), publications (*Candide*, 1759), and events (Volume 7 of the *Encyclopedia* is banned, 1757).

## C. Matching Exercise: Historical Actors

_____ Denis Diderot
_____ Philosophe
_____ François Quesnay
_____ Frederick the Great
_____ Wolfgang Amadeus Mozart
_____ Immanuel Kant
_____ Jean-Jacques Rousseau
_____ John Wesley
_____ Georges-Louis Buffon
_____ Cesare Beccaria

A. Although he never broke with the Anglican Church, this English preacher attempted to bring ordinary people back to religion by providing them with a more immediate and emotionally satisfying religious experience.

B. Through his scientific studies of plants and animals (and hopscotch!), this French researcher helped to link the Scientific Revolution to the Enlightenment.

C. This French economist was a physiocrat who argued that the grain trade should be freed from arbitrary price controls.

D. This ruler of Prussia declared himself the "first servant" of his people and brought Voltaire to his court. Despite his pretensions at being an "enlightened" monarch, he was primarily concerned with increasing his own power.

E. The foremost proponent of German idealism, this philosopher emphasized the importance of reason in the acquisition of knowledge, but his insistence on the importance of subjective experience undermined the rational objectivity and universalism of the High Enlightenment.

F. Inspired by the humanitarian spirit of the Enlightenment, this Italian noble called for the reform of the European justice system in a work that convinced some enlightened monarchs to ban torture.

G. This short-lived German composer shared the Enlightenment belief in progress and human perfectibility and, despite his musical genius, earned only a precarious living from a combination of aristocratic patronage and public concerts.

H. A thinker and a writer, he was known throughout Europe by his French name as an exemplar of Enlightenment ideas.

I. This contentious Swiss thinker argued with most of the major Enlightenment authors, but his writings—which emphasized the importance of emotion and nature—had a crucial impact on late eighteenth-century political and social theory.

J. Of humble origins, this French author championed the Enlightenment cause by acting as editor of the *Encyclopedia*, for which he was briefly imprisoned.

## IMPORTANT HISTORICAL FACTS: STUDY-DRILL ANSWERS

### A. Multiple Choice

1. D. human beings are born without any preconceived ideas.
2. A. the Church.
3. C. Portugal.
4. B. Methodism.
5. D. the Inquisition.
6. A. salonières.
7. B. enlightened absolutism.
8. C. Austrian Jews and Protestants.
9. C. free the Russian serfs.
10. B. free market competition.

**B. Chronological Relationships**

1. Locke. *An Essay Concerning Human Understanding* (1690).

   Montesquieu. *The Spirit of the Laws* (1748).

   Diderot, ed. *The Encyclopedia* (beginning in 1751).

   Voltaire. *Candide* (1759).

   Rousseau. *The Social Contract* (1762).

   Rousseau. *Émile* (1762).

   Beccaria. *On Crimes and Punishment* (1764).

   Gibbon. *The History of the Decline and Fall of the Roman Empire* (beginning in 1776).

   Kant. *Critique of Pure Reason* (1781).

   Mozart. *The Magic Flute* (1791).

**C. Matching Exercise: Historical Actors**

J   Denis Diderot

H   Philosophe

C   François Quesnay

D   Frederick the Great

G   Wolfgang Amadeus Mozart

E   Immanuel Kant

I   Jean-Jacques Rousseau

A   John Wesley

B   George-Louis Buffon

F   Cesare Beccaria

# 11 Eighteenth-Century Dynastic Rivalries and Politics

## 1. CHAPTER OUTLINE

I. THE EIGHTEENTH-CENTURY STATE SYSTEM was beset by conflicts, the result of global and dynastic rivalries.
  A. GLOBAL RIVALRIES, created by competing colonial claims, led to conflicts between Britain and France and Britain and Spain.
  B. THE HANOVERIANS AND THE STUARTS IN GREAT BRITAIN: The accession of the Hanoverian Dynasty in Great Britain was accompanied by war within the kingdom, as Jacobites sought to recapture the crown for the Catholic Stuarts.
  C. THE PRUSSIAN-AUSTRIAN DYNASTIC RIVALRY IN CENTRAL EUROPE came to a head in 1740, when two dynamic monarchs—Maria Theresa of Austria and Frederick II of Prussia—acceded to their respective thrones.

II. CONFLICTS BETWEEN THE GREAT POWERS occurred when states seeking to expand their power and territory were confronted by states wishing to maintain the balance of power.
  A. THE WAR OF THE AUSTRIAN SUCCESSION broke out between Prussia and Austria after Frederick the Great seized Silesia from Maria Theresa, but the conflict quickly expanded to include the other European Great Powers.

  B. THE SEVEN YEARS' WAR began as a new conflict between Prussia and Austria, but a "diplomatic revolution" brought France in on the Austrian side and Britain in on the Prussian side. The war took on global proportions as Britain and France fought in India and North America.
  C. ARMIES AND THEIR TACTICS IN THE EIGHTEENTH CENTURY: The officer corps remained a noble preserve, but the European military continued to modernize. Armies became larger and more efficient, but warfare was also more "civilized" (with fewer civilian casualties) than it had been during the Thirty Years' War.
  D. NAVIES were expanded and improved, but few significant naval battles took place during the eighteenth century.

III. POLITICAL CHANGE IN GREAT BRITAIN: During the eighteenth century, the role of Parliament—and especially the House of Commons—steadily increased.
  A. THE GROWING POWERS OF CENTRAL GOVERNMENT IN BRITAIN supported the creation and consolidation of the British Empire. Statesmen like Robert Walpole stabilized government financing and used patronage to build governing coalitions.

**115**

B. THE ROLE OF THE HOUSE OF COMMONS became increasingly important during the eighteenth century, but corrupt electoral practices and inadequate representation of emerging industrial districts compromised the integrity of the system.

C. THE DEVELOPMENT OF PARTY POLITICS IN THE 1760S: WHIGS AND TORIES solidified their positions, emerging as more recognizably modern political "parties." The Tories tended to support the monarchy, the titled aristocracy and the Anglican Church, while the Whigs formed a "loyal opposition."

D. THE RISE OF BRITISH NATIONALISM was fueled by Britons' pride in their governmental and financial institutions, by their economic investment in the British Empire, and by their shared duties (including universal taxation) and liberties.

IV. CHALLENGES TO ESTABLISHED AUTHORITY emerged throughout Western Europe in the 1760s and 1770s.

A. BRITISH RADICALS, led by MP and journalist John Wilkes, agitated for increased civil liberties (including freedom of the press) and greater political representation for ordinary people.

B. AMERICAN REVOLUTIONARIES protested British domination, and, in 1776, declared the thirteen colonies' independence from Britain. The colonists eventually defeated the British army, and American independence was recognized in 1783.

C. In France, conflict arose between THE PARLEMENTS AND THE FRENCH MONARCHY. Although the parlements often defended elite interests, they came to be seen as representatives of popular resistance to monarchical despotism. Despite Turgot's concerted effort to reform the French tax system—in desperate need of an overhaul—opposition from all sectors of society forced his resignation.

D. OTHER MOVEMENTS FOR REFORM appeared throughout Europe—in Greece and the Dutch United Provinces, for example—but most were repressed by local elites or foreign armies.

V. FADING POWERS: THE OTTOMAN EMPIRE AND POLAND

A. THE DECLINE OF TURKISH POWER IN EUROPE was the result of an overextended empire and largely incompetent leadership on the part of the sultans.

B. THE DISAPPEARANCE OF POLAND stemmed from Polish nobles' refusal to accept political and social reforms and from the greediness for territory of the kingdom's more powerful neighbors: Austria, Prussia, and Russia.

VI. CONCLUSION

## 2. HISTORICAL GEOGRAPHY

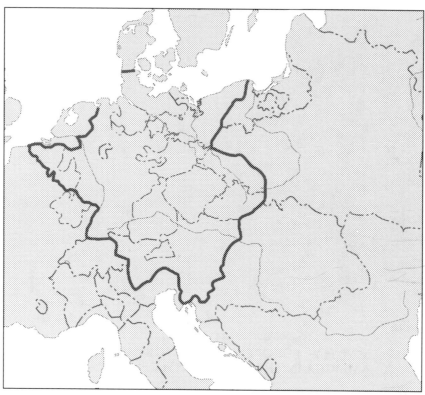

**MAP 11.1   CENTRAL EUROPE IN THE EIGHTEENTH CENTURY**

**Map Exercises**

Familiarize yourself with the maps provided in your text, and then attempt to locate the following places on Blank Maps 11.1 and 11.2.

CENTRAL EUROPE IN THE 18TH CENTURY

| | |
|---|---|
| Austria | Hungary |
| Austrian | Munich |
| Netherlands | Ottoman Empire |
| Berlin | Poland |
| Bohemia | Prussia |
| Brandenburg | Rhine River |
| Danube River | Russia |
| Dutch United | Saxony |
| Provinces | Silesia |
| Elbe River | Transylvania |
| Hanover | Vienna |

EUROPEAN HOLDINGS IN NORTH AMERICA IN THE 18TH CENTURY

| | |
|---|---|
| Acadia | Mississippi River |
| Boston | Montréal |
| Canada | Newfoundland |
| Caribbean Sea | New Orleans |
| Cuba | New Spain |
| Florida | New York |
| Fort Albany | Québec |
| Great Lakes | St. Lawrence River |
| Havana | St. Louis |
| Louisiana | Thirteen Colonies |

**MAP 11.2   EUROPEAN HOLDINGS IN NORTH
AMERICA IN THE EIGHTEENTH CENTURY**

**Map Questions**
What territories did Prussia gain
during the course of the eighteenth
century?

How did British, French, and Spanish
holdings in the New World change
over the course of the eighteenth
century?

What did Austria, Prussia, and
Russia each gain from the partitions of
Poland?

## 3. PEOPLE AND TERMS TO IDENTIFY

| | | |
|---|---|---|
| George III ~ *Hanoverian* | "Diplomatic Revolution" of 1756 | Stamp Act |
| War of Jenkins' Ear | | Thomas Paine |
| George I | Press-gangs | Battle of Yorktown |
| Jacobites | South Sea Bubble | Parlements |
| Maria Theresa | Robert Walpole | Jansenists |
| Frederick II | Rotten Boroughs | Flour War |
| Balance of Power | Whigs and Tories | Dutch Patriot Party |
| War of the Austrian Succession | Political Party | Stanislas Poniatowski |
| Seven Years' War | "Privileged Island" | Partitions of Poland |
| | "Wilkes and Liberty" | |

## 4. STUDY QUESTIONS

1. How did colonial rivalries affect relations between the European Great Powers during the eighteenth century?

2. Why did the crown of Great Britain pass to a German branch of the English royal family in 1714? *Historical Continuities:* What were the seventeenth-century origins of Jacobite resistance to this dynastic settlement?

3. What caused the War of the Austrian Succession? Why did other European nations join in?

4. What caused the Seven Years' War? In what sense was it a "global" war?

5. *Historical Continuities:* How did eighteenth-century warfare differ from warfare in the previous two centuries?

6. What role did Robert Walpole play in the increasing centralization of British government?

7. What caused the development of party politics in Britain in the 1760s?

8. What were the root causes of British nationalism? *Historical Continuities:* What general conditions do you expect will be necessary to the appearance of nationalism as a European-wide phenomenon in the nineteenth century?

9. Why did the American colonies break away from British rule?

10. Why did the French parlements emerge as leaders in the movement to limit absolutist monarchy?

11. What role did taxation play in the growing opposition to the French monarchy?

12. Why were reform movements in places like Greece and the Dutch United Provinces less successful than those in Britain and America?

13. What caused the decline of Ottoman Turkey and the disappearance of Poland? *Historical Continuities:* How might these developments be expected to affect relations between the European Great Powers?

## 5. ANALYZING ART AND ARTIFACTS

What do eighteenth-century artistic depictions of warfare tell you about attitudes toward war? What can you learn about actual military practice from these images?

## 6. TECHNOLOGY AND HISTORY

How did military technologies change during the eighteenth century?

## 7. HISTORICAL ANALYSIS: INTERPRETIVE ESSAYS

1. Was Great Britain justified in considering itself a "privileged island" during the eighteenth century?

2. Why did war break out between the major European powers so often during the eighteenth century?

3. Compare and contrast the social origins and political perspectives of the "conservative" supporters of order and the "radical" supporters of reform in eighteenth-century Europe.

4. *Historical Continuities:* How did events in the eighteenth century lay the foundations for the rise of democracy in the nineteenth and twentieth centuries?

5. *Historical Continuities:* You are Stanislas Poniatowski and have just been named king of Poland. Having reviewed Chapters 9, 10, and 11 of your text, write up a "modernization" plan for the Polish kingdom that incorporates the most important economic, social, intellectual, and political advances of eighteenth-century Europe (and that will promote the survival of Poland as an independent nation).

## 8. HISTORICAL VOICES: WAR IN THE OLD WORLD AND REVOLUTION IN THE NEW WORLD

### A. Voltaire on the Plight of the Soldier

The bite of Voltaire's satirical wit extended beyond religion to the military and politics. In the following excerpt from his most famous piece of writing, the short novel *Candide* (1759), Voltaire takes aim at the deceptive practices of military recruiters and the brutality of military discipline.

The "Bulgarian" army into which Candide is recruited is, in reality, the Prussian army of Frederick the Great at the time of the Seven Years' War, which was going on as Voltaire wrote. (The name "Bulgarian" is a crude joke: Voltaire intends to suggest that Frederick and his troops were prone to "buggery.") Frederick, who was very concerned with improving the quality of his troops, had created special regiments of six-foot-tall soldiers, which explains why the recruiters are so interested in Candide's height. Similarly, the brutal beating Candide receives for deserting is simply an exaggerated form of punishments imposed on real deserters from the Prussian army.

However, if Frederick the Great's military policies are satirized in this passage, Voltaire's real intent in *Candide* was to condemn the "heroic butchery" of warfare in general. When Candide finally escapes from the Bulgarian army, he discovers that its enemies, the "Abares" (the French), are equally as bloodthirsty. The real victims of war are ordinary soldiers, who die by the thousands as their kings look on at this "entertainment," and civilians, whose villages are burned and pillaged and who are themselves raped and slaughtered by the "Bulgarian heroes" and the "heroic Abares."

### FROM *Candide* by Voltaire

... [Candide] took up his stand at the door of an inn. He had not been long there, before two men dressed in blue, fixed their eyes steadfastly upon him. "Faith, comrade," said one of them to the other, "yonder is a well made young fellow, and of the right size." Upon which they made up to Candide, and with the greatest civility and politeness invited him to dine with them. "Gentlemen," replied Candide, with a most engaging modesty, "you do me much honor, but upon my word I have no money." "Money, sir!" said one of the blues to him, "young persons of your appearance and merit never pay anything; why, are not you five feet five inches high?" "Yes, gentlemen, that is really my size," replied he, with a low bow. "Come then, sir, sit down along with us; we will not only pay your reckoning, but will never suffer such a clever young fellow as you to want money. Men were born to assist one another." ... His generous companions next entreated him to accept of a few crowns, which he readily complied with, at the same time offering them his note for the payment, which they refused, and sat down to table. ... We ask you whether you have not a great affection for the king of the Bulgarians?" "For the king of the Bulgarians?" said Candide, "oh Lord! not at all, why I never saw him in my life." "Is it possible! oh, he is a most charming king! Come, we must drink his health." "With all my heart, gentlemen," says Candide, and off he tossed his glass. "Bravo!" cry the blues; "you are now the support, the defender, the hero of the Bulgarians; your fortune is made; you are in the high road to glory." So saying, they handcuffed him, and carried him away to the regiment. There he was made to wheel about to the right, to the left, to draw his rammer, to return his rammer, to present, to fire, to march, and they gave him thirty blows with a cane; the next day he performed his exercise a little better, and they gave him but twenty; the day following he came off with ten, and was looked upon as a young fellow of surprising genius by all his comrades.

Candide was struck with amazement, and could not for the soul of him conceive how he came to be a hero. One fine spring morning, he took it into his head to take a walk, and he marched straight forward, conceiving it to be a privilege of the human species, as well as of the brute creation, to make use of their legs how and when they pleased. He had not gone above two leagues when he was overtaken by four other heroes, six feet high, who bound him neck and heels, and carried him to a dungeon. A court-martial sat upon him, and he was asked which he liked better, to run the gauntlet six and thirty times through the whole regiment, or to have his brains blown out with a dozen musket-balls? . . . he determined, in virtue of that divine gift called free will, to run the gauntlet six and thirty times. He had gone through his discipline twice, and the regiment being composed of 2,000 men, they composed for him exactly 4,000 strokes, which laid bare all his muscles and nerves from the nape of his neck to his stern. As they were preparing to make him set out the third time our young hero, unable to support it any longer, begged as a favor that they would be so obliging as to shoot him through the head; the favor being granted, a bandage was tied over his eyes, and he was made to kneel down. At that very instant, his Bulgarian majesty happening to pass by made a stop, and inquired into the delinquent's crime, and being a prince of great penetration, he found, from what he heard of Candide, that he was a young metaphysician, entirely ignorant of the world; and therefore, out of his great clemency, he condescended to pardon him, for which his name will be celebrated in every journal, and in every age. A skillful surgeon made a cure of the flagellated Candide in three weeks by means of emollient unguents prescribed by Dioscorides. His sores were now skinned over and he was able to march, when the king of the Bulgarians gave battle to the king of the Abares.

*Source:* Voltaire. *Candide.* In *The Works of Voltaire: A Contemporary Version*, vol. 1, pp. 65–68. Trans. William F. Fleming. New York: E. R. DuMont, 1901.

### Questions

How does Candide come to serve in the "Bulgarian" army? Why does he desert?

According to this passage, how was discipline maintained within the eighteenth-century military?

Why would you expect an Enlightenment philosophe like Voltaire to oppose war?

## B. The American Colonists Declare Their Independence

The growing alienation between Britain and its North American colonies finally culminated in a definitive rupture in 1776. On July 4th, representatives of the thirteen colonies gathered at Philadelphia during the Second Continental Congress and openly declared their break with the home country.

The "Declaration of Independence," drafted by Thomas Jefferson and revised by the other members of the Continental Congress, was deeply imbued with the political thought of the Enlightenment. Drawing on the writings of John Locke and Montesquieu and on the British Bill of Rights, the declaration was intended to explain and justify the American colonists' actions to the world. The American Revolution, the colonists argued, was not simply the result of specific and local abuses, but was also an expression of all human beings' universal and "self-evident" right to resist oppression.

While Jefferson's arguments were derived from pre-existing political theory, the declaration presented these ideas in a uniquely elegant, forceful, and succinct style. A rallying cry for the thirteen colonies in their successful bid for independence, it would also serve as an inspiration to subsequent revolutionaries, especially in the Portuguese and Spanish colonies of Latin American.

### FROM *The Unanimous Declaration of the Thirteen United States of America* drafted by Thomas Jefferson

When, in the course of human events, it becomes necessary for one people to dissolve the political bands which have connected them with another, and to assume, among the powers of the earth, the separate and equal station to which the laws of nature and of nature's God entitle them, a decent respect to the opinions of mankind requires that they should declare the causes which impel them to the separation.

We hold these truths to be self-evident, that all men are created equal; that they are endowed by their Creator with certain unalienable rights; that among these, are life, liberty, and the pursuit of happiness. That, to secure these rights, governments are instituted among men, deriving their just powers from the consent of the governed; that, whenever any form of government becomes destructive of these ends, it is the right of the people to alter or to abolish it, and to institute a new government, laying its foundation on such principles, and organizing its powers in such form, as to them shall seem most likely to effect their safety and happiness. Prudence, indeed, will dictate that governments long established, should not be changed for light and transient causes; and, accordingly, all experience hath shown, that mankind are more disposed to suffer, while evils are sufferable, than to right themselves by abolishing the forms to which they are accustomed. But, when a long train of abuses and usurpations, pursuing invariably the same object, evinces a design to reduce them under absolute despotism, it is their right, it is their duty, to throw off such government, and to provide new guards for their future security. Such has been the patient sufferance of these colonies, and such is now the necessity which constrains them to alter their former systems of government. The history of the present king of Great Britain is a history of repeated injuries and usurpations, all having, in direct object, the establishment of an absolute tyranny over these States. . . .

In every stage of these oppressions, we have petitioned for redress, in the most humble terms; our repeated petitions have been answered only by repeated injury. A prince, whose character is thus marked by every act which may define a tyrant, is unfit to be the ruler of a free people.

Nor have we been wanting in attention to our British brethren. We have warned them, from time to time, of attempts made by their legislature to extend an unwarrantable jurisdiction over us. We have reminded them of the circumstances of our emigration and settlement here. We have appealed to their native justice and magnanimity, and we have conjured them, by the ties of our common kindred, to disavow these usurpations, which would inevitably interrupt our connections and correspondence. They, too, have been deaf to the voice of justice and consanguinity. We must, therefore, acquiesce in the necessity, which denounces our separation, and hold them, as we hold the rest of mankind, enemies in war, in peace, friends.

We, therefore, the representatives of the United States of America, in General Congress assembled, appealing to the Supreme Judge of the

World for the rectitude of our intentions, do in the name, and by the authority of the good people of these colonies, solemnly publish and declare, That these United Colonies are, and of right ought to be, free and independent States; that they are absolved from all allegiance to the British crown, and that all political connexion between them and the state of Great Britain, is, and ought to be, totally dissolved; and that, as free and independent States, they have full power to levy war, conclude peace, contract alliances, establish commerce, and to do all other acts and things which independent States may of right do. And, for the support of this declaration, with a firm reliance on the protection of Divine Providence, we mutually pledge to each other, our lives, our fortunes, and our sacred honor.

*Source:* "The Unanimous Declaration of the Thirteen United States of America." In: S. M. Johnson [John Fulton?], *Free Government in England and America*, pp. 461–462, 464. New York: Carleton, 1864.

### Questions

Why was this declaration written?

Review the Locke and Montesquieu readings (Chapters 6 and 10) and identify the specific ideas borrowed from these texts by Jefferson.

In what sense is this document a quintessential product of the Enlightenment?

## 9. IMPORTANT HISTORICAL FACTS: STUDY DRILLS

### A. Multiple Choice

1. In 1739, Great Britain and Spain went to war over shipping rights in the colonies. This was known as
   A. the War of Spanish Succession.
   B. the Battle of Culloden Moor.
   C. the Seven Years' War.
   D. the War of Jenkins' Ear.
2. This monarch took power as the result of a "Pragmatic Sanction":
   A. Empress Maria Theresa
   B. Empress Catherine the Great
   C. Queen Anne
   D. King George I
3. The War of the Austrian Succession started because Frederick the Great seized
   A. Poland.
   B. Bohemia.
   C. Austria.
   D. Silesia.
4. This financial scandal had a serious impact on British politics and government financing:
   A. The Flour War
   B. The East India Company
   C. The Stamp Act
   D. The South Sea Bubble

5. The distinguishing feature of the British Whigs was
   A. the extent to which Parliament could set limits to the monarch's power.
   B. support for king, aristocracy, and church.
   C. the desire to see a Catholic on the throne.
   D. support for popular democracy.
6. During the reign of George III, all of the following happened *except:*
   A. Britain lost the Thirteen Colonies.
   B. John Wilkes attacked the government in his newspaper, the *North Briton.*
   C. The Jacobites were defeated at the Battle of Culloden Moor.
   D. A nationalist cult developed around the British monarchy.
7. The Stamp Act was intended to
   A. supplement British government revenues.
   B. force the Thirteen Colonies into rebellion.
   C. provide the East India Company with an outlet for surplus tea.

D. found a postal system in the American colonies.

8. Written in 1776, this pamphlet helped to convince the Continental Congress to declare the Thirteen Colonies' independence from Britain:
   A. Rousseau's *Social Contract*
   B. Paine's *Common Sense*
   C. Edmund Burke's *Thoughts on the Cause of the Present Discontents*
   D. Issue 45 of John Wilke's *North Briton*

9. In France, the primary role of the parlements was to
   A. settle religious disputes.
   B. register royal edicts.
   C. represent the common people.
   D. levy taxes.

10. The disappearance of Poland as an independent state was the result of all of the following *except*
    A. Poland's military weakness.
    B. Polish nobles' opposition to Stanislas Poniatowski's liberal constitution.
    C. Catherine the Great's efforts to protect Polish sovereignty.
    D. Austrian, Prussian, and Russians desire for new territory.

**B. Chronological Relationships**

1. Identify the date at which each of the following events occurred and list them in chronological order:
   The Seven Years' War ends.
   The South Sea Bubble bursts.
   The American colonists declare their independence.
   A poor harvest and anger over Turgot's financial reforms spark a "flour war" in France.
   Maria Theresa and Frederick II inherit the thrones of Austria and Prussia, respectively.
   George I, the first Hanoverian, becomes king of Great Britain.
   Poland disappears as an independent kingdom.
   The War of the Austrian Succession ends.
   British troops are defeated at Yorktown.
   The Jacobites are defeated at the Battle of Culloden Moor.

2. Name the rulers of the following countries in the year 1776 and identify the dynasty to which they belonged:
   Austria
   France
   Great Britain
   Prussia
   Russia

**C. Fill in the Blanks**

1. The _____ were British supporters of the Catholic Stuart dynasty and engaged in several unsuccessful revolts against the ruling Hanoverians during the first half of the eighteenth century.

2. Whenever any single European Great Power threatened to upset the _____ by seeking to increase its territory, the other European states rushed to intervene.

3. The _____ was arguably the first global conflict, involving confrontations between France and England in North America, the Caribbean, and India, and between all of the major European powers on the continent.

4. The _____ involved a major transformation of the European alliance system. Fearful of Prussian expansionism, France and Austria united to battle Frederick the Great, who then turned to France's enemy, Great Britain, for support.

5. Due to harsh shipboard conditions, European navies often had trouble recruiting sailors. They therefore resorted to the use of _____, which coerced unfortunate men— many of whom subsequently deserted—into service.

6. Parliament's claim to represent the British people was undermined by the existence of _____, districts in which the re-election of incumbents went virtually unchallenged due to the presence of few (or even no) eligible voters.

7. In the 1760s British radicals rallied to the cry of _____, insisting on greater freedom of the press and various parliamentary reforms.

8. Although the British crown would not recognize American independence until 1783, the war for independence had effectively ended two years earlier, when Lord Cornwallis surrendered at _____ .

9. The French parlements' opposition to the monarchy was political and economic, but it also had religious ramifications. Many *parlementaires* were _____ or supported these dissidents in their struggles against the pope and the French crown.

10. In the Dutch United Provinces in the 1780s, the _____ , a radical political organization supported by artisans, demanded democratic reforms and briefly expelled stadholder William V.

## IMPORTANT HISTORICAL FACTS: STUDY-DRILL ANSWERS

### A. Multiple Choice
1. D. the War of Jenkins' Ear.
2. A. Empress Maria Theresa
3. D. Silesia.
4. D. The South Sea Bubble
5. A. the extent to which Parliament could set limits to the monarch's power.
6. C. The Jacobites were defeated at the Battle of Culloden Moor.
7. A. supplement British government revenues.
8. B. Paine's *Common Sense*
9. B. register royal edicts.
10. C. Catherine the Great's efforts to protect Polish sovereignty.

### B. Chronological Relationships
1. 1714 George I, the first Hanoverian, becomes king of Great Britain.
   1720 The South Sea Bubble bursts.
   1746 The Jacobites are defeated at the Battle of Culloden Moor.
   1740 Maria Theresa and Frederick II inherit the thrones of Austria and Prussia, respectively.
   1748 The War of the Austrian Succession ends.
   1763 The Seven Years' War ends.

1775 A poor harvest and anger over Turgot's financial reforms spark a "flour war" in France.
1776 The American colonists declare their independence.
1781 British troops are defeated at Yorktown.
1795 Poland disappears as an independent kingdom.

2. Austria:   Maria Theresa [Habsburg]
   France:    Louis XVI     [Bourbon]
   Great
     Britain: George III    [Hanoverian]
   Prussia:   Frederick     [Hohen-
                the Great    zollern]
   Russia:    Catherine     [Romanov]
                the Great

### C. Fill in the Blanks
1. Jacobites
2. Balance of power
3. Seven Years' War
4. "Diplomatic revolution" of 1756
5. Press-gangs
6. rotten boroughs
7. "Wilkes and Liberty!"
8. Yorktown
9. Jansenists
10. Dutch Patriot Party

# 12

# *The French Revolution*

## 1. CHAPTER OUTLINE

I. THE OLD REGIME IN CRISIS: The French Revolution, while not inevitable, was the predictable outcome of a set of inter-related eighteenth-century developments.

   A. LONG-TERM CAUSES OF THE FRENCH REVOLUTION included Enlightenment political thought, which emphasized equality before the law and was critical of monarchical despotism; growing tensions between nobles and bourgeois; and increasing peasant anger over poor harvests, exploitation by noble landowners, and vexing feudal obligations.

   B. THE FINANCIAL CRISIS that precipitated the Revolution was the result of the government's inability to pay off an excessive national debt. When the king's ministers proposed fiscal reforms to an "assembly of notables," these nobles refused to accept any taxation of their property.

II. THE FIRST STAGES OF THE REVOLUTION

   A. Faced with a growing "noble revolt," the king finally submitted to CONVOKING THE ESTATES-GENERAL. After considerable debate over voting procedures, the Estates-General met, but the representatives of the third estate soon broke away to form a National Assembly.

   B. STORMING OF THE BASTILLE: Worried about the security of the National Assembly, the ordinary people of Paris rose up in revolt

and assaulted the Bastille in search of weapons.

   C. THE GREAT FEAR AND THE NIGHT OF AUGUST 4: French peasants then joined the Revolution as well, storming seigneurial châteaux and sparking panic in rural regions. The National Assembly responded by abolishing the "feudal regime."

III. CONSOLIDATING THE REVOLUTION: Over the following two years, the National Assembly laid the foundations for a new, constitutional monarchy.

   A. THE DECLARATION OF THE RIGHTS OF MAN AND CITIZEN set forth the general principles of the new order, including equality before the law and the sovereignty of the nation.

   B. When the king resisted the National Assembly's proposals, Parisian women marched to Versailles and forced the royal family—"THE BAKER, THE BAKER'S WIFE, AND THE BAKER'S LITTLE BOY"—to come to Paris.

   C. REFORMING THE CHURCH AND CLERGY: The National Assembly brought the Church under state control, appropriating its property—which was used to back a new paper money—and requiring that priests accept the Civil Constitution of the French Clergy.

   D. THE REFORMS OF 1791 included a new constitution. Voting rights were granted to affluent men, but women, slaves in the colonies, and many workers were excluded from the ranks of the "active" citizens.

E. RESISTANCE AND REVOLUTION: Opposition to the Revolution began to surface, especially in the south and west, but this only served to further radicalize many supporters of the Revolution, especially the Parisian *sans-culottes*.

F. The royal family's attempted FLIGHT TO VARENNES failed, and increased popular hostility toward the monarchy.

IV. WAR AND THE SECOND REVOLUTION: The revolutionary left, fearful of invasion by foreign and émigré armies, went to war and replaced the monarchy with a republic.

A. REACTIONS TO THE FRENCH REVOLUTION IN EUROPE were mixed. Liberals like Thomas Paine and Mary Wollstonecraft greeted it with enthusiasm; conservatives like Edmund Burke criticized it. When the kings of Austria and Prussia expressed their willingness to support Louis XVI, the Assembly declared war on Austria.

B. The pressures and anxieties of war led to A SECOND REVOLUTION. The king was deposed in 1792, and, after a French victory at Valmy, a republic was declared. Louis XVI soon went to the guillotine, and divisions deepened in France, even among revolutionaries, and especially as military reversals heightened the population's insecurity.

C. In 1793, a full-scale COUNTER-REVOLUTION broke out in western France.

D. Faced with foreign invasion and civil war, the radical Jacobin-controlled government implemented THE TERROR. Under the leadership of the Committee of Public Safety, the revolutionary government

centralized its operations and used forceful measures to put down the Vendéan and Federalist revolts, to win the war, and to bring radical revolutionaries under control. At the same time, leaders like Robespierre and Saint-Just sought to replace Old Regime culture with a new republican culture.

V. During THE FINAL STAGES of the Revolution, the government of the Terror was replaced by the Directory.

A. In THERMIDOR (July 1794), moderates in the government, fearful of being the next victims of the Terror, overturned the Committee of Public Safety. Robespierre went to the guillotine, and the radical revolution was ended.

B. THE DIRECTORY: POLITICS AND SOCIETY: The new government represented a reaction against the asceticism of the Terror, and benefited the rich both politically and financially. With the end of price controls, a harsh winter in 1795, and continuing war, the poor suffered great hardships.

C. INSTABILITY continued as the war dragged on and the Directory was assailed by royalists on the right and radicals on the left. General Napoleon Bonaparte was victorious in Italy, but other ventures proved less successful.

D. In 1799, on THE EIGHTEENTH BRUMAIRE (November 9), Sieyès and Bonaparte staged a coup d'état against the Directory. Sieyès hoped that a new government with a stronger executive and support from the military might help to stabilize the French economy.

VI. PERSPECTIVES ON THE FRENCH REVOLUTION

A. EUROPEAN RESPONSES TO THE REVOLUTION: While the French revolutionary armies were often welcomed by Europeans in the territories these armies sought to "liberate," French rule often stimulated discontent and an increased sense of national identity among subject populations.

B. HISTORIANS' VIEWS OF THE REVOLUTION differ, ranging from older Marxist approaches to more recent "political culture" interpretations, but all agree that the French Revolution has had a major impact on modern history.

## 2. HISTORICAL GEOGRAPHY

**Map Exercises**

Familiarize yourself with the maps provided in your text, and then attempt to locate the following places on Blank Maps 12.1 and 12.2.

REVOLUTIONARY FRANCE

| *Provinces:* | *Cities:* | *Departments:* |
|---|---|---|
| Alsace | Bordeaux | Gironde |
| Brittany | Caen | Vendée |
| Dauphiné | Lyon | |
| Franche- | Marseille | *Rivers, etc.:* |
| Comté | Paris | Loire River |
| Languedoc | Toulon | Quiberon |
| Normandy | Varennes | Bay |
| Provence | Versailles | Seine River |

THE EXPANSION OF REVOLUTIONARY FRANCE

Adriatic Sea
Avignon
Batavian Republic
Cisalpine Republic
Corsica
Fleurus
Helvetic Republic
Ionian Islands
Jémappes
Ligurian Republic
Republic
  of Lucca
Nice
Parma
Parthenopean
  Republic
Piedmont
Roman Republic
Kingdom of
  Sardinia
Savoy
Grand Duchy of
  Tuscany
Valmy

**Map Questions**

What was the French revolutionaries' intent in replacing provinces with departments?

What new territories did France acquire between 1789 and 1799?

Locate the centers of counter-revolutionary and federalist activity in revolutionary France.

## 3. PEOPLE AND TERMS TO IDENTIFY

Louis XVI
Marie-Antoinette
The Estates-General
The National Assembly
The Bastille
Jean-Paul Marat
Émigrés
*Assignats*
The Civil Constitution of
  the Clergy
Georges-Jacques Danton
Olympe de Gouges
Jacobins
*Sans-culottes*
Girondins
Edmund Burke
Declaration of Pilnitz
Valmy
Vendée
*Levée en masse*
The Terror
Committee of Public
  Safety
Enragés
Maximilien Robespierre
De-christianization
Thermidor
The Directory
Eighteenth Brumaire

## 4. STUDY QUESTIONS

1. What caused the French monarchy's financial crisis of the 1780s? *Historical Continuities:* How had the French state financed its operations since 1500? What weaknesses were inherent in this system?

2. What was the National Assembly and why was it formed?

3. Why did ordinary French people support the efforts of the National Assembly? How did they express their support?

4. What was the "Great Fear"? What caused it and why was it significant?

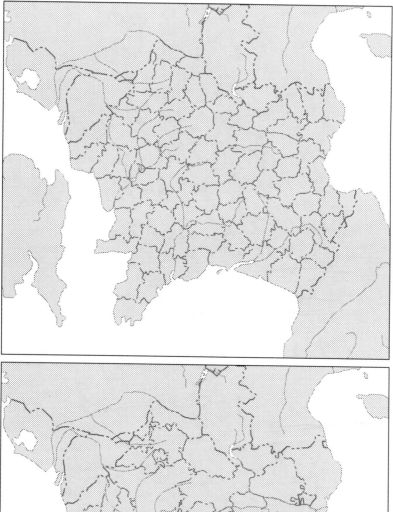

**MAP 12.1   REVOLUTIONARY FRANCE**

**MAP 12.2    THE EXPANSION OF REVOLUTIONARY FRANCE**

5. How did revolutionary legislation affect the practice of religion in France?

6. How did Europeans react to the French Revolution? Why were the governments of the other European nations so hostile to the Revolution?

7. What caused the French Revolution to enter a second, more radical phase?

8. From what disadvantages did the French revolutionary armies suffer going into war with Austria? Why were they so surprisingly successful?

9. What characterized the regions in which counter-revolutionary movements emerged?

10. What was the Terror? What caused it? Why did it end?

11. What were the weaknesses of the Directory? In what areas was it successful?

12. How did Napoleon seize power? Why was he able to do this?

13. *Historical Continuities:* What long-term impact do you expect French rule might have on conquered populations?

## 5. ANALYZING ART AND ARTIFACTS

What kind of emotional response is Jacques-Louis David's *Death of Marat* (p. 532 in the textbook) intended to elicit in the viewer? In what sense is this a "heroic" portrayal of the slain political leader? What is the political significance of this portrait?

How were ordinary supporters of the Revolution depicted in popular images of the period?

## 6. TECHNOLOGY AND HISTORY

Why do you think French revolutionaries introduced the guillotine (p. 528 in the textbook) as a means of execution? In what way was the guillotine a "humane" form of capital punishment? In what sense might its use be said to reflect Enlightenment values?

## 7. HISTORICAL ANALYSIS: INTERPRETIVE ESSAYS

1. What long-term conditions contributed to discontent with the French monarchy? What specific short-term factors precipitated the French Revolution?

2. Analyze the French Revolution as a fundamental change in European political culture. You may wish to contrast Old Regime political models with the new models of state and government formulated in "The Declaration of the Rights of Man and Citizen."

3. To what extent was the French Revolution a victory for liberty, equality, and fraternity?

4. *Historical Continuities:* What general, long-term trends in European history can explain the outbreak of revolutions (both successful and unsuccessful) in the latter part of the eighteenth century?

5. *Historical Continuities:* What different political lessons might nineteenth-century Europeans draw from the French Revolution in all its stages?

## 8. HISTORICAL VOICES: MEN, WOMEN, AND THE FRENCH REVOLUTION

### A. The Rights of Man, The Rights of Woman

Like the representatives of the thirteen American colonies, the French members of the revolutionary National Assembly felt called upon to justify their actions to the world and to present a public declaration of their principles and goals. On August 26, 1789, they decreed the "Declaration of the Rights of Man and Citizen" as the preamble to a yet-to-be-written French Constitution. Following the line of political thought pioneered by Locke and elaborated by Montesquieu, Rousseau, and Jefferson, the French declaration represented a distillation of the fundamental premises of classical liberalism and became a rallying cry for liberal thinkers and activists throughout Europe.

Two years later, in 1791, the political activist Olympe de Gouges (1755–1793) published her own declaration of the "Rights of Woman." Modeled on the "Declaration of the Rights of Man and Citizen," de Gouges' revision was intended as a protest against the exclusion of French women from the ranks of those citizens whose rights had been guaranteed in 1789. Identifying a contradiction in the liberalism of the French revolutionaries, de Gouges argued that the tyrannical power of men over women was as objectionable as the despotism of the French monarchy. Her support for Marie Antoinette earned de Gouges the enmity of the revolutionary government, and she went to the guillotine in 1793, charged with the crime of being a royalist.

FROM *The Declaration of the Rights of Man and Citizen*

The representatives of the French people, constituted as the National Assembly, considering that ignorance, neglect or contempt for the rights of man are solely responsible for public misfortunes and the corruption of governments, have resolved to set forth the natural, inalienable and sacred rights of man in a solemn declaration, to the end that it may serve all the members of the body politic as a constant reminder of their reciprocal rights and duties; that the acts of the executive and legislative powers may be all the more respected because they can be constantly compared with the end of all political institutions; and that the demands of the citizens, grounded henceforth on simple and incontestable principles, should always tend to the maintenance of the Constitution and the common good.

Consequently the National Assembly, in the presence and under the auspices of the Supreme Being, recognizes and declares the following rights as belonging to man and the citizen:

1 Men are born free and remain free and equal in their rights. Social distinctions can only be founded on public utility.

2 The aim of every political association is the maintenance of the natural and imprescriptible rights of man. Those rights are those of liberty, property, security and resistance to oppression.

3 The fundamental source of all sovereignty resides in the nation. No body nor any individual may exercise any authority which does not derive explicitly from the sovereign nation.

FROM *Declaration of the Rights of Woman and Citizen* by Olympe de Gouges

The mothers, daughters, sisters, representatives of the nation, ask to constitute a National Assembly. Considering that ignorance, forgetfulness or contempt of the rights of women are the sole causes of public miseries, and of corruption of governments, they have resolved to set forth in a solemn declaration, the natural, unalterable and sacred rights of woman, so that this declaration, being ever present to all members of the social body, may unceasingly remind them of their rights and their duties; in order that the acts of women's power, as well as those of men, may be judged constantly against the aim of all political institutions, and thereby be more respected for it, in order that the complaints of women citizens, based henceforth on simple and indisputable principles, may always take the direction of maintaining the Constitution, good morals and the welfare of all.

In consequence, the sex superior in beauty and in courage in maternal suffering recognizes and declares, in the presence of and under the auspices of the Supreme Being, the following rights of woman and of the woman citizen:

*Article I.* Woman is born free and remains equal to man in rights. Social distinctions can be based only on common utility.

*Article II.* The aim of every political association is the preservation of the natural and imprescriptible rights of man and woman. These rights are liberty, prosperity, security and above all, resistance to oppression.

*Article III.* The source of all sovereignty resides essentially in the Nation, which is nothing but the joining together of Man and Woman; no body, no individual, can exercise authority that does not emanate expressly from it.

4 Liberty consists in being able to do anything which does not harm another: thus each man's exercise of his natural rights has no limits but those which guarantee the other members of society the enjoyment of these same rights. These limits can only be determined by the law. . . .

6 The law is the expression of the general will. Every citizen has the right, in person or by representation, to participate in the legislative process. The law must be the same for all, whether it punish or protect. Every citizen, being equal in its eyes, is equally admissible to every dignity, office and public employment in accordance with his ability and with no other distinction than that of his virtue and talent. . . .

10 No one must be troubled on account of his opinions, even his religious beliefs, provided that their expression does not disturb public order under the law.

11 Free expression of thought and opinions is one of the most precious rights of man. Accordingly every citizen may speak, write and publish freely, subject to the penalties for the abuse of this freedom provided for by the law. . . .

*Article IV.* Liberty and justice consist in giving back to others all that belongs to them; thus the only limits on the exercise of woman's natural rights are the perpetual tyranny by which man opposes her; these limits must be reformed by the laws of nature and of reason. . . .

*Article VI.* Law must be the expression of the general will: all citizens, men and women alike, must personally or through their representatives concur in its formation; it must be the same for all; all citizens, men and women alike, being equal before it, must be equally eligible for all high offices, positions and public employments, according to their abilities, and without distinctions other than their virtues and talents. . . .

*Article X.* No one ought to be disturbed for one's opinions, however fundamental they are; since a woman has the right to mount the scaffold, she must also have the right to address the House, provided her interventions do not disturb the public order as it has been established by law.

*Article XI.* The free communication of ideas and opinions is one of the most precious rights of woman, since this freedom ensures the legitimacy of fathers toward their children. Every woman citizen can therefore say freely: I am the mother of a child that belongs to you, without being forced to conceal the truth because of a barbaric prejudice; except to be answerable for abusers of this liberty as determined by law. . . .

*Source:* "The Declaration of the Rights of Man and Citizen." In *The French Revolution: The Fall of the Ancien Regime to the Thermidorian Reaction, 1785–1795*, pp. 114–117. Ed. and tr. John Hardman. New York: St. Martin's Press, 1982.

*Source:* Olympe de Gouges. "Declaration of the Rights of Woman and Citizen." In *European Women: A Documentary History, 1789–1945*, pp. 63–66. Eds. Eleanor S. Riemer and John C. Fout. New York: Schocken Books, 1980.

## Questions

To what extent do these two documents draw on pre-existing political theory? How do they compare with the American "Declaration of Independence"?

How does Olympe de Gouges' reworking of the "Declaration of the Rights of Man and Citizen" transform its meaning?

How do you think male revolutionaries would have responded to de Gouges' declaration?

## B. British Responses to the French Revolution: The Debate Between Edmund Burke and Mary Wollstonecraft

Born in Ireland, Edmund Burke (1729–1797) came to London as a young man to begin a successful career as a political writer and journalist. He was elected to Parliament in 1765 and served as a Member of Parliament for the next thirty years. Although he supported the American colonists in their conflict with Britain, he was fiercely critical of the French Revolution and of its British supporters. *Reflections on the Revolution in France,* written in 1790 in response to a French friend's letter, is an extended critique of specific aspects of the French Revolution, but it is also a general treatise that analyzes the foundations and functioning of state and society. In his championing of slow and cautious amelioration of existing political structures—as opposed to sudden, revolutionary change—and in his insistence on the importance of maintaining social hierarchies based on birth and wealth, Burke is often identified as the founding father of modern conservative political thought.

Burke's work elicited a passionate response from the British partisans of the Revolution, and no fewer than thirty "Answers to Burke" were published in the years following the appearance of *Reflections on the Revolution in France.* While Thomas Paine's *The Rights of Man* is the best known of these responses, Mary Wollstonecraft's *Vindication of the Rights of Men* was one of the earliest, and earned Wollstonecraft a prominent place in British liberal intellectual circles. Wollstonecraft (1759–1797), now famous for her *Vindication of the Rights of Woman,* a key text in the origins of modern feminism, derived her feminist theory from her classical liberalism. Like de Gouges, Wollstonecraft supported the French Revolution because she believed it would further the cause of human rights in general.

### FROM *Reflections on the Revolution in France* by Edmund Burke

The people of England will not ape the fashions they have never tried, nor go back to those which they have found mischievous on trial. They look upon the legal hereditary succession of their crown as among their rights, not as among their wrongs; as a benefit, not as a grievance; as a security for their liberty, not as a badge of servitude. They look on the frame of their commonwealth, *such as it stands,* to be of inestimable value; and they conceive the undisturbed succession of the crown to be a pledge of the stability and perpetuity of all the other members of our constitution. . . .

You will observe, that from Magna Charta to the Declaration of Right, it has been the uniform policy of our constitution to claim and assert our liberties, as an *entailed inheritance* derived to us from our forefathers, and to be transmitted to our posterity; as an estate specially belonging to the people of this kingdom, without any reference whatever to any other more general or prior right. By this means our constitution preserves an unity in so great a diversity of its parts. We have an inheritable crown; an inheritable peerage; and a House of Commons and a people inheriting privileges, franchises, and liberties, from a long line of ancestors.

The policy appears to me to be the result of profound reflection; or rather the happy effect of following nature, which is wisdom without re-flection, and above it. A spirit of innovation is generally the result of a selfish temper, and confined views. People will not look forward to posterity, who never look backward to their ancestors. Besides, the people of England well know, that the idea of inheritance furnishes a sure principle of conservation, and a sure principle of transmission; without at all excluding a principle of improvement. It leaves acquisition free; but it secures what it acquires. Whatever advantages are obtained by a state proceeding on these maxims, are locked fast as in a sort of family settlement; grasped as in a kind of mortmain for ever. By a constitutional policy working after the pattern of nature, we receive, we hold, we transmit our government and our privileges, in the same manner in which we enjoy and transmit our property and our lives. The institutions of policy, the goods of fortune, the gifts of Providence, are handed down to us, and from us, in the same course and order. Our political system is placed in a just correspondence and symmetry with the order of the world, and with the mode of existence decreed to a permanent body composed of transitory parts; wherein, by the disposition of a stupendous wisdom, moulding together the great mysterious incorporation of the human race, the whole, at one time, is never old, or middle-aged, or young, but, in a condition of unchangeable constancy, moves on through the varied tenor of perpetual decay, fall, renovation, and progression. Thus, by preserving the method of nature in the conduct of the state, in what we improve, we are never wholly new; in what we retain, we are never wholly obsolete. By adhering in this manner and on those principles to our forefathers, we are guided not by the superstition of antiquarians, but by the spirit of philosophic analogy. In this choice of inheritance we have given to our frame of polity the image of a relation in blood; binding up the constitution of our country with our dearest domestic ties; adopting our fundamental laws into the bosom of our family affections; keeping inseparable and cherishing with the warmth of all their combined and mutually reflected charities, our state, our hearths, our sepulchres, and our altars. . . .

## FROM *A Vindication of the Rights of Men* by Mary Wollstonecraft

The birthright of man, to give you, Sir, a short definition of this disputed right, is such a degree of liberty, civil and religious, as is compatible with the liberty of every other individual with whom he is united in a social compact, and the continued existence of that compact.

Liberty, in this simple, unsophisticated sense, I acknowledge, is a fair idea that has never yet received a form in the various governments that have been established on our beauteous globe; the demon of property has ever been at hand to encroach on the sacred rights of men, and to fence round with awful pomp laws that war with justice. But that it results from the eternal foundation of right—from immutable truth—who will presume to deny, that pretends to rationality—if reason has led them to build their morality and religion on an everlasting foundation—the attributes of God? . . .

I perceive, from the whole tenor of your Reflections, that you have a mortal antipathy to reason; but, if there is any thing like argument, or first principles, in your wild declamation, behold the result:—that we are to reverence the rust of antiquity, and term the unnatural customs, which ignorance and mistaken self-interest have consolidated, the sage fruit of experience: nay, that, if we do discover some errors, our *feelings* should lead us to excuse, with blind love, or unprincipled filial affection, the venerable vestiges of ancient days. These are gothic notions of beauty—the ivy is beautiful, but, when it insidiously destroys the trunk from which it receives support, who would not grub it up?

Further, that we ought cautiously to remain for ever in frozen inactivity, because a thaw, whilst it nourishes the soil, spreads a temporary inundation; and the fear of risking any personal present convenience should prevent a struggle for the most estimable advantages. This is sound reasoning, I grant, in the mouth of the rich and short-sighted.

*Sources:* Edmund Burke. *Reflections on the Revolution in France,* 1790. In *The Works of the Right Honourable Edmund Burke,* vol. 4, pp. 27, 35–37. London: Oxford University Press, 1907.
  Mary Wollstonecraft. *A Vindication of the Rights of Men,* pp. 7–10. Delmar, NY: Scholars' Facsimiles and Reprints, 1975.

### Questions

Why does Burke reject the "right to revolution"? What is Wollstonecraft's response to this argument?

What makes Burke a "conservative"? Wollstonecraft a "liberal"?

What does Burke mean when he calls British liberties an "entailed inheritance"? Why does Wollstonecraft reject this idea?

## 9. IMPORTANT HISTORICAL FACTS: STUDY DRILLS

### A. Multiple Choice

1. In the late eighteenth century, the French monarchy was weakened by all of the following *except*
   A. a clergy hostile to the monarchical principle.
   B. an inept king and an unpopular queen.
   C. inadequate and inequitable taxation.
   D. a nobility eager to hold on to its privileges.
2. The third estate included all of the following *except*
   A. peasants.
   B. urban workers.
   C. priests.
   D. lawyers.
3. During the "Great Fear"
   A. French nobles attempted to flee the country.
   B. peasants were stirred to action by rumors of an aristocratic "famine plot."
   C. representatives of the third estate took an oath on a tennis court.
   D. the Bastille, a prison-fortress, was attacked by Parisians.
4. An ardent advocate of women's rights, she wrote *The Declaration of the Rights of Woman and Citizen,* and went to the guillotine during the Terror:
   A. Marie Antoinette
   B. Joan of Arc
   C. Charlotte Corday
   D. Olympe de Gouges
5. A *sans-culotte* could be identified by
   A. his fancy knee britches.
   B. his inherited wealth.
   C. his opposition to the Revolution.
   D. his tendency to call everyone "citizen."
6. Confronted with outbreaks of civil war in the provinces, the revolutionary government decreed mass conscription in 1793, calling on all loyal revolutionaries to take arms in support of the nation. This was known as
   A. the *levée en masse.*
   B. the Festival of Reason.
   C. the Seigneurial Reaction.
   D. the Assembly of Notables.
7. On September 20, 1792, the revolutionary army won its first significant victory, inspiring Goethe to declare, "a new epoch is beginning." The battle that turned the tide for the French, and prepared the way for the proclamation of the First French Republic, was known as
   A. the Vendée.
   B. Valmy.
   C. Varennes.
   D. the September Massacres.

8. Created by the Convention in March of 1793, this twelve-member body governed France during the Terror and included Robespierre as one of its leading figures:
   A. The Directory
   B. The National Assembly
   C. The Committee of Public Safety
   D. The Patriot Party
9. The radical revolutionary campaign to shut down religious institutions and destroy religious symbols that began in late 1793 was known as
   A. the Law of Suspects.
   B. the Civil Constitution of the Clergy.
   C. the Counter-Revolution.
   D. de-christianization.
10. The French established "Sister Republics" in all but
    A. Naples and Milan.
    B. Switzerland.
    C. Russia.
    D. The Netherlands.

## B. Chronological Relationships

Arrange the following events in chronological order and explain the causal relationship between each matched set:

The French REPUBLIC is declared.
The counter-revolutionary VENDÉE rebellion begins.
The National Assembly abolishes the "FEUDAL regime."
France declares WAR on Austria.
The meeting of the ESTATES-General.
The government of the DIRECTORY is established.
The fall of the BASTILLE.
In THERMIDOR, Robespierre goes to the guillotine.
The Convention institutes "TERROR" against the enemies of the Revolution.
The meeting of the Assembly of NOTABLES.

1. _____
2. _____
Relationship:

3. _____
4. _____
Relationship:

5. _____
6. _____
Relationship:

7. _____
8. _____
Relationship:

9. _____
10. _____
Relationship:

## C. Fill in the Blanks

1. Scheduled to meet on May 1st, 1789, the _____ would be made up of representatives selected from the nobility, the clergy, and "everybody else."
2. In search of guns and ammunition, the people of Paris attacked and captured _____ on July 14, 1789.
3. On the basis of land confiscated from the Catholic Church, the French revolutionary government issued a paper currency known as _____.
4. A populist orator who had denounced the distinction between "active" and "passive" citizens, _____ went to the guillotine for his "indulgent" belief that the Terror was no longer necessary.
5. The _____ were republicans, many of whom hailed from the Bordeaux region, and who agitated for a revolutionary war against the tyranny of European monarchs and nobles.
6. In the _____ King Leopold II of Austria and King Frederick William II of Prussia expressed their mutual desire to see order restored in France, generating anxiety about foreign invasion in France, and providing ammunition for those French revolutionaries who wished to go to war against the European monarchies.
7. In March 1793, a full-scale insurrection against the Revolution broke out in western France. This counter-revolutionary uprising was known as the _____.

*enragés*

8. The most radical of the revolutionary factions, the _____ called for strict enforcement of maximum limits on bread prices and intensification of the "de-christianization" campaign, but their leaders were struck down by the Committee of Public Safety.

9. Known as "The Incorruptible," _____ came to be feared as the mastermind of the Terror, and he was ousted from power in the month of "Thermidor."

10. On the _____ [November 9, 1799] the young Corsican general, Napoleon Bonaparte, staged a coup d'état (with his co-conspirator, Sieyès), overthrowing the Directory and taking effective control of the French government.

## IMPORTANT HISTORICAL FACTS: STUDY-DRILL ANSWERS

### A. Multiple Choice
1. A. a clergy hostile to the monarchical principle.
2. C. priests.
3. B. peasants were stirred to action by rumors of an aristocratic "famine plot."
4. D. Olympe de Gouges
5. D. his tendency to call everyone "citizen."
6. A. the *levée en masse.*
7. B. Valmy.
8. C. The Committee of Public Safety
9. D. de-christianization.
10. C. Russia.

### B. Chronological Relationships
1. NOTABLES / 2. ESTATES
3. BASTILLE / 4. FEUDAL
5. WAR / 6. REPUBLIC
7. VENDÉE / 8. TERROR
9. THERMIDOR / 10. DIRECTORY

### C. Fill in the Blanks
1. Estates-General
2. Bastille
3. assignats
4. Georges-Jacques Danton
5. Girondins
6. Declaration of Pilnitz
7. Vendée Rebellion
8. enragés
9. Maximilien Robespierre
10. Eighteenth Brumaire

# 13 *Napoleon and Europe*

## 1. CHAPTER OUTLINE

I. NAPOLEON'S RISE TO POWER was made possible by the French Revolution.
   A. THE YOUNG BONAPARTE was born in Corsica only shortly after it became French territory, and attended military school in France.
   B. NAPOLEON AND THE REVOLUTION: Siding with the Jacobins, Napoleon served as an officer in the revolutionary army and soon became commander of the Army of Italy.

II. CONSOLIDATION OF POWER: After campaigns in Italy and Egypt, Napoleon returned to France, where he helped to stage the Eighteenth Brumaire coup d'état against the ruling Directory.
   A. The ESTABLISHMENT OF THE CONSULAT involved the creation of a strong executive authority, headed by First Consul Napoleon.
   B. In the interests of ending religious discord, Napoleon negotiated and signed THE CONCORDAT with the pope in 1802.
   C. NAPOLEON'S LEADERSHIP: An "ever-restless spirit," Napoleon was a hardworking executive, but refused to delegate authority and became increasingly tyrannical and bellicose during the course of his reign.
   D. WARS OF CONQUEST AND EMPIRE: Having declared himself emperor, Napoleon once again went to war with Europe. After a series of brilliant campaigns, France ruled over the largest European empire since that of Rome.
   E. THE CORSICAN WARRIOR: Napoleon's military successes were based less on originality than on innovative implementation of strategy and tactics developed in the eighteenth century. Relying on "citizen-soldiers," Napoleon created a large, flexible, and highly mobile military machine.

III. THE FOUNDATIONS OF THE FRENCH EMPIRE
   A. INSTITUTIONAL FOUNDATIONS: IMPERIAL CENTRALIZATION was imposed in all matters of state, including finance and education.
   B. LEGAL FOUNDATIONS: THE NAPOLEONIC CODE provided a uniform law code for all of France (and much of the rest of Europe). Despite its social conservatism, especially regarding women and children, it formalized many of the legal gains of the revolutionary era.
   C. SOCIAL FOUNDATIONS OF THE EMPIRE: THE IMPERIAL HIERARCHY created by Napoleon was based not on inheritance but on service to the state. While reestablishing a titled elite, Napoleon preserved a certain degree of social mobility.

IV. THE TIDE TURNS AGAINST NAPOLEON: An overextended empire and ill-considered military

campaigns would eventually bring
Napoleon down.

A. THE CONTINENTAL SYSTEM
was designed to strangle British
trade, but this policy was never
successful, and Britain remained
committed to defeating France.

B. Seeking to defeat Great Britain's
ally Portugal, Napoleon found
himself embroiled in THE
PENINSULAR WAR, which
tied down French troops in
Spain and Portugal from 1808
to 1813.

C. STIRRINGS OF NATIONALISM
IN NAPOLEONIC EUROPE:
Especially in the Italian and
German states, French invasion
stimulated a new sense of national
identity—and a desire for freedom
from French rule.

D. MILITARY REFORMS IN
PRUSSIA AND AUSTRIA were
undertaken in response to
devastating defeats by the French
armies.

E. THE EMPIRE'S DECLINE AND
THE RUSSIAN INVASION: In the
face of growing resistance to his
rule in France, Napoleon invaded
Russia with his Grand Army. The
Russians retreated, leaving
Moscow in flames, and forcing
Napoleon to march his troops back
to France in the bitter Russian
winter.

F. THE DEFEAT OF NAPOLEON
came in 1814, when Austria,
Britain, Prussia, and Russia
successfully united against France.

V. MONARCHICAL RESTORATION
AND NAPOLEON'S RETURN

A. Napoleon was sent into exile by
the victorious allies and THE
BOURBON RESTORATION was
greeted with relief by most French
people. However, many came to
resent Louis XVIII's support of
"Ultra-royalist" policies.

B. THE 100 DAYS: In a bold move,
Napoleon escaped from Elba and
returned to France, where he
regained the support of his faithful
army and the general public. He
ruled for 100 days, but was
decisively defeated by an allied
army at Waterloo.

VI. NAPOLEON'S LEGACY: Napoleon
left behind him a Europe much
transformed by war, political and
legal changes, and developing
nationalism. He claimed to have
sought the good of France and of
Europe, but his personal ambition
brought much death and disorder to
the continent—and bequeathed a
heroic myth to subsequent
generations.

## 2. HISTORICAL GEOGRAPHY

**Map Exercises**

Familiarize yourself with the maps
provided in your text, and then attempt to
locate the following places on Blank Map
13.1.

NAPOLEONIC BATTLES

| | |
|---|---|
| Austerlitz | Moscow |
| Borodino | Paris |
| Dresden | Smolensk |
| Friedland | Trafalgar |
| Jena | Ulm |
| Leipzig | Wagram |
| Lisbon | Waterloo |
| Madrid | |

ITALY DURING THE NAPOLEONIC ERA

| | |
|---|---|
| Campo Formio | Kingdom of |
| Corsica | Naples |
| Elba | Piedmont |
| Florence | Rome |
| Illyrian Provinces | Sardinia |
| Kingdom of Italy | Savoy |
| Milan | Sicily |
| Naples | Venice |

**Map Questions**

How was the map of the German states
redrawn during the Napoleonic era?

What territories did the Napoleonic
Empire include at its greatest expanse?

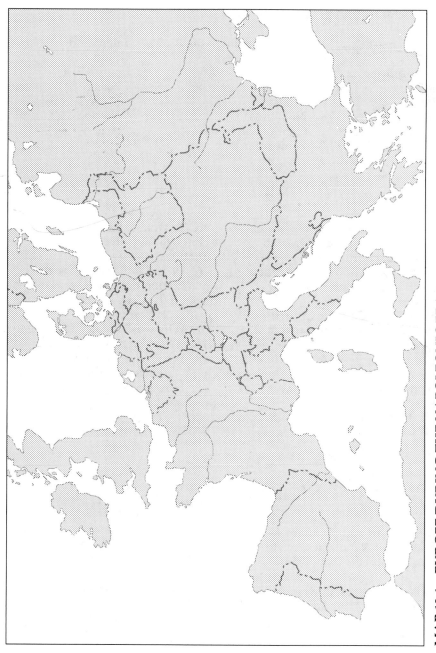

**MAP 13.1 EUROPE DURING THE NAPOLEONIC ERA**

## 3. PEOPLE AND TERMS TO IDENTIFY

Napoleon Bonaparte
Consulat
"Authority from above,
    confidence from below"
Concordat
Duke of Enghien
Toussaint L'Ouverture
Battle of Trafalgar

Confederation of the Rhine
Citizen-soldiers
Napoleonic Code
"A career open to all
    talents"
Notables
Continental System
Peninsular War

Talleyrand
Grand Army
Louis XVIII
Charter
100 Days
Waterloo

## 4. STUDY QUESTIONS

1. What factors in Napoleon's background help to explain his rise to power? *Historical Continuities*: To what extent was his dramatic ascent a product of the French Revolution?

2. Why did Napoleon negotiate a Concordat with the Catholic Church? *Historical Continuities:* To what extent was this agreement typical of previous arrangements made between French monarchs and the Church?

3. Why did France go back to war again in 1805?

4. How did Napoleon win so many battles?

5. To what extent was "centralization" a characteristic of all of Napoleon's initiatives?

6. Describe the type of social organization promoted by Napoleon through the Civil Code and through his creation of a service elite.

7. Why was Napoleon unable to defeat either Great Britain or Spain?

8. What were the distinctive characteristics of German nationalism?

9. How was Napoleon defeated? Was this defeat inevitable?

## 5. ANALYZING ART AND ARTIFACTS

How did fine art and popular representations of Napoleon serve to support (or deflate) the Napoleonic legend?

*Historical Continuities:* In what sense is David's *Bonaparte Leaping the St. Bernard* (p. 585) "romantic"? How does it depart

from the classicism of David's earlier painting, *The Death of Marat* (p. 532)?

## 6. TECHNOLOGY AND HISTORY

To what extent were Napoleon's military successes the result of technological innovations?

## 7. HISTORICAL ANALYSIS: INTERPRETIVE ESSAYS

1. Write an essay defending one of the following statements:
    Napoleon was an imperialist tyrant.
    Napoleon was one of the greatest
        rulers who ever lived.
2. What effect did Napoleon's reign have on Europe as a whole?

3. *Historical Continuities:* Did Napoleon end or continue the French Revolution?

4. *Historical Continuities:* In what sense might Napoleon's government be considered the first "modern" (as opposed to early modern) regime?

## 8. HISTORICAL VOICES: THE NAPOLEONIC LEGACY

### A. Napoleon Regulates Marriage and the Family

The French Civil (or "Napoleonic") Code and the French Penal Code, promulgated in 1804 and 1810 respectively, contributed to the completion of the codification of law begun at the time of the Revolution of 1789. The Napoleonic Code served as the foundation for the civil law not only of France but also of Louisiana and much of continental Europe and Latin America.

If the Napoleonic Code ratified many of the civil liberties gained during the revolutionary period, it also reestablished the legal authority of fathers and husbands, which had been substantially diminished during the revolutionary era. Rejecting the liberal feminism of thinkers like the Marquis de Condorcet and Olympe de Gouges, Napoleon and his legal consultants gave the political and economic inequality of women (and children) a firm basis in law. Similarly, Napoleonic lawmakers gave legal sanction to the sexual double standard, establishing harsh penalties for a married woman's adulterous relations but turning a blind eye to her husband's sexual adventures, except in the most extreme cases. Similarly, an unwed mother was prohibited from seeking child support from the father of her child unless she could prove that she had been the victim of an abduction.

### FROM Napoleon's Civil Code of 1804

Article 19. A French woman who marries a foreign national takes her husband's nationality. If she becomes a widow, she recovers her French nationality if she is living in France, or if she returns to France with the King's authorization and having declared that she wishes to establish permanent residency in the country.

Article 37. Witnesses to civil proceedings must be male, [and] at least twenty-one years of age. . . .

Article 108. A married woman can have no other domicile than that of her husband. . . .

Article 144. A man younger than eighteen years of age, and a woman younger than fifteen years of age, cannot enter into a marriage contract. . . .

Article 148. A son under the age of twenty-five, and a daughter under the age of twenty-one, cannot enter into a marriage contract without the consent of his or her father and mother; in case of disagreement, the consent of the father suffices. . . .

Article 212. Husband and wife owe each other faithfulness, support, and assistance.

Article 213. A husband owes protection to his wife, a wife obedience to her husband.

Article 214. A wife is obligated to live with her husband, and to follow him wherever he judges it appropriate to reside: A husband is obligated to receive his wife [in his domicile] and to furnish her with all that is necessary for her survival, in accordance with her faculties and station.

Article 215. A wife cannot file a civil suit without the authorization of her husband, even if she is a public merchant, or is not in a joint-property marriage, or is legally separated from her husband. . . .

Article 229. A husband can file for divorce on the grounds of the adultery of his wife.

Article 230. A wife can file for divorce on the grounds of the adultery of her husband, if her husband has kept his mistress in the conjugal domicile. . . .

Article 340. Paternity suits are forbidden. In the case of abduction, if the period at which time the abduction took place corresponds with that of conception, the abductor can, at the request of the interested parties, be declared the father of the child.

### FROM **Napoleon's Penal Code**

Article 337. A wife convicted of adultery will be subject to a prison sentence of at least three months and of no more than two years.

Her husband retains the right to end this imprisonment by consenting to take his wife back.

Article 338. The accomplice of an adulterous wife will be punished with a comparable term of imprisonment, and, in addition, a fine of between 24,000 and 480,000 francs.

The only proofs which can be admitted as evidence against the accused accomplice are, besides being caught in the act, those resulting from letters or other documents written by the accused.

Article 339. A husband who has kept his mistress in the conjugal domicile, and who has been convicted as a result of his wife's legal complaint, will be punished with a fine of between 24,000 and 480,000 francs.

*Sources:* Petits Codes Dalloz. *Code Civil annoté d'après la doctrine et la jurisprudence,* 56th ed., pp. 15, 45, 87, 94, 96, 118, 119, 125, 175. Trans. Kathleen M. Nilan. Paris: Jurisprudence Générale Dalloz, 1957.

Petits Codes Dalloz. *Code Pénal annoté d'après la doctrine et la jurisprudence,* pp. 226, 227. Trans. Kathleen M. Nilan. Paris: Jurisprudence Générale Dalloz, 1954.

### *Questions*

By what logic did the Civil Code establish that a French woman who married a non-French husband would lose her French citizenship?

Given the disabilities imposed on women by the Civil Code, why do you think that women were allowed to marry at an earlier age than men?

To what extent do the Civil and Penal Codes represent an attempt to regulate female sexuality?

### B. The Napoleonic Legend

Admired and reviled during his lifetime, Napoleon continued to elicit adoration and outrage after his death. Seen by some French moderates as the savior of the Revolution, he was hated by liberals for his autocracy and by conservatives for his opportunism. Whether loved or hated, his meteoric career cast a long shadow on European culture and politics throughout the nineteenth century.

The first generation of romantics was torn between its admiration for Napoleon's heroism and his almost superhuman individual capacities and its contempt for his failure to either uphold the liberal gains of the Republic or restore the Monarchy and his often brutal and exploitative treatment of subject populations. Both liberals and royalists found much to praise and criticize, but few could resist the temptation to mythologize the life and actions of this great man.

The following selection of French assessments of Napoleon demonstrates the diversity of responses to the legacy of the emperor. The first citation, written by Germaine de Staël (1766–1817), an ardent liberal and an early proponent of romanticism in France, reveals de Staël's dislike for Napoleon, mingled though it is with a certain grudging admiration for the political finesse of the man who banished her from Paris for her opposition to his political regime. In the second, René de Chateaubriand (1768–1848), another early French romantic, but one who felt a deep sentimental attachment to both legitimism and Catholic Christianity, describes his own mixed feelings about Napoleon. Chateaubriand rallied to Napoleon's government as a result of the Concordat with the pope, and he served Napoleon as ambassador to Rome, but he resigned in 1804, after the execution of the duke d'Enghien on trumped-up charges. The final passage, the poem "The Grandmother's Tale," by the very successful songwriter Pierre-Jean de Béranger (1780–1857), presents a more populist portrait of the emperor. Here Napoleon appears as a man of the people, the "little corporal," who led France to victory, but whose successes did not distance him from the concerns of common folk. While de Staël's and Chateaubriand's comments on Napoleon reflect the often critical opinions of the educated elite, Béranger's poem clearly exhibits the lingering sympathy for the emperor among many members of the general public.

### FROM *Ten Years of Exile* by Germaine de Staël

Bonaparte's government is characterized by a profound contempt for all of the intellectual riches of human nature: virtue, the dignity of the soul, religion, enthusiasm, these are, in his eyes, the *eternal enemies of the continent,* to avail myself of his favorite expression. He would like to reduce man to nothing but force and cunning, and would name everything else stupidity or madness. Above all others, the English irritate him because they have discovered a means of achieving success with honesty, a thing which Napoleon would like to make people think is impossible. This beacon of light in the world hurt his eyes from the first days of his reign; and unable to destroy it with his weapons, he has never ceased to direct against it all of the artillery of his false reasoning.

I do not believe that Bonaparte, having taken over as head of state, had at that time formed the plan of establishing a universal monarchy. But I do believe that his intent was captured in what he said to a man I count among my friends, a few days after the 18th of Brumaire: "One must," he said, "do something new every three months if one wants to capture the imagination of the French nation. With her, he who does not move forward is lost." He promised himself to encroach each day a bit further on the liberty of France, and on the independence of Europe, but, without losing sight of his final goal, he knew how to adapt himself to circumstances. He circumvented an obstacle, when that obstacle was too strong; he stopped completely when the opposing wind was too violent. That man, at bottom so impatient, has the talent of waiting things out when necessary. He takes this from the Italians, who know how to restrain themselves in order to attain their passions' goal, as if they had cold-bloodedly chosen this goal. It is through the art of alternating between cunning and force that he subjugated Europe. . . .

### FROM *The Memoirs of Chateaubriand* by René de Chateaubriand

A monstrous pride and an incessant affectation spoil Napoleon's character. At the time of his dominion, what need had he to exaggerate his stature, when the God of Armies had furnished him with the war chariot "whose wheels are living"?

He took after the Italian blood; his nature was complex: great men, a very small family upon earth, unhappily find only themselves to imitate them. At once a model and a copy, a real personage and an actor representing that personage, Napoleon was his own mime; he would not have believed himself a hero, if he had not dressed himself up in a hero's costume. . . .

That Bonaparte, following up the successes of the Revolution, everywhere disseminated principles of independence; that his victories helped to relax the bonds between the peoples and the kings, and snatched those peoples from the power of the old customs and the ancient ideas; that, in this sense, he contributed to the social enfranchisement: these are facts which I do not pretend to contest; but that, of his own will, he laboured scientifically for the political and civil deliverance of the nations; that he established the narrowest despotism with the idea of giving to Europe and to France in particular the widest Constitution; that he was only a tribune disguised as a tyrant: all this is a supposition which I cannot possibly adopt.

Bonaparte, like the race of princes, desired nothing and sought nothing save power, attaining it, however, through liberty, because he made his first appearance on the world's stage in 1793. The Revolution, which was Napoleon's wet-nurse, did not long delay in appearing to him as an enemy; he never ceased beating her. . . .

The Emperor meddled with everything; his intelligence never rested; he had a sort of perpetual agitation of ideas. In the impetuousness of his nature, instead of a free and continuous train, he advanced by leaps and bounds, he flung himself upon the universe and shook it; he would have none of it, of that universe, if he was obliged to wait for it: an incomprehensible being, who found the secret of debasing his most towering actions by despising them, and who raised his least elevated actions to his own level. Impatient of will, patient of character, incomplete and as though unfinished, Napoleon had gaps in his genius: his understanding resembled the sky of that other hemisphere under which he was to go to die, the sky whose stars are separated by empty spaces.

### From *The Grandmother's Tale*. by Pierre-Jean de Béranger

His fame shall never pass away!
　Beside the cottage-hearth the hind
　No other theme shall list to find
For many and many a distant day.
When winter nights their gloom begin,
　And winter embers ruddy glow,
Round some old gossip closing in,
　They'll beg a tale of long ago—
"For all," they'll say, "he wrought us ill,
　His glorious name shall ne'er grow dim,
The people love, yes, love him still,
　So, Grandmother, a tale of him,
　　　A tale of him!"

"One day past here I saw him ride,
　A caravan of kings behind;
　The time I well can call to mind,
I hadn't then been long a bride.
I gazed out from the open door,
　Slowly his charger came this way;
A little hat, I think, he wore,
　Yes, and his riding coat was grey.
I shook all over as quite near,
　Close to this very door he drew—

'Good-day,' he cried, 'good-day, my
          dear!' "—
  "What, Grandmother, he spoke to you,
    He spoke to you?"

"The following year I chanced to be
  In Paris; every street was gay,
  He'd gone to Notre Dame to pray,
And passed again quite close to me!
The sun shone out in all its pride,
  With triumph every bosom swelled,
'Ah, what a glorious scene!' they cried,
  'Never has France the like beheld!'
A smile his features seemed to wear,
  As on the crowds his glance he threw,
For he'd an heir, at last, an heir!"—
  "Ah, Grandmother, what times for you,
    What times for you!"

"Then came for France that dreadful day
  When foes swept over all the land;
  Undaunted he alone made stand,
As tho' to keep the world at bay!—
One winter's night, as this might be,
  I heard a knocking at the door;
I opened it; great heavens! 'twas he!
  A couple in his wake, no more;
Then sinking down upon a seat,
  Ay, 'twas upon this very chair,
He gasped 'Defeat! ah God, defeat!' "—
  "What, Grandmother, he sat down *there*,
    He sat down *there*?"

"He called for food; I quickly brought
  The best I happened to have by;
  Then when his dripping clothes were dry,
He seemed to doze awhile, methought;
Seeing me weeping when he woke,
  'Courage,' he cried, 'there's still a chance;
I go to Paris, one bold stroke,
  And Paris shall deliver France!'
He went; the glass I'd seen him hold,
  The glass to which his lips he'd set,
I've treasured since like gold, like gold!"—
  "How, Grandmother, you have it yet,
    You have it yet?"

"'Tis there. But all, alas, was o'er;
  He, whom the Pope himself had crown'd,
  The mighty hero world-renown'd,
Died prisoner on a far-off shore.
For long we none believed the tale,
  They said that he would reappear,
Across the seas again would sail,

> To fill the universe with fear!
> But when we found that he was dead,
> When all the shameful truth we knew,
> The bitter, bitter tears I shed!"—
> "Ah, Grandmother, God comfort you,
> God comfort you!"

*Sources:* Madame la baronne de Staël. *Dix Années d'exil.* In *Oeuvres complètes de Mme la baronne de Staël, publiées par son fils,* vol. 15, pp. 14–15. Trans. Kathleen M. Nilan. Paris: Treuttel and Würtz, 1821.
François René, vicomte de Chateaubriand. *The Memoirs of Chateaubriand,* vol. 3, pp. 199–201. London: Freemantle and Co., 1902.
Pierre-Jean de Béranger. "The Grandmother's Tale." In *Songs of Béranger,* pp. 56–59. Trans. William Toynbee. London: Walter Scott, 1892.

### Questions

What did de Staël and Chateaubriand admire about Napoleon? Why did they ultimately reject him?

Why do you think the grandmother in Béranger's poem feels such sympathy for Napoleon?

With which of these three assessments do you most agree? Why?

## 9. IMPORTANT HISTORICAL FACTS: STUDY DRILLS

### A. Multiple Choice

1. Napoleon Bonaparte was, by birth
   A. Genoese.
   B. French.
   C. Corsican.
   D. English.
2. In his role as executive, Napoleon exercised "authority from above," but he allowed the French people to demonstrate their "confidence from below" through
   A. public demonstrations.
   B. democratic elections of government officials.
   C. plebiscites.
   D. an uncensored press.
3. The duke of Enghien died because
   A. Napoleon needed an excuse to declare himself emperor.
   B. he had conspired to return the Bourbons to the throne of France.
   C. he had fought in the Battle of Waterloo.
   D. he had violated the Napoleonic Code.
4. The French sugar island of Haiti first gained its independence under the leadership of
   A. Pascale di Paoli.
   B. Toussaint L'Ouverture.

   C. the Notables.
   D. Spanish guerrillas.
5. The Napoleonic Code did all of the following *except*
   A. establish a uniform code of law for all of France.
   B. guarantee freedom of religion.
   C. guarantee women voting rights.
   D. protect property rights.
6. Napoleon's motto, "a career open to all talents," demonstrated his support for
   A. absolute social equality.
   B. the abolition of all titles and similar social distinctions.
   C. university-level education for all French people.
   D. social mobility based on ability and service to the state.
7. At the beginning of the 1812 campaign against Russia, the "Grand Army" consisted of
   A. 40,000 troops.
   B. 100,000 troops.
   C. 300,000 troops.
   D. 600,000 troops.
8. After Napoleon's defeat in 1814, he was replaced on the French throne by
   A. Talleyrand.
   B. Louis XVIII.

C. Sieyès.
D. the Duchess of Parma.
9. Napoleon's return to power in 1815 was known as
    A. the Bourbon Restoration.
    B. the Directory.
    C. the Concordat.
    D. the 100 Days.
10. Napoleon's last battle was fought at
    A. Waterloo.
    B. Austerlitz.
    C. Trafalgar.
    D. St. Helena.

## B. Chronological Relationships

1. List the following military events in chronological order. In a brief sentence explain their historical significance.
    The Peace of Amiens
    The Battle of Austerlitz
    The Battle of Friedland
    The Battle of Jena
    The Battle of the Nile
    The Peninsular War
    The Invasion of Russia
    The Siege of Toulon
    The Battle of Trafalgar
    The Battle of Wagram
    The Battle of Waterloo
2. *Historical Continuities:* Draw a timeline detailing the changing political regimes in France during the period between 1789 and 1815.

## C. Fill in the Blanks

1. The government known as the _____ was established in France in 1799, after Napoleon and his co-conspirators staged a coup d'état.
2. In an effort to make peace with the Catholic Church, Napoleon negotiated and signed an agreement with the pope known as a _____

3. Although Admiral Nelson would die as a result of wounds suffered during the _____, this naval engagement brought a decisive end to French hopes of invading England.
4. In an effort to consolidate his German holdings, Napoleon abolished the Holy Roman Empire and replaced it with the _____.
5. During the French Revolution and the reign of Napoleon, mercenaries were replaced by _____, troops who fought not for money but out of commitment to the French nation.
6. As opposed to the titled nobles of the Old Regime, who inherited their status, the _____ of the Napoleonic era earned their place in the elite through service to the state.
7. Napoleon's _____ was intended to "strangle" British commerce by depriving it of European markets, thereby forcing the British government to negotiate an end to its war with France.
8. When Napoleon attempted to capture both Spain and Portugal for the French Empire, his army met with considerable resistance from guerrilla fighters and became embroiled in the long _____.
9. A former bishop, _____ served as Napoleon's minister of foreign affairs until 1807. A proponent of the "party of peace," he helped to negotiate the restoration of Bourbon rule in 1814.
10. Although "Ultra-royalists" like the count of Artois wished to reestablish an absolute monarchy in 1814, Louis XVIII agreed to rule as a constitutional monarch, guaranteeing the maintenance of representative government and "public liberties" in the _____.

# IMPORTANT HISTORICAL FACTS: STUDY-DRILL ANSWERS

## A. Multiple Choice

1. B. French.
2. C. plebiscites.
3. A. Napoleon needed an excuse to declare himself emperor.
4. B. Toussaint L'Ouverture.
5. C. guarantee women voting rights.
6. D. social mobility based on ability and service to the state.
7. D. 600,000 troops.
8. B. Louis XVIII.
9. D. the 100 Days.
10. A. Waterloo.

**B. Chronological Relationships**

1. The Siege of Toulon (1793)
   The Battle of the Nile (1798)
   The Peace of Amiens (1802)
   The Battle of Trafalgar (October 21, 1805)
   The Battle of Austerlitz (December 2, 1805)
   The Battle of Jena (1806)
   The Battle of Friedland (1807)
   The Peninsular War (1808–1813)
   The Battle of Wagram (1809)
   The Invasion of Russia (1812)
   The Battle of Waterloo (1815)
2. 1789–1792 The Constitutional Monarchy
   1792–1795 The First French Republic
   1795–1799 The Directory
   1799–1804 The Consulate
   1804–1814 The First Empire
   1814      First Bourbon Restoration
   1814–1815 100 Days
   1815–1830 Second Bourbon Restoration

**C. Fill in the Blanks**

1. Consulat
2. Concordat
3. Battle of Trafalgar
4. Confederation of the Rhine
5. Citizen-soldiers
6. Notables
7. Continental System
8. Peninsular War
9. Talleyrand
10. Charter

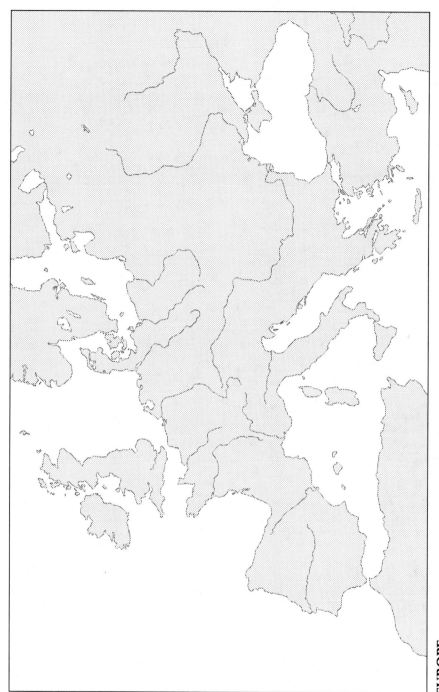

**EUROPE**

THE WORLD